COLLEGES THAT CHANGE LIVES

40 Schools That Will
Change the Way You Think
About College

Fourth Edition

LOREN POPE

REVISED BY HILARY MASELL OSWALD

D0179748

PENGUIN BOOKS

PENGUIN BOOKS
Published by the Penguin Group
Penguin Group (USA) Inc.,
375 Hudson Street, New York, New York 10014, U.S.A.
Penguin Group (Canada), 90 Eglinton Avenue East, Suite 700, Toronto,
Ontario, Canada M4P 2Y3 (a division of Pearson Penguin Canada Inc.)
Penguin Books Ltd, 80 Strand, London WC2R 0RL, England
Penguin Ireland, 25 St Stephen's Green, Dublin 2,
Ireland (a division of Penguin Books Ltd)
Penguin Group (Australia), 250 Camberwell Road, Camberwell,
Victoria 3124, Australia (a division of Pearson Australia Group Pty Ltd)
Penguin Books India Pvt Ltd, 11 Community Centre,
Panchsheel Park, New Delhi - 110 017, India
Penguin Group (NZ), 67 Apollo Drive, Rosedale, Auckland 0632,
New Zealand (a division of Pearson New Zealand Ltd)
Penguin Books (South Africa) (Pty) Ltd, 24 Sturdee Avenue,
Rosebank, Johannesburg 2196, South Africa

Penguin Books Ltd, Registered Offices:
80 Strand, London WC2R 0RL, England

First published in Penguin Books 1996
First revised edition published 2000
Second revised edition published 2006
This third revised edition published 2012

13 15 17 19 20 18 16 14 12

Copyright © Loren Pope, 1996, 2000, 2006
Copyright © The Estate of Loren Pope, 2012
All rights reserved

Library of Congress Cataloging-in-Publication Data

Pope, Loren.
Colleges that change lives : 40 schools that will change the way you think about
colleges / Loren Pope ; revised by Hilary Masell Oswald.
p. cm.
Includes index.
ISBN 978-0-14-312230-2 (pbk.)
1. Universities and colleges—United States—Directories.   2. School
environment—United States.   3. College choice—United States.   I. Title.
L901.P58 2012
378.73—dc23
2012020978

Printed in the United States of America
Set in Fairfield LT STD • Designed by Elke Sigal

*To Viola, the copyreader and critic of my choice,
and Ann Garman Rittenberg, former client
(good small college, Eckerd), who now has her own literary
agency, and who got me off dead center.* —LP

———————

*For Richard and Karen Masell,
my first and best teachers, with love.* —HMO

A Note About This Edition

Loren Pope twice oversaw the revision of *Colleges That Change Lives*, the last edition published in 2006. His mission and perspective guided this fully updated and rewritten edition. Readers will find quintessential Pope-esque quotes from previous editions preserved in this one—a gentle attempt to keep Loren Pope's important message, as only he could deliver it, in these pages.

Contents

SOUTH

MIDWEST

SOUTHWEST

WEST

COLLEGES THAT CHANGE LIVES

Getting Beyond the Hype

(or Why You Can Relax and Enjoy Your College Search)

Let's begin by agreeing that college should change your life.

It's a catchy idea (and not a bad book title), so hang on to it for a minute and contemplate: What does it mean to find a college that changes your life?

The answer depends on you, but for all college-bound teens, the idea of a transformative college experience is an invitation to be bold. Don't fall for Ivy worship. Don't listen to the blather about "best" schools whipped up by the rankings game. Don't let your older friends' descriptions of frat parties and football games define what college should be for you.

Be bold. Set your expectations high.

It won't be easy. The national conversation about higher education is obsessed with outcomes: What do you *get* for your four (or five or six) years in college? A little piece of paper that says you did what the college told you to do? A bigger paycheck? An entrée into grad school? A photo op with the college president?

This question makes sense in light of how expensive a college degree is. But it misses an essential point: College isn't just about the end result. It's also about the means, the process, the path you take to earn your degree, whom you meet, and who inspires and mentors you. If the path is right for you, you'll get the piece of paper, the bigger paycheck, the acceptance to grad school, the photo op with the president, and more—you'll be a sharper, wiser, and better-prepared adult.

To find a life-changing college, you must pay attention to *how* a college educates its undergraduates. Scratch the surface of the Ivies, their clones, and most large universities, and you'll be surprised at what you find. Undergraduates are generally ignored. There are few rewards for teaching, so professors do little of it. If they do, you'll see them only behind a lectern. At a large state university, your adviser won't know much about you, except that you need to register for Biology 102 next semester. If you can't get a course, even if it's necessary for other classes you must take, you'll just have to wait until the next time it's offered. There's little chance anyone will advocate for you, and when the time comes to find a professor to guide you toward your next steps—graduate school, a job, a year as part of a volunteer corps—you'll have a hard time finding anyone who knows you well enough to give advice or write a letter of recommendation on your behalf.

Dr. William Deresiewicz, a writer and former Yale professor of English, wrote in *The American Scholar* in 2008, "There are due dates and attendance requirements at places like Yale, but no one takes them very seriously. Extensions are available for the asking; threats to deduct credit for missed classes are rarely, if ever, carried out. In other words, students at places like Yale get an endless string of second chances."

The Ivies inculcate feelings of security and entitlement. "Getting through the gate is very difficult, but once you're in, there's almost nothing you can do to get kicked out," Dr. Deresiewicz writes. Students conflate their success (or supposed success) with their worth and value, so failure is terrifying.

Therein lies the rub: "[I]f you're afraid to fail, you're afraid to take risks, which begins to explain the final and most damning disadvantage of an elite education: that it is profoundly anti-intellectual. This will seem counterintuitive. Aren't kids at elite schools the smartest ones around, at least in the narrow academic sense? Don't they work harder than anyone else—indeed, harder than any previous generation? They are. They do. But being an intellectual is not the same as being smart. Being an intellectual means more than doing your homework."

Dr. Deresiewicz's coup de grâce is a condemnation of professors at Ivies and their ilk: "Throughout much of the 20th century, with the growth of the humanistic ideal in American colleges, students might have encountered the big questions in the classrooms of professors possessed of a strong sense of pedagogic mission. Teachers like that still exist in this country, but the increasingly dire exigencies of academic professionalization have made them all but extinct at elite universities."

The former professor is not the only one to bemoan the quality of education at big-name schools. Every so often, an administrator at an Ivy or a flagship public university publicly confesses his or her institution's sins: We aren't paying attention to undergraduates; we are graduating people who aren't any sharper or inspired than they were when they arrived here; we've sacrificed learning at the altar of research.

Then these contrite administrators point to liberal arts colleges and say, "We need to be more like them." The Ivies and large universities are great places to go to graduate school (after all, their focus is on grad students!), but for the very best undergraduate education, seek out a small liberal arts college.

Here's why. The colleges in this book have one primary mission: educate the undergraduate. Each appeals to a slightly different type of teenager, but they all share a mission to raise students' trajectories and develop thinkers, leaders, and moral citizens.

The little-known truth is that these colleges have been on the cutting edge of higher education for decades. Many of them have outperformed most of the rankings sweethearts in the percentages of graduates who become America's scientists and scholars. Their students have won Fulbrights, Rhodeses, Goldwaters, Watsons, and other prestigious postgraduate scholarships far out of proportion to their sizes and selectivity. And their graduates get accepted to medical, dental, law, and graduate schools at rates that far outpace the national averages.

These colleges not only equip their students to live full lives, but they also work their magic on a wide range of students. The list includes colleges for the venturesome, the do-it-yourselfers, those who need structure or nurture or both, the late bloomers, the naïfs, and those who need a second chance.

Every one of these catalytic places will push and stretch you beyond what you think possible; they'll let you slip and slide and they'll help you find your footing, but they won't let you hide from your potential or yourself.

Almost all of them accept more than half of their applicants, and they attract strikingly different kinds of kids. Their programs range from the choose-your-own-adventure challenges of Marlboro and New College to the prescribed, no-electives approach of the Great Books curriculum at St. John's.

Their power is in how they teach. The focus is on the student, not the faculty; he is heavily involved in his education. There are no passive ears; students and faculty work so closely together, they even coauthor publications. Teaching is an act of love. Students and professors develop a mentor relationship in class, and professors become students' hiking companions, intramural teammates, dinner hosts, and friends. Learning is collaborative rather than competitive; values are central; community matters. These colleges are places of great coherence, where the whole becomes greater than the sum of its parts.

It is these circumstances that develop leaders, people who can land on their feet, who are bold and imaginative, and who can see the big picture.

These colleges are places where people will listen to you. Not because all of your ideas are brilliant. (They're not.) Not because people are pandering to you. (They're not.) People—professors, peers, administrators—will listen to you because it's an essential part of learning. So many institutions of higher education in this country expect you only to listen—as you sit in a class of hundreds of students. But doesn't it make you wonder how students in these classes test their own ideas?

It's a powerful thing to present your idea to an expert and hear,

"Yes, you're on to something!" or "No, I don't think you've got much to stand on. Let's talk about a different route." That's the stuff of life. And when you must get your own job, you won't last long if the only thing you know how to do is present someone else's ideas.

So let these schools inspire you. Dare to imagine your college years as a billion interactions that draw out your talents, ignite new passions, challenge your assumptions, nurture your hopes, and teach you how to own your place at the table when you're done.

WHY YOU CAN (AND SHOULD) IGNORE THE RANKINGS

Imagine that someone asked you to rate NFL, NBA, NHL, and MLB teams on one scale. Are the Colts better than the Yankees? How would you convert triples to fourth-down conversions or break-aways to free throws?

You couldn't—no one could. Yet when publications rank colleges and universities, they're essentially engaging in this kind of absurdity. How can anyone measure what happens in a small philosophy class in Hoboken against what happens in a large Biology 101 lecture in Portland? And where does the individual student's growth come into play?

No matter the absurdity, publications make these comparisons all the time, based on criteria dreamed up by their editors, many of whom never talk to an administrator, professor, or student before crowning champions and runners-up. Statisticians measure mostly input factors—incoming students' SAT scores and class ranks, selectivity, professors' salaries—many of which are totally irrelevant to education. They know nothing about what happens to young minds and souls in the four years of college. Judging the quality of a college by the grades and scores of the freshmen it admits is like judging the quality of a hospital by the health of the patients it admits. What happens during the stay is what counts.

Rankings have fallen over the edge of misleading into the sea of ridiculousness. You can find out which are the best "jock schools" and which are "dodgeball targets," places characterized by "reefer madness" or "palatial dorms." Every year, the media report on the biggest party school. (Doesn't it make you wonder exactly how that's determined? Is someone measuring students' average blood-alcohol levels on a series of Saturday nights?)

So why do we pay attention? Rankings proliferated in the absence of clear research about the effects and value of higher education. Statistics like SAT scores and professors' salaries are much easier to quantify than life-changing classes or personal epiphanies. And college is expensive: We want the best outcome, the best return on our investment, and the rankings make it seem so easy. But they jinx college choices year after year because they don't— they can't—tell *you* what's best for *you*.

You have better options for evaluating the power of a particular college's teaching, though not all colleges participate. One is the National Survey of Student Engagement (NSSE, pronounced "Nessie," like the Loch Ness monster). Each year, NSSE randomly surveys freshmen and seniors at four-year colleges across the country to find out how often they participate in activities that research has shown are linked to learning, such as studying, continuing class discussions outside class, receiving prompt feedback from professors, and using opportunities for collaboration with faculty. It also assesses how well the college uses its resources to get students engaged in these activities. NSSE allows schools to compare their results with those of similar colleges, so schools know how they are faring.

The other tool is the Collegiate Learning Assessment (CLA), a three-part test that asks students to answer realistic problems that require them to assess the value and importance of various pieces of information. Researchers evaluate students' written responses to the problems and "assess their abilities to think critically, reason analytically, solve problems and communicate clearly and cogently," the CLA says. The assessment measures students' growth over time and compares results across schools.

NSSE and CLA don't release their reports to the public, but if your prospective colleges participate—and many in this book do— you can ask to see the results. They're far better measures of a college's efficacy than the rankings.

WHY SELECTIVITY IS JUST
SMOKE AND MIRRORS

Thanks to ranking systems that give high marks to schools for refusing admission to the majority of applicants, we've been taught that selectivity equals value or prestige or rigor. That's bunk.

But lots of people—and colleges—buy it. When colleges report their acceptance rates, they calculate those rates based on all of the students who sent in *any part* of the application. That calculation makes their prospective pool bigger and their resulting acceptance rate lower: If you have a pool of one hundred applications and you accept twenty of them, you're more selective than if you have a pool of fifty applicants and you accept twenty of them.

This method is misleading because students don't always complete their applications. Here's an example: Emma uses the Common App to apply to six colleges. She sees that Awesome College allows her to apply for free, so she checks Awesome College's box because she figures, "Why not?" But Awesome College has a supplement, which Emma doesn't finish because she wasn't very interested in Awesome College in the first place, and she's tired of writing essays about which character from her favorite book is most like her.

But Awesome College still counts Emma as an applicant, even though there's no way she could have actually gotten in because she didn't finish her application. See the problem?

So for this book, every college has recalculated its acceptance rates based on its pool of completed applications. In each chapter, you'll also find admitted students' average high-school GPAs on a 4.0 scale and the standardized test scores for the middle 50 percent of accepted students. (The reported SAT ranges are math and critical reading scores combined and don't include writing.) Those numbers give you a much better understanding of your chances of admission *if you actually finish your application.*

Better still, admissions officers at these colleges won't toss out your application if you have lower-than-desired test scores or you don't fit their academic profile perfectly. They're eager to know you and figure out if you'll succeed at their college, and they're willing to take chances on students who show potential and curiosity. And as of 2011, thirteen of them are test optional, which means that they don't require standardized test scores for admission: Agnes Scott, Clark, Denison, Earlham, Goucher, Guilford, Juniata, Knox, Lawrence, Marlboro, McDaniel, St. John's, and Ursinus. (Home-schooled students still might have to submit scores; check with the colleges that interest you.)

These schools' philosophy is countercultural, and the implications are huge: Your SAT score, your class rank, and your GPA do not determine your fate! That's good news for teenagers who haven't hit their academic strides, and it's also important news for those who have. In interviews with more than a thousand students at these colleges, I found both types of students. The late bloomers said that with patient guidance and gentle nudges from faculty members, they discovered their own talents and passion for learning. And students who were academic rock stars in high school gushed that these schools taught them how to think and take smart risks.

In short, you don't have to be one of the jittery millions of students anxiously fattening résumés to impress some high-status school that won't do nearly as much for you as the catalytic college that really wants you.

WHY A LIBERAL ARTS EDUCATION IS ESSENTIAL

"Liberal arts" has nothing to do with a college's political bent or its sculpture program. It refers to an educational philosophy that embraces the value and importance of studying core academic subjects, typically comprising the humanities (literature, history, fine arts, languages, religion, and philosophy) and the sciences (natural sciences, math, and social sciences).

The ancient Greeks dreamed up the idea of liberal learning. Sons of wealthy families studied such things as logic and astronomy, not trades, as the lower classes did. The Greeks saw this education as essential to society: These young men would grow up to debate laws in the assembly, hold sway over their communities, lead their fellow citizens during wartime, and influence ideas of beauty and goodness. Their education was a cultural inheritance expected to cultivate their intellect and their virtue. "Liberal" refers to these young men's freedom, political and economic, to get such an elite education.

Liberal arts colleges today depend on the same philosophy: Citizens ought to be educated in ideas and ways of knowing that aren't tied to doing one particular job. And even though the liberal arts tradition is more than 2,500 years old, it's more practical today than ever.

Liberal learning teaches students to investigate and understand the world: microorganisms and macroeconomics, the essence of a poem and the validity of political rhetoric, theories of chemical reactions and reactions to artistic expression. It builds nimble minds and creates independent thinkers.

It also builds the skills employers say they want. In 2009, as the economy sank into a recession, the Association of American Colleges and Universities (AAC&U) commissioned a survey of 302 private-sector employers to ask what they valued in employees. When asked where colleges should place the most emphasis,

- 89 percent said effective oral and written communication;
- 81 percent said critical thinking and analytical reasoning skills;
- 79 percent said knowledge and skills applied to real-world settings;
- 75 percent said connections between choices or actions and ethical decisions;
- 71 percent said teamwork and the ability to collaborate;
- 70 percent said the ability to innovate and be creative.

They might as well have written the marketing material for liberal learning.

If the first decade of the new millennium taught us anything, it's that the world is a wild, raucous place where almost anything can happen. And in such a place, nobody can tell you precisely how your career will go. Nobody can give you the facts you need to do your job ten years from now because nobody knows what your job will be ten years from now. A liberal education gives you skills you will always need to be an adaptive learner, an effective communicator, and a sharp-idea generator.

And then there are the personal benefits of liberal learning in the information age. Our digital idolatry has cost us focus. It has turned communication into fleeting 140-character messages and status updates of little consequence. It has diminished our need and ability to contemplate. It has unraveled the definition of community and allowed us to define friendships by clicks of a mouse. Of course, you can be a liberal arts student and love technology. None of these schools calls you to be a Luddite. But the richness and depth of your learning will enhance the things that this era of ubiquitous information and social media might cost us: patience, intimacy, an appreciation of nuance, a desire for truth, a sharp eye, and a tender heart.

It sounds lofty, but a liberal education doesn't just prepare you for work. It prepares you for life and all the things life comprises. It teaches you how to tell the truth from the slop. It equips you to vote, make good choices, influence your community, raise your kids, take smart risks, and keep learning long after the days when you're reading books simply because a professor put them on a syllabus.

Emerson wrote, "'What will you have?' quoth God. 'Pay for it and take it.'" These are places eager and eminently able, if you are willing to pay with hard work, to empower you to take it all—and carry it with you the rest of your life.

Required Reading:
College Myth Busters

You're not as smart as you think you are if you believe:

- your college should be bigger than your high school;
- a name-brand college will give you a better education and ensure your success;
- a university will offer more than a good small college;
- you should go where your friends are going;
- you don't need to reflect on who you are, what you want, or what the college offers.

Here's why these myths don't hold up.

1. The Best-Sized College

Most good colleges have populations of no more than three thousand students for a reason: College is a time to explore and get to know yourself, your talents, and your interests. A small, familial community is more conducive to such an experience. What's important is not the number of people but the people themselves, the sense of community.

Good small colleges strive for all the variety they can get—in admissions decisions, course offerings, and extracurricular activities. Public institutions admit by formula, and large private universities tend to be compartmentalized by specialties.

And let's remember: Even if you attend a school of 1,200 students, every year, 300 of those students leave and 300 new ones show up.

So in the course of your college career, you'll come into contact with 2,100 people. Do you have 2,100 Facebook friends?

2. The Best Jump Start in Life

For undergraduates, nothing replaces the distinctive combination of dedicated, talented, accessible professors and opportunities for new academic and personal experiences. Ivy on the walls does not. An 8 percent acceptance rate does not. Classmates with perfect SAT scores do not.

Need proof? No problem. Researchers at the National Bureau of Economic Research, a nonprofit, nonpartisan organization that examines how the economy works, conducted a long-term study of 6,335 college graduates' SAT scores and postgraduation income. Here's what they discovered: Earning a degree from a college where students have higher SAT scores didn't lead to higher income over time. A closer predictor of postgraduation income was the SAT scores at schools students applied to but didn't attend—either because of rejection or by their own choice. The researchers conclude, "Evidently, students' motivation, ambition and desire to learn have a much stronger effect on their subsequent success than average academic ability of their classmates."

If you have those qualities—or you'd like to have those qualities—choose a liberal arts college like the ones profiled here. At nearly every campus in this book, faculty members who have taught at Ivy schools or other prestige-soaked places said the work of their upper-class students is as good as that of students in Ivy upper classes. The fact that many of these colleges consistently outperform the Ivy types in producing scholars and scientists speaks for itself.

3. The University as Slack-Filled Merchandise

Halfway through the interviews for this edition, I could read a professor's curriculum vitae and guess how he'd answer my question about why he chose to teach at a liberal arts college instead of a research-driven university. If he had earned his bachelor's degree at a university, he would say that he had felt adrift or frustrated during parts of his undergraduate career. He would add that only by luck and his own persistence had he found his way to an academic department where he found his passion.

On the other hand, if a professor had earned her undergraduate degree at a liberal arts college, she would tell me her experience had been so formative and powerful, she wanted to be a part of creating those experiences for her students.

In both camps, professors described the ways the university shortchanges the undergraduate. "It was clear to me [in graduate school] that there was something very wrong with institutions where faculty had pressure not to spend time with students," says Dr. Holly Sypniewski, a classics professor at Millsaps. At Hendrix, Dr. Sasha Pfau gave the second verse of the same song: "I taught a freshman writing class [while earning my PhD at the University of Michigan], and I was horrified when I realized that I was the only person my students knew in a position of authority to help them solve problems."

And Dr. Patrick McDonald, a math professor at New College of Florida, was an instructor at the Ohio State University while he earned his PhD: "I wouldn't call what I was doing 'teaching.' I was talking at a group of several hundred students, none of whom I knew. Whether they learned anything, I don't know."

Large universities offer you less while claiming to do more. How? By not letting you get involved in your own education; by making you a passive ear in huge lecture classes; by consigning most of the teaching to graduate students and part-timers. You may never see a professor outside of class; you may never have a discussion in class; you may never even write a paper. That is not what an education should be, nor is it preparation for a changing world. Furthermore, chances are very good you'll spend five or more years getting this degree: In 2011, the average four-year graduation rate for *undergraduates* at public universities offering bachelor's, master's, and doctoral degrees—in other words, research-driven institutions—was 29.4 percent. The six-year rate? Just over 54 percent.

Outside of class, your chances of getting a leadership role are slim to none unless you're a shining star—an aggressive shining star. More likely you are sentenced to being a spectator. The salve has to be the Roman circus of the big football weekend. Remember: no matter where you enroll in college, you can buy tickets to the nearest Division I football game. You can't buy tickets to a real education.

4. The Cost of Being a Teenage Sheep

Going where your friends go—or worse yet, your boyfriend or girlfriend goes—is a common mistake. Don't be afraid to leave your friends. You'll make new ones at college, especially at places in this book, where nearly all freshmen show up not knowing a soul.

This blunder costs you the opportunity to do the soul-searching that is essential to choosing a college. Your dreams and motivations aren't the same as your friends', and sacrificing the essential parts of yourself for a little extra time with your high-school buddies is a terrible mistake.

Yes, it's a big jump from high school to college, especially if you're considering a residential college away from home. But the students at the schools in this book are fanatical about their campus communities. "You find your best friends here," said a woman at Juniata College in Pennsylvania. At Agnes Scott in Decatur, Georgia, a woman said, "We care so deeply about each other; we take care of each other." When I asked a group of students at Austin College in Texas what's best about their college, they couldn't decide if they liked their classmates or their professors best. One student settled the matter: "Let's just say the people. The people are the best part." His classmates agreed enthusiastically.

5. The Importance of Examining Yourself and the College

A college education is the only significant asset you'll have your entire life. Nothing lasts as long or stands to serve you as powerfully as what you learn in these four years.

So picking a college is a crucial decision that will affect the quality of your future. Your college career can be the most exciting four years of your life, or you can plod through (for five or more years), largely untouched and unaffected, unnoticed by anyone, entirely unchanged.

Look at yourself honestly. Why, really, are you going? For fun or for some other reason? What are your abilities and strengths? What are your weaknesses? What do you want out of life? Are you supremely confident or unsure of yourself? Are you a self-starter or in need of nurture and structure? Are you socially self-sufficient, or do you need warm, familial support? In your wildest dreams, what does college enable you to do?

Only after you've thought about the answers can you choose a college that fits you. How? Spend a weekday and a night on campus as part of the community. Go to two or three classes; ask a few dozen students and two or three professors the questions most important to you; observe interactions in the cafeteria; see how students talk to one another (or not) as they walk across campus.

Short on questions? These should get you started.

For students:
- What would you change about the college?
- How has your experience here affected you?
- If you e-mail a professor, how long does it take her to reply?
- Where do you go for help?
- Would you call your teachers your friends?
- Who gives you advice about your future?
- If you have a crazy idea for a new club or a new course, does someone take you seriously enough to listen to you?
- When's the last time a professor mentioned an internship, research opportunity, study-abroad term, or other special opportunity to you?

For professors:
- Why did you choose this college, and why have you stayed?
- How would you describe the students here?
- What's distinctive about the college and your department?
- Why do you think I should enroll here?

In short, don't go as a supplicant. Don't worry that people will think you're nosy or pushy. They won't! If they're proud of their school and they've had a good experience, they'll be eager to brag about it. If their experiences are mediocre, they'll be happy to complain.

Our national obsession with rankings often focuses college-bound teens' attention on whether they can get in. And while you should pay attention to a college's academic profile to see if you're a good fit—not just for admission but also for four years of growth—you should also remember that the act of choosing goes both ways. The college chooses you, but you ultimately choose the college. Don't get so caught up in the status game that you forget to do your research, so that when the time comes, you can find the right fit.

Taking Your Learning Disability to College

(and Why You're Going to Love It!)

The good news first: The colleges in this book aren't like high school. For a lot of reasons, most high schools emphasize a particular type of performance. You memorize. You repeat. You learn the quadratic formula, when NATO was established, who Robert Frost is. But perhaps you don't think about why or how he took the road less traveled or what difference it made for him.

The colleges in this book free you from that type of environment. They emphasize what a student at Kalamazoo College called the "so what?" factor: Learning isn't about memorizing information for the sake of vomiting it back up on a test. Instead, these colleges want you to take information you learn and apply it. Connect it to other ideas. Ask questions. Come up with your own ideas.

And if you have a learning disability, you might be very good at these activities.

Here's why: Neurologists have discovered that many learning disabilities are simply biological differences in the way the brain's two hemispheres connect. Dyslexics, for example, tend to have a tough time with left-brain activities, such as processing fine details and component parts of a whole. This is why dyslexics struggle with reading: Identifying the component parts (letters) and then combining them into a meaningful whole (words) is generally a left-brain task. The right brain processes big-picture ideas. It's the hemisphere that helps us make connections among different ideas or items and put a thing into context. Some of the world's greatest innovators, entrepreneurs, and creative forces are dyslexic, their success tied directly to the exceptional ways their brain's right hemispheres process information.

Drs. Fernette and Brock Eide, experts in how the brain learns and processes information and authors most recently of *The Dyslexic Advantage* (Hudson Street Press, 2011), make the compelling argument that dyslexia isn't a disability: It's a totally different way of processing information, one that doesn't align well with the ways most students in most K–12 schools are asked to think. Their book is full of stories of successful dyslexics: best-selling novelist Vince Flynn, singer-songwriter John Lennon, paleontologist Jack Horner, financial-services guru Charles Schwab, actor Anthony Hopkins, cell phone pioneer Craig McCaw, along with many other thriving entrepreneurs, lawyers, inventors, and doctors. Their success isn't a coincidence, the Eides argue. Rather, it's tied to the ways dyslexics think.

The good doctors identify four broad areas where dyslexics excel; they call these skills MIND strengths. *M* stands for material reasoning, particularly 3-D spatial relationships and how things interact in space and motion. *I* represents interconnected reasoning, or the ability to see how different ideas relate to one another and to identify the most relevant (but not most obvious) connections. *N* signifies narrative reasoning, skills that enable a person to draw "mental scenes" from the past to give meaning to information and imagine other possibilities. And *D* stands for dynamic reasoning, or the ability to make best-case guesses about a situation when a definite solution isn't yet clear.

The world puts a premium on the visual, spatial, conceptual, and creative abilities so characteristic of dyslexics and other students who think differently. With computers doing the routine work, the intelligence most in demand is the one that can most creatively and effectively find and make use of information, not the one with the greatest store of it.

And that's one of the great strengths of these catalytic colleges, one where they easily outdo the famous ones. The emphasis at large universities, particularly in early courses, is on repetition of information, mere memorization. At these liberal arts colleges, professors will ask you to examine and apply that information. How you get it—by reading from the book or by using text readers or recordings—doesn't much matter.

What's more, says Dr. Fernette Eide, "Personal memory is often really strong with these students. If they can connect with and be inspired by a mentor, they tend to have better recall." Small class sizes and relationships with professors can make a big difference in all students' learning, but these small-college benefits might be especially helpful for learning-disabled students.

Many of these schools also rely on hands-on learning: labs, fieldwork, creative and group projects—tasks well suited to students with LDs. "If [dyslexic students] have to go to the library, they might struggle; they can't skim or search for things easily. If they go out into the field and interview people, it's a totally different thing. They blossom," says Dr. Eide.

Of course, not all of the colleges in this book are great places for students with LDs; the fit depends on the type of disability. St. John's Great Books curriculum could be overwhelming for students who struggle with reading. Reed, Hillsdale, Marlboro, and New College also have significant reading loads. Cornell College's distinctive one-course-at-a-time curriculum might not be a good fit for a student who needs more time to process information, since each course lasts only eighteen days.

But there are likely several good-fit schools for you among these colleges, given how diverse and student-centered they are. Here's how to prepare yourself for success and find a place that will support your learning style.

START MANAGING YOUR LD NOW

Parents tend to be "in charge" of high-school students' LDs: attending Individualized Education Program (IEP) or 504 meetings, overseeing medication, advocating for their children, and providing kicks in the pants to keep their kids on task and on time.

Unless you plan to take your parents to college with you, it's a good idea to start taking responsibility for your LD. Start by reflecting on the accommodations that are most helpful to you. Read your IEP. Attend an IEP or 504 meeting. It's time to know thyself. By the time you pack up your car to move to campus, you should be able to explain how you learn best and what you need from your professors in order to succeed.

If you take medication but you don't know much about it, now's the time to learn. Read the labels. Understand the dosages and side effects. Ask your doctors to explain what each drug does. If you leave home for college, you'll need to be able to manage your meds on your own. Practice now.

TELL THE COLLEGES ABOUT YOUR LD *DURING* YOUR COLLEGE SEARCH

Colleges cannot deny you admission because of your learning disability, and it's important—vital, really—for you to know whether a college offers the types of accommodations that you need.

Here's the tricky part: Each college determines its own requirements for documentation, and each college decides whether and what kinds of accommodations it will offer you. Just because you had accommodations in high school doesn't mean you'll get the same or any accommodations in college.

When you're planning your visit to campus, ask the admissions counselor to arrange an interview with the director of the disabilities resource center, which goes by different names at different places but performs the same role: coordinating accommodations for students who need them. Find out what types of technology, resources, and services are available. Ask about what types of documentation you need to qualify for accommodations. Speak with students with LDs who use the center's services. Pay attention to the physical space. Is it pleasant, or is it stuffed in the basement of an academic building?

Many students are tempted to shrug off the LD "label" and just be "normal" college students. First, let me assure you, there are no "normal" students. Everyone has strengths and weaknesses, which college tends to draw out more readily than high school does. More important, the leap from high school to college is large, even at the colleges in this book, which have very good programs and support for first-year students. Now is not the time to try going it on your own for two key reasons.

First, accommodations are not retroactive—that is, you can't go back to your professor after you've bombed a test and say, "Well, here's the thing: I have a learning disability, and if I had had extra time, I'm very sure I would have aced this puppy." Second, unlike K–12 schools, colleges don't have a legal obligation to go out of their way to identify and help students with LDs. If you don't tell them, they'll never know, and you could miss out on the help you need to achieve your highest potential.

MENTION YOUR LD IN YOUR APPLICATION

The colleges in this book, and others that share their inclusive philosophy, want to get to know you, including the ways your learning disability has influenced your academic record. Maybe you weren't diagnosed until sophomore year, so your freshman grades are weak. Maybe you had trouble getting your medication right at the start of junior year, so you had a bumpy quarter. Maybe you didn't take any foreign-language courses because you have a language-based or hearing disability, so your school waived the requirement.

Be brief but specific. Include a sentence or two about how you learn best and why you believe the college is a good fit for you.

SUBMIT YOUR OFFICIAL DOCUMENTATION SOON AFTER YOU SEND YOUR ENROLLMENT DEPOSIT

You'll probably send it to the disability services center, not the admissions office. Follow up to make sure the office received it, and then arrange a time to chat about your accommodations long before you show up on the first day of freshman orientation.

Your information is very safe. Your professors won't get any specific information about your diagnosis, only that you qualify for specific accommodations, so there's really no reason not to reveal your LD to your college.

BE HOPEFUL!

Students with LDs are often called "late bloomers," which might make you cringe. But you should embrace it: Late blooming is a bonus. (Really!) In nature, the most sophisticated kinds of life take the longest to mature.

Until a couple of decades ago, scientists believed that the human brain was mostly "wired" by the time a person was three years old; by a person's tenth birthday, they thought, her brain was fully mature. Then scientists made the revolutionary discovery that you are not born with all the gray cells you will ever have; you grow billions more. The brain, like other parts of the body, continues to grow into old age, renewing itself. And hard work stimulates it, which means learning-disabled students often outperform students for whom reading and math come easily.

This late-blooming phenomenon might mean that students with LDs could benefit from a gap year—a break between the end of high school and the beginning of college. It's not leisure time; you could work to save money or take on a long-term service project. If you consider this option, you should still apply to colleges your senior year of high school. Once you select a school, you can defer your enrollment for a year.

These colleges are willing to help you because they want you to succeed. Nobody's betting on your failure. Quite the opposite is true: Because federal aid is not keeping up with the rising costs of higher education, colleges are pouring more institutional dollars into each student. If you're admitted to a college in this book, that college wants you to enroll—guaranteed. In most cases, they're betting thousands of dollars a year that you'll succeed. What's more, the administrators and professors at these schools chose small, liberal arts environments because they believe in the power of this learning model for a broad range of students.

Allegheny College

Meadville, Pennsylvania

"Attractive Allegheny, founded in 1815, is a shining example
of what the exciting colleges in this book are doing to prepare
their students for a new kind of world, things that make most
of the prestige institutions looks stodgy."

—LOREN POPE

In the lush, rolling hills of northwest Pennsylvania, in little Meadville, ninety miles from Pittsburgh, Allegheny College builds on
its long history of strong liberal arts education while preparing students for exciting futures. It's no wonder that Allegheny has a distinguished record of producing scientists and business leaders.

At the heart of Allegheny's curriculum is the requirement that
every student choose a major in one of three divisions (natural sciences, social sciences, or humanities) and a minor in another.
(Alternatively, a student can double major in academic areas from
two different divisions.) A student must also complete at least two
courses in the third division. It sounds simple, but the requirement
prevents one of higher education's biggest vices: education that

trains a student for only one field, when the reality is that most of today's college kids will have as many as seven different careers.

Allegheny students don't have to worry about being pigeon-holed, academically or otherwise. Their breadth of learning is at the heart of liberal arts education and is essential to building skills that will serve these students for the rest of their lives: critical thinking, oral and written communication, problem solving, and confidence to bring new ideas to the table.

Students profess loving their lives at Allegheny. "I'm not just one thing," says a senior political science and environmental studies double major who plays football and follows the prelaw track. "Nobody here is one-dimensional, and I think that makes us all eager to learn more about each other and ourselves." Students are eager to explain all of the things they do on campus—what they study, what they play, how they lead, where they volunteer. They seem to be enthusiastic not because they're padding résumés but because they're genuinely delighted by all facets of their work.

The college also boasts a strong seminar series, the backbone of the curriculum. Each freshman takes a topical seminar her first two semesters; the goal is to boost her writing and speaking skills so she's equipped to handle the rigor of upper-level courses. Her freshman seminar professor becomes her adviser until she declares a major—by the end of her sophomore year.

The seminar series continues with a sophomore seminar, a more intense course often tied to the student's intended major, also designed to hone writing and analytical-thinking skills. Junior year, each student takes a seminar related to research methods in his major and begins to develop the thesis for his senior comprehensive project, a capstone experience during which he conducts original research in his major field and writes a substantive paper. (We're talking about one hundred pages or so.) He'll top it off with an oral defense in front of his professors and an audience of his peers.

It's no small feat "to comp"—a homegrown verb that means "to be in the midst of working on a senior project." (If you hear a student say she has been "decomped," she means that she has finished her oral defense.) Students are thrilled and a bit overwhelmed by their comps, but by the time they are seniors, they're eager for the challenge. Alumni frequently say that their comps infused them with confidence and showed them just how far they had developed in their ways of thinking. "I feel like Allegheny refines and refines and asks more and more of its students—really pushing us to the edges of what's possible—and then reveals to us what we're capable of," says an alumna now in a graduate program for international studies. "When I got to graduate school, I felt so at ease, not just because I could handle the content but because I knew how to learn and analyze. I trusted myself, and I think that my comp really proved to me exactly what I could do. I finished my oral defense and thought, 'Did I really do that?' It was a high."

The college is building on this legacy with a strong push to add more international experiences or study-away opportunities for students. ("Study away" refers to off-campus learning that happens in the United States.) Its three-week May term is rife with courses that include travel overseas—to China, Ghana, Greece, Turkey, Turks and Caicos Islands, and Ukraine, among other places. Students can study abroad for a semester in programs on six continents, and in 2011 the college was considering adding a requirement that all students study away before graduation.

Allegheny is also boosting its commitment to interdisciplinary study, important because students ought to learn how to think about issues and solve problems from a variety of perspectives. Two programs, in their infancy in 2011, have captured students' and professors' imaginations: The new Global Health minor integrates courses in environmental science, epidemiology, political science, economics, history, religious studies, and philosophy. Students must also study away to get real-life understanding of health issues in other parts of the world.

The second program, Journalism in the Public Interest, builds on Allegheny's history of producing journalists, starting when Ida Tarbell graduated in 1880. She went on to write *The History of the Standard Oil Company*, an exposé of John D. Rockefeller's business practices and personal qualities. (Tuck that tidbit away for your next *Jeopardy!* tournament.) The program combines journalism courses with classes in political science, economics, and philosophy—a boon for students because journalists ought to be able to understand and communicate ideas in context.

Of course, the success of all of these things—a strong core curriculum, a thoughtful seminar program, new and exciting off-campus and interdisciplinary programs—depends on high-quality teaching. In this category, Allegheny delivers.

As at other student-centered colleges, professors earn tenure based on teaching *and* research. There is great interest in the art of teaching and in collaborating to boost opportunities for students. "Simply put: If you don't want to teach, this isn't the place for you," says President James Mullen.

Students confirm the president's claim. They gush, "It's easy to build rapport with professors" and "I go to office hours just to hang out." One young woman whose father is a music professor swore she would never enroll at Allegheny. "I wanted to go away for college, just like everyone else," she says. But she took a few classes on campus during her senior year of high school and got hooked: "The classes sealed it for me. The professors were amazing."

Students chat just as eagerly about the Allegheny community. Their mantras: "It feels like home," and "It's my favorite place on earth." A black student, a junior English major, says that Allegheny "embraces your full identity." A senior says, "You feel comfortable being passionate about the things you love." The college's ethnic diversity has grown in recent years, and in 2011 the college hired a chief diversity officer. Several students mention that the campus community is deeply involved in conversations about how to support students from a range of backgrounds, ethnicities, and sexual orientations.

Students also say they feel the college has reached a point where it is time to address tolerance and diversity with more candor than in the past, but nobody feels that the community is in crisis—or anything close. An African American student explains, "This is the first time I've felt my skin color. Allegheny is willing to talk about otherness, and it's been awesome. I feel like we're really forward-moving and in a safe place to discuss big issues of identity, both mine as an individual and this campus's identity as a large group of individuals living together."

Dean of students Joe DiChristina calls the campus ethos "an ethic of care about others," which extends beyond the Allegheny campus. The relationship between Meadville and the college has warmed up in recent years, students and staff say; students are thinking more about what they can do for Meadville and less about what Meadville can do for them. "You don't come to Allegheny for Meadville," a sophomore says, "but a lot of us have built really satisfying relationships with nonprofits or locals. I think it's more educational to live in a place that's not all picture-perfect homes. We have those, but we also have economic problems and people who are in need." Perhaps it was fitting that during these interviews a few students across the cafeteria were wearing T-shirts that read, "I Heart Meadville."

In many ways, the college emphasizes the moral life. Allegheny is one of twenty-seven schools in the country to have a Bonner Scholars program and one of forty-seven schools to have a Bonner Leaders program. Both programs provide financial support for students with financial need and commitments to community service. The programs' influence on campuses is notable: Even though the percentage of Bonner participants is small, their focus on the community seems contagious. At Allegheny, about 60 percent of students volunteer their time and talent.

Perhaps this care for others stems from the college's long history of doing just that: Allegheny has a legacy of providing low-income students access to a top-notch college education. Dr. James Bulman, an English professor, theorizes: "We tend to attract students who are less privileged. They come wide-eyed, hungry, not terribly sophisticated, but smart and ambitious. And they're much more socially concerned than students at other places, like Brown," where his son went to school.

Students abide by an academic honor code that requires honest work—no lying, cheating, or plagiarizing—and asks students to report infractions they observe. What's notable here is that students—not administrators holed up in an ivory tower—developed the code, and every three years the student body votes on whether to preserve it. Each time the referendum has come up, the code has passed by a strong majority. Students and faculty say they believe the code works, and students profess loving it—especially since it leads to take-home tests and exams that aren't proctored.

It's clear why Allegheny students are a happy group. Of Allegheny freshmen, 87 percent return for sophomore year—and in recent years, 100 percent of black students have returned. The college gets high marks from students for being a place where they can feel comfortable taking risks to discover the areas—academic, athletic, political, artistic, you name it—where they thrive.

The most common complaint is the workload. "The hardest I've ever worked in my life was for a class here. I got a B. I was so proud and a little devastated," says a senior majoring in environmental studies and political science. A sophomore says that she appreciates how professors emphasize learning instead of grades. "I got a C– on my first English paper, and I was like, 'What?' But I think I learned more from that one paper than I did my whole senior year of high school. I had to learn how to make an argument with my writing, and I did. My high-school self would have been totally freaked out over that grade, and of course I still want to do well, but there's more to school than acing tests."

The setting for all of this good work is a beautiful campus of brick paths, vibrant flower beds (when the snow isn't falling), and renovated historical buildings. The campus gives the impression that the college's keepers care about the students' home away from home—especially important because Allegheny requires students to live on campus all four years.

In the first decade of the new millennium, Allegheny invested about one hundred million dollars in its campus facilities. The new Vukovich Center for Communication Arts, opened in 2009, is a glass-and-steel marvel that houses state-of-the-art media production facilities, rehearsal spaces, and a 250-seat theater that would make any aspiring actor salivate. The architectural firm that designed the building counts the Santa Fe Opera House and the restoration of Carnegie Hall among its triumphs. The scientists got a major boon too: The renovated Carr Hall, home of the environmental science and physics programs, offers expanded space for faculty-student collaboration and more lab space for research.

Another of the college's shining assets is ACCEL (Allegheny College Center for Experiential Learning), which houses its career services center. ACCEL is also command central for internships, off-campus study, community service, and preprofessional studies (premed, prelaw, or education). Its airy, welcoming space is in a building near the center of campus, and every student from a random sample of passersby raved about ACCEL.

As many as 80 percent of graduates do internships before they leave Allegheny; the national average is 55 percent. What's more, ACCEL doles out between $110,000 and $140,000 a year to help students cover travel and living expenses while they're interning, and every student can apply for one grant a year, an opportunity that encourages students to dream big. Recent internships include a stint in Greece to study sea-turtle reclamation, a trip to the Black Forest Writing Seminars in Germany, work with the National Coalition for the Homeless in Washington, D.C., and a project in Hawaii studying dolphins and sea lions.

Allegheny also does an excellent job preparing premed students, not merely for medical school but also for careers in medicine. The premed program offers ten students a year the opportunity to rotate through departments of the local hospital, giving them up-close-and-personal looks at what a career in medicine would be like. Another program pairs premed students with alumni who are doctors in nearby metropolitan areas (Cleveland, Akron, Pittsburgh, and Buffalo); for three weeks in the summer, students spend twenty hours a week with doctors. The reason: It's easy to romanticize medicine by shadowing a doctor for a few hours a day, but after sixty hours, students have a much clearer idea if that professional path appeals to them. If a student decides she wants to go to med school, she has a good shot at getting in: Allegheny has an average acceptance rate of 80 percent, more than twice the national average.

Like all of the colleges in this book, Allegheny accepts a wide range of students and helps them discover and develop their talents. It offers admission to 60 percent of applicants, and those who enroll have an average GPA of 3.8. The middle 50 percent score between 24 and 29 on the ACT and 1100 and 1300 on the SAT (math and critical reading combined), and 76 percent are in the top quarter of their high-school classes. But if you've had a few blips on your high-school record, don't shy away from Allegheny: The admissions staff is looking for potential, for students who can succeed in this type of college but who might not have blossomed yet.

And there's more good news: Allegheny does a fine job offering aid to admitted students. The average financial aid package in the 2010–2011 school year was more than $28,000 (well over half the sticker price), and loans made up about 17 percent of that amount. The same year, Allegheny awarded $33 million in institutional grants and scholarships to help make the college affordable. One unique element of its scholarship program is that students who earn Trustee Scholarships, worth five thousand to twenty thousand dollars a year, are guaranteed that money for all four years; the college doesn't want to discourage students from taking academic risks for fear of losing their scholarships. It also recently introduced the Bicentennial Scholarship in honor of its two hundredth anniversary in 2015. The amount: $2,015 a year.

It's fitting for the college to reflect on its history. It was a frontier school two centuries ago, a place on the edge of the unknown, founded because "westerners" wanted a college education of a similar caliber to the education offered at New England schools. The irony is thick: Today Allegheny shuns the ethos of prestige places (many of them in the Northeast) and delivers an education at least on par with—and perhaps better than—those places. It is still turning out pioneers who look at the world and know they have the skills, knowledge, and confidence to shape it.

Clark University

Worcester, Massachusetts

"Clark ... [has] something rare anywhere, but unique in New England: a four-star academic experience in a major research university that gives a B student the chance to do undergraduate research on big league projects. And several years later, when Clark alumni wind up with PhDs as tenured faculty members at top universities, the point is proven."

—LOREN POPE

What happens when you take the best of a liberal arts college and the best of a research university and mash them together?

You get Clark.

The university is in a field by itself: It is devoted to educating undergraduates across disciplines, so they're broad thinkers who have sharpened their skills against ideas in humanities, sciences, and social sciences. But it's also devoted to Research—capital *R*—so those same undergraduates are deeply engaged in cutting-edge discoveries alongside their professors and graduate students.

Clark was founded in 1887, making it the second-oldest graduate institution in the country after Johns Hopkins. It opened a liberal arts college in 1902 with a commitment to combining research and undergraduate training rather than polarizing the two, as is done elsewhere.

Clark's legacy is long and storied. Its first president was G. Stanley Hall, who founded the American Psychological Association. At

President Hall's invitation, Sigmund Freud introduced America to psychoanalysis in a series of lectures at Clark (before Freud decided he hated America and retreated to Austria). A. A. Michelson, the first American Nobel Prize winner in the sciences, held a post at Clark; so did Robert Goddard, inventor of rocket technology. And the university's researchers have touched ideas and products that are part of our public discourse and daily lives: Clark researchers developed the formula for the windchill factor, contributed to the chemistry behind the birth control pill, first discovered how brain tissue regenerates itself, and participated in the United Nations program to develop a long-term strategy for addressing HIV/AIDS.

Today, Clark's 2,200 undergrads and 900 graduate students team up with professors to continue tackling big ideas and solving major problems. They take seriously the college's motto ("Challenge convention. Change our world."), and many of them make an important link between their own learning and their power to do good in the world.

Undergraduates begin their college careers with a shared intellectual experience grounded in liberal studies. The required course work is broken into two components. First, students must take two courses that cultivate critical thinking skills: one that teaches students how to connect critical-thinking and writing skills, and a formal-analysis course that places special emphasis on logical and algebraic modes of thinking.

The second curricular component is a series of "perspectives" courses that introduce students to the different ways in which various disciplines define thinking, learning, and knowing. Everyone takes courses in the arts, comparative global cultures, history, language and cultures, scientific study, and values (as reflected in personal behavior, institutional norms, and public policy). It's important to note that Clark's introductory classes aren't as small as those at the other colleges in this book; at Clark, you could have a class of as many as 150 students, which would break down into smaller groups, led by graduate teaching assistants, for discussion or lab.

As a student progresses in her career at Clark, she begins to narrow her academic focus and has opportunities to conduct research. Because Clark is working on major research grants with teams of scholars, some of them international, a student gets a real taste of the pace, methodology, and questions that are driving some of the biggest ideas in their fields. "We see undergraduates as a real asset because they ask innovative questions and can make interdisciplinary connections that aren't always obvious to professor and grad students who are steeped in our disciplines," says dean of research Nancy Budwig, PhD.

And if a student finds his passion in academia and meets academic standards, he can have a fifth year at Clark tuition free to earn his master's degree. This opportunity is available to about 25 percent of Clark undergrads.

Professors express great satisfaction in having found a place where they fold their teaching into their research and vice versa. "I wanted a place where there was magic in the classroom, where everyone is engaged," says Dr. Jeffrey Arnett, a developmental psychologist. He taught at a small liberal arts college in the South where the teaching load was heavy and limited his research and at a large public university in the Midwest where "teaching was clearly secondary; promotions and other rewards were not based on teaching." Clark is the perfect balance, he says.

Take a close look at professors' credentials. Many of them earned their doctoral degrees at the finest graduate universities in the country. Over and over again, they mention how Clark embodies the best parts of those universities but offers something more: students who are less polished, less interested in grades, and more interested in finding meaningful work.

Dr. William Fisher, director of the International Development, Community, and Environment Department (IDCE), taught at Columbia, Princeton, and Harvard before coming to Clark. "When I first considered coming to Clark, I asked my colleagues at Harvard about it. They had sent their kids here, had research partners here," he says. "I was seeking interdisciplinary collaboration, and I wanted students interested in making a change in the world. I got both. At Harvard, I had amazing undergraduate students. Clark students are just as smart, but they haven't had the same educational benefits. They have amazing potential, and this is a place where that potential can be developed."

"Our top students can compete with any in the country," says Dr. Colin Polsky, a geographer. "On balance, the first-year class isn't as prepared as you might expect or want, but by junior or senior year, the majority of them have evolved so dramatically, it's gratifying to see."

Clearly, Clark isn't an elitist place. It accepts about 68 percent of its applicants, the middle 50 percent of whom have GPAs between 3.2 and 3.8 and SATs (critical reading and math) between 1100 and 1300. About a third come from Massachusetts; 10 percent, from foreign countries; and approximately 15 percent of students are ethnic minorities. A full 90 percent of freshmen come back for their sophomore year, and three-quarters graduate in four years.

In 2011 the university's administrators and faculty were deeply engaged in a conversation about how to make sure that every Clark student had the kind of transformative experiences that lead to intellectual fulfillment and the skills they need to compete in the global marketplace. So Clark turned its research lens on itself, delving into what was happening with and to the students who seemed the most transformed by their education.

Teams of professors and administrators talked to these students and alumni to find out about the specific educational experiences that propelled students forward at Clark. "We found that students were flourishing when they were in situations with two characteristics: First, they had found ways to center their education on an issue or topic that they were passionate about," says President David Angel, PhD. "Their education was connecting to their hearts as well as their heads. Second, it was important that they exceeded their own expectations of themselves. They went outside traditional incentives—grades or validation from professors—and were driven by something bigger."

The university's keepers also talked to employers about what they need from college graduates they hire. "They all affirmed the value of liberal education as a foundation for success. They validated the skills liberal learning hones best: critical thinking, ability to write and speak well, creative thinking," President Angel says. Employers also want skills that aren't as easily proven: resilience, courage to make value-based decisions, and persuasiveness.

So the university is reengineering its liberal arts curriculum to connect traditional academic work with problem-solving situations where students will practice and hone this whole range of skills. Part of the process is finding ways to demonstrate and measure the results rigorously. "We're utterly convinced here that this work will be nationally influential," President Angel says. "We want to show that there is a way for colleges and universities to build and measure these capabilities that we're talking about."

It's worth keeping an eye on Clark to see whether its curricular changes fulfill this ambitious vision. Meanwhile, students and alumni think the university already delivers on its promises.

Students cite two primary reasons for coming to Clark: the research model and the chance to earn a master's degree for free in Clark's fifth-year program. But they stay because they build strong relationships with their fellow Clarkies—a nickname they embrace.

A fifth-year student earning a master's degree in biology says he likes "the sense of family" best. His parents both went to Dartmouth—"which is all about connections, right?" But at Clark, he says, "You work with your professors and you make those connections yourself. My parents and I don't feel like I'm missing anything by not following in their footsteps, and actually, I think I'm learning things here, like building my own résumé and not assuming that I'm entitled to a job or a graduate grant simply because of where I've gone to school."

Students point to two features of Clark that complement each other: First, they describe the campus as laid-back. "Other places, students are fulfilling a role," says a senior from Denver. "You don't have to worry about fitting a mold here." A student from Zambia agrees: "My international friends love it here for that reason. It's just 'be who you are.'" This acceptance is important because of the second component of life here: the freewheeling exchange of ideas.

"We can get into really heated discussions, and after class we say to each other, 'Want to go get lunch?'" says a senior from Massachusetts. "We take our work seriously, but we don't take ourselves too seriously."

They also mention Clark's well-earned reputation as a liberal place. When asked if the college has political diversity, a student jokes, "I know one Republican and two Libertarians." Another says that she feels that Clark could use a broader range of political thought. Students are split on whether conservatives and moderates would feel comfortable on campus; some point out that Clark welcomes varying viewpoints, but others suggest that it might be hard to be part of such a small minority at an outspoken place.

Clark activism fits well in its surroundings. The university's location is an important part of its identity, but not because the neighborhood is idyllic; just the opposite. Clark is in a run-down part of Worcester, a postindustrial city about forty miles from Boston. The location might turn off prospective students, but Clarkies view it as an opportunity. "Clark exists in the real world," says an alumna who now works for the admissions office. Students, staff, and professors participate in the community, developing programs, giving their time and talent, and using their research methods and tools to find solutions to the real problems just outside its wide-open gates.

There's something powerful about the juxtaposition of a high-caliber education and a community in need. Clark's culture assumes that if you are fortunate enough to get this kind of education, you have a responsibility to do what you can to use it to mitigate others' suffering. But the service here isn't perfunctory; it's born of inspiration.

Stop any student you meet on campus and ask how she changes her world. You might hear about the student who started a group-mentoring program for local high-school students, the goal of which is to introduce these teens to college life in hopes of encouraging them to graduate from high school and enroll in college. Another group developed a curriculum that helps high-school students deal with bullying, thoughts of suicide, stereotypes, and other social challenges. Students persuaded the university to stop using minerals mined in the Congo because they're mined in situations of armed conflict and human-rights abuses. "We rally around issues the way some schools rally around their football teams," says a junior who volunteers at the university's sexual health clinic. "It's a way to find your passion and your close friends." Another woman says advocacy work "shaped what I want to do with my life. Now I know I want to work on international development issues."

Clark supports their ideas. Students say it's easy to start an organization and there's never a shortage of interested participants. And for true innovators, there's the Eureka Idea Contest, an annual competition that invites students to dream up solutions to campus problems. Students vote, and the winner gets funding to implement the change. One year, the victor opened a thrift shop across the street from campus to absorb the stuff college students frequently discard at the end of each academic year. Another bright idea was buying bicycles for the campus police, who had been cruising campus in SUVs. "It just felt really anti-Clark to have such obvious examples of wastefulness here," says a junior from New Jersey.

Clark also supports healthy discourse. In 2006 the university launched a program called Difficult Dialogues, funded by a grant from the Ford Foundation. Part of its impetus was a general malaise on campus: Students weren't discussing issues of importance; professors hesitated to raise hot-button issues in class or even with one another. It seemed that Clarkies needed to learn how to listen, converse, and approach topics that are inherently divisive, hard, and complicated.

Difficult Dialogues teaches those skills through a range of programs. Each semester, the university chooses a single issue and presents talks, panel discussions, arts events, and opportunities for reflection on the topic. The program also gives the campus community tools to communicate effectively, so that when conflict arises, the members of Clark's community know how to respond. It has infused Clark with a healthy willingness to talk about controversial ideas, just as the students mention.

Clark's alumni express gratitude for their years at Clark. A 2001 graduate from Amman, Jordan, who makes a point of explaining he was not much of a student, says that Clark was "a profound life experience for me. It was a place where I felt I could bring about change, and it really left me wanting more out of life." Another alumnus, who graduated in 2007, describes himself as a "straight B/C student in high school." After a rough first year at Clark, "I realized my own accountability. Clark gave me a chance to learn from my mistakes, and my résumé and my character grew." Today he teaches fourth grade at an inner-city school. "I hated school as a kid, and that's why I teach. I know now what learning can do for you."

And a 2010 graduate summarizes a story told again and again on Clark's campus and among alumni: "I always did well [in high school], but none of us cared. We never talked about what we were learning. At Clark, I met people who were actually interested in what they were studying. It was cool to be interested in ideas. I learned that what I have to say is valuable, and even if I'm wrong, I know how to learn from that. The person I am today is a much better person than the girl who showed up here as a freshman."

Juniata College

Huntingdon, Pennsylvania

Juniata is not on every high-school senior's lips, but it deserves to be. It is an incubator of high achievers and producer of happy alumni, thanks to its clear mission to help its 1,600 undergraduates discover and sharpen their talents and raise their sights. "Our students don't always know how good they are," says Dr. James Lakso, the provost and an economist. "Our faculty does a very good job of elevating students' goals and expectations."

To wit: Among its alumni are Dr. William Phillips, corecipient of the Nobel Prize for physics in 1997, five members of the National Academy of Sciences, and deans at top research universities and medical clinics. They include leading news executives, MTV cinematography award winners, the developer of Teflon, and Dr. William von Liebig, inventor of the Dacron tubing used in blood-vessel and heart replacement. Juniata's impressive science center is named for him.

So it's no surprise that Juniata students express hope and eagerness when they talk about their future. "It feels like the whole school is set up just to make sure we succeed," says a senior from New Jersey. "We're learning what we need to learn, and our professors are always saying, 'Did you hear about that internship?' or 'I have this colleague who needs a research assistant this summer. Want to go?'"

Experiential opportunities are top notch at Juniata. If you visit (and you should), conduct this little experiment: Ask any student you meet about internships, study abroad, and research opportunities. It's almost guaranteed you'll hear an impressive and fascinating list of such experiences from anyone you meet here. (And you'll get to experience one of Juniata's best qualities: a friendly, enthusiastic student body.)

The backbone of learning here is a broad liberal arts curriculum that encourages interdisciplinary study. Juniata students don't declare majors. Instead, they have Programs of Emphasis (POEs). A student can choose a "designated" POE—which works like a traditional major with requirements determined by departments— or an individualized POE, an interdisciplinary program that the student designs with input from faculty. About a third of students choose this route, which gives them chances to explore and make connections among seemingly disparate topics.

And each student gets guidance from not one but two advisers. One is a professor in her POE; the other can be a second professor or a beloved staff member. The system underscores the college's emphasis on students: The whole community exists to help them achieve.

The unofficial mantra on campus is "challenge and support." Professors' expectations are high, and even if a student arrives without much self-motivation, the campus culture will strengthen it. "People want to do well here. I don't think there are any students who are bored or not paying attention," says a junior from Pennsylvania. "I just don't know anyone who isn't excited about what they're learning. It's so different from high school—awesomely different." A student who says he was a mediocre student at a middling public high school adds, "If high school had been like Juniata, I would have been the valedictorian."

The source of this spirit is teachers' interest in students and their work. As at other colleges in this book, Juniata's faculty is committed to improving its teaching methods. Professors share ideas informally and visit one another's classes to get ideas and give feedback. They also have brown-bag lunches regularly, during which they share ideas about what works in their classes and what doesn't.

"There's no fear of reprisal," Dr. Lakso says, because everyone shares the same goal. By 2011, the college had raised nearly one million dollars for a new Center for Teaching and Learning, where professors will collaborate to keep improving their teaching.

This emphasis is important for undergraduates: At large research universities, many of which don't value teaching the way small liberal arts colleges do, professors might never discuss best practices in teaching. On almost every campus in this book, professors mention how disappointed their dissertation committees were when as newly minted PhDs they declared their intention to teach—a reflection of teaching's low status at many research universities. Such places are good at creating new knowledge, but they aren't nearly as committed to teaching or mentoring undergraduates. At Juniata and places like it, teachers who are very good want to get even better, and you cannot underestimate the influence of talented, passionate teachers on students of all types.

Juniata students feel this commitment deeply. They rave about their professors, often letting their conversation veer off into an exchange about specific teachers: "You have to take a class with him!" or "Our class is going to her house for dinner this week!" There seems to be a healthy balance of affection and respect among professors and students.

And the whole campus feels like a genuinely friendly place. Students greet one another as they pass on the sidewalks; the chatter in the cafeteria is lively; professors and students chat casually in hallways. It's no wonder the most common answer by far to a question about what they love best about Juniata is "community." Some students even theorize that the college's small-town location fosters that sense of camaraderie in a way that a spot in a big city might not.

Juniata's home is Huntingdon, a town of about 6,500 people in central Pennsylvania's pretty Allegheny Mountains. If you're up early—try it at least once when you're a college student—you might catch the fog rolling off the hills to blanket the campus. The college is close to Huntingdon's downtown core, blocks of restaurants, bars, shops, and small businesses. It's also close to outdoor recreational sites, including thousands of miles of hiking and biking trails and the area's impressive Raystown Lake, with its 118 miles of shoreline. Several students mention that they manage the stress of college life by heading off for a day of fishing and swimming in the warm months and cross-country skiing in the winter.

About 60 percent of Juniata's 1,600 students come from Pennsylvania, but the student body represents thirty-seven states and thirty-eight foreign countries—a number that has grown in the last ten years. About 70 percent of applicants are accepted; the middle 50 percent of them have scored between 1080 and 1280 on the SAT (critical reading and math) and had an average high-school GPA of 3.75.

Juniata owns and operates a 385-acre field station on the lake, about a thirty-minute drive from campus. The field station is an ideal spot for hands-on learning, and professors from seven different departments, particularly in the sciences, use it regularly for classes. The college maintains a fleet of five powerboats and a slew of canoes, and the property's buildings include a multipurpose learning center and two residential lodges, where students stay as part of the Sense of Place semester. This program, hosted by the environmental studies department, gives a very small group of students an intimate look at the region's environmental, social, and ecological issues and how they're connected.

The field station is only one part of Juniata's strong science program. Among scientists and scholars (and graduate schools), Juniata has an excellent and well-deserved reputation in the sciences that stretches back decades. The equipment is state-of-the-art *and*—this is an important distinction—available for student use. The science building was designed to foster student-professor collaboration. An example: Study areas adjoin faculty offices, so students can ask questions as they work on their homework or analyze lab results. "We try to encourage students, to model for them what it means to be a scientist in the liberal arts context, and that means interacting quite a lot," says Dr. Richard Hark, chair of the chemistry department. "This is a collegial place, and that collegiality extends to relationships with students." About 75 percent of chemistry majors go on to graduate school, making Juniata fourth in the nation in the percentage of graduates earning PhDs in chemistry.

The prehealth tracks, including premed, prevet, and predental, are just as strong. Not only are the courses excellent preparation for entrance exams and professional school, but Juniata also does a very good job advising these students and helping them discern what they'd like to do. For example, every prehealth student shadows a professional in the field because the experience helps her understand if the work appeals to her. If she decides it does, Juniata has excellent acceptance rates: In 2011, 100 percent of students who applied to dental school were accepted, as were 75 percent of students who applied to med school, 100 percent of vet-school applicants, 100 percent of physical therapy applicants, and 100 percent of students who applied to public-health programs. It's important to note that because Juniata is a small school, these pools of students can be quite small, so the numbers can skew significantly from year to year. (If there are only two applicants to vet school and one gets in, the acceptance rate drops to 50 percent.) But a close look at Juniata's acceptance rates over many years shows that it has long been a jumping-off point for many health professionals.

Better still, Juniata's culture of support extends even to the prehealth sciences, notorious at other places for being cutthroat. "We never slam kids. If they have bad grades, we find out why," says Dr. Debra Kirchhof-Glazier, director of the health professions program. "Every prehealth kid gets the same support from us." If a student's grades suggest he won't get into medical, vet, or dental school, but he wants to try, the committee will advise him as thoughtfully as it does the highest-performing candidates. And for the few students who aren't admitted, Dr. Kirchhof-Glazier and her colleagues are very good at suggesting other paths within the health-sciences field.

Dr. Kirchhof-Glazier sounds like her colleagues in other departments when she says, "I know a lot of people [in my discipline], so if a kid wants to research, we make it happen." Juniata's standing internships include a 240-hour stint with a group of family physicians in Altoona, about forty minutes from campus, where students can learn alongside medical residents and even spend some time with the local hospital's trauma team; a paid pediatric internship in the summer with a Juniata alumna; and a nine-day intensive internship in January at a nearby hospital, where students can observe surgeries and shadow a range of specialists.

All of these features should be enough to make any student considering health sciences look closely at Juniata. But here's the icing on the cake: Juniata believes so strongly in the value of studying abroad that even students on the health-sciences track can go abroad for a full year. The college has worked out a smart, careful plan for these students so they finish the professional-school prerequisites and submit applications on time. Students can't be more effusive about this opportunity because they say they couldn't find another college that was as supportive of their desire to go abroad. "I knew [when I was looking for colleges] that college might be the only time in my life I could go live somewhere else as a student, not a tourist," says a sophomore premed student. "Every other school sort of acted like it was a huge inconvenience for them to support me, and then I got to Juniata, and someone actually said to me, 'You're going to be a better doctor if you've lived among people who aren't like you and if you've faced challenges that make you think creatively. We think every future doctor should go abroad.' I was blown away by that kind of thinking. But now I know that's Juniata. It's all about possibility here. It's all about people saying, 'What are your biggest dreams? Let's see how we can help you get there.'"

In keeping with Juniata's commitment to experiential learning, the college's study-abroad program is another of its crown jewels. It has developed thirty-three exchange programs with universities in sixteen countries, not only sending Juniata students and faculty abroad but also bringing international students and professors to campus, opening up opportunities for horizon-expanding learning and conversation. The exchange model also means that any student's financial aid travels with him or her; a student doesn't pay any more money to attend classes in Japan than she does to attend classes in Huntingdon (with the exception of a plane ticket). For students who need funding to help pay for travel, the college offers grant money.

It might be easy to assume Juniata's only strength is science. Not true. Education majors rave about how much time they get in classrooms long before they have to do their student teaching. Politics majors swear they have the most invigorating classes on campus. Students interested in digital media show off the college's digital media studio, where students create the majority of publications and videos for promoting the college and on-campus events.

Business and economics students brag about the Center for Entrepreneurial Leadership, which rewards students for developing businesses. The center offers loans, grants, and help for students developing business plans, and the college even owns a building—a former elementary school—that provides space for students to work.

But the most fanatical students might be in the theater department. In true Juniata fashion, the program is not what you might expect. There are only two theater professors; the rest of the teachers are professionals who come to campus for short periods of time—up to six or seven weeks—to provide intensive instruction. As a result, the program exposes students to a broad swath of artistic expression and skills: mime, circus arts, acting for the camera, improvisation, dance and movement, set design, lighting, costume design—the list goes on. "Students get to hone what kind of artist they are by the time they leave," says Kate Clarke, a theater professor. Plus, the department does a lot of "devised work"—new plays developed alongside students. "There are a lot of opportunities to create," Ms. Clarke adds. Her students nod eagerly.

Alumni have long been supportive of Juniata, thankful for the ways it vaulted them into lives more enriching than they could have dreamed as eighteen-year-olds. You might not find a more representative story than this one, from a 1992 graduate who was a first-generation college student. He's now a physician and playwright who produces plays that address issues raised during his life as a doctor.

He says he came to Juniata when he was seventeen and his family was "devastated emotionally and financially" by the death of his father at age forty. He chose Juniata because it was close to home and because it had an excellent med-school acceptance rate.

"What I had not expected," he says, "was the degree to which Juniata would change my life and enable me to make use of my grief." He credits the college, more than any other piece of his education or medical training, with teaching him skills he needs to deal with the "triumphs and tragedies" of his profession. "Because of my experience in theater at Juniata, I was better able to understand myself, my family, and my future patients. . . . I have no doubt in my mind that Juniata College forever changed my life and transformed me from a grieving adolescent into a medical doctor who has never forgotten the lessons learned in Huntingdon, Pennsylvania. I remain forever grateful to the mentoring and challenges that Juniata presented to me. I feel almost blessed to have found such an extraordinary place."

Marlboro College

Marlboro, Vermont

"You will find the Marlboro adventure far more intense and intellectually demanding than Harvard, any other Ivy, or Ivy clone. There simply is no comparison."

—LOREN POPE

At first glance, Marlboro looks like a homey, nurturing place in the country. Atop a hill near the artsy community of Brattleboro in southern Vermont, its three-hundred-acre campus looks out over the postcard-perfect Green Mountains. Many of Marlboro's white frame buildings were once barns, and its classrooms have the feel of one-room schoolhouses, well-crafted and simple. The whole place seems like a stop along the road less traveled (which is appropriate, given that one of the college's founders was Robert Frost's advisee at Amherst College).

But its looks are deceiving. Marlboro's academic program is rigorous. The college might look low-key, but that's because Marlboro has figured out something most universities in this country have not: The essential work of teaching and learning doesn't have to be fancy—in fact, it probably shouldn't be—but it does take a lot of energy and focus on the part of students and professors. The rest is just fluff.

Marlboro was founded in 1947 by World War II veterans who wanted to create a college where students learned "mind on mind." It's an apt description. The college has no core requirements; instead, its three hundred students sharpen their intellect and skills by following their curiosity and seeking guidance from professors. For their part, faculty members develop courses based on student interest and their own curiosity and research. The result is a lively, dynamic community of thinkers whose members push one another to explore.

After studying broadly the first two years, a student develops his own Plan of Concentration, an area of academic focus that almost always crosses disciplines. The student works with faculty advisers to create his plan, which often changes and deepens as the learning progresses, raising new questions and the need to explore new areas.

A completed plan comprises three parts: a paper (ranging from twenty pages to more than one hundred), a project (a creative work or original research experiment, for example), and an independent project (often a reflective piece to accompany the academic work, completed without any direct help from professors). The student must also pass an oral defense of his plan before he can graduate. His committee includes his faculty advisers plus an outside expert: a professor from another college, a scientist from a research lab, or maybe a playwright from New York. The outside examiner puts students and professors on the same side of the fence, since the examiner is evaluating the professors' efficacy as teachers and advisers.

The outside examiners often give better grades than do the Marlboro faculty. A Cornell professor says the plan he examined compared very favorably with the work of Cornell's top honors students in English. An MIT professor kicks it up a notch, saying that a senior physics student's knowledge of relativity was "greater than that of all but the rarest MIT graduate."

Part of the magic is in the college's sense of intellectual adventure. "Our curriculum supports the process of discovery," says Dr. Richard Glejzer, the college's dean of faculty. "We talk a lot among the faculty about that balance between flexibility and guidance, giving students room to explore but also giving them good advice for their future."

Most students say they came to Marlboro for the academic program. "It's exhilarating," says a junior from Nashville. Another woman, a senior working on a play about losing her mother, says, "The plan isn't just an academic accomplishment. It's an opportunity to explore something I care about. No matter what you're doing, it's driven by passion."

Whatever their plans, all Marlboro graduates have proved to themselves (and professors, who are "not easy graders," according to students) that they can define a problem, set clear limits on an area of inquiry, analyze the object of study, evaluate the result, and report thoughtfully on the outcome. No matter where they go from here—for 70 percent of them, it's graduate school—those skills will be integral to their success.

The academic program is a main attraction for faculty members too. Dean Glejzer acknowledges that the college asks a lot of its teachers; many of them are one-person "departments," though there's such a strong interdisciplinary focus that professors would find that description misleading. Professors say they love that the college leaves them room to explore right alongside students. "One has complete autonomy here. I have wide-ranging interests; I don't want to be someplace where I have to teach the same courses over and over again," says Dr. William Edelglass, a philosopher.

That's not a risk at Marlboro. Curiosity rules here, so as professors research in their fields and as their knowledge and interests grow, so do courses. And if a student can't find a course about a topic that interests her, she can request a tutorial, a one-on-one or small-group class that relies more heavily on students' independence in reading, researching, and analyzing. Tutorials often meet once a week for an hour or two to discuss the week's work; the rest is up to the student.

The only other graduation requirement—aside from completing the necessary number of credits—is the Clear Writing Requirement. Every student takes a writing-intensive course, a description that's misleading because almost every course at Marlboro involves writing. Every freshman must submit twenty pages of good, strong writing before the end of the year. Clear writing isn't just correct grammar and spelling; it's the ability to make and sustain an argument or idea, and it ensures that Marlboro graduates can think clearly and communicate well, hallmarks of a liberal arts education.

Despite the college's emphasis on self-directed learning and individual passion, Marlboro has the heart of a true community. Its founders provided for a self-governing community modeled on the New England town meeting. Everyone is on a first-name basis (even President Ellen McCulloch-Lovell is simply "Ellen"), and everyone has an equal vote. Once a month, the whole community gathers in the dining hall, a converted cow barn, to discuss campus business. The idea is to give students a sense of political agency, to reveal to them the power and responsibility of a citizen in a democracy.

And as in a democracy, the stakes are high. Students sit on faculty hiring committees, and each student gets a vote equal to each professor's. What's more, students sit on every faculty review committee; that means that when a professor is up for tenure or a promotion, students are part of every single conversation. "There's never a time in any meeting when the so-called grown-ups would say, 'All right, it's time for the students to leave.' We're full members in every sense," says a senior from Vermont.

Does it work? "It has the classic flaw of any democracy: the voters," says a senior from Virginia (who is studying political theory and biology). "There's a constant push to get people involved, but I love it." He adds that community governance has made him skeptical of "get out the vote" campaigns. "I'm more about 'get out the educated vote' campaigns. Anything less is a popularity contest."

So it's clear why the governance structure is so important here, and not just for the day-to-day management of the community. It develops citizens who understand the power and function (and dysfunction) of participatory government.

Students rave about it (notable because these students are not prone to bouts of sentimentality). "It's the reason I came," and "It's amazing," they say over and over again. "Even in seasons that are political, people want to talk. I suppose that could go badly, but we process as a community. At our core, we are a community that cares about each other," says a senior from Delaware.

It might seem strange to marry an academic program built on self-directed learning and a governance structure reliant on participation by the whole community. But both have to do with expectation, says President McCulloch-Lovell. "There's still a strong belief here that young people rise to expectation," she says. "We expect you to act like an adult and take responsibility for your education. Seniors tell me every year, 'My faculty expected more of me than I knew I could do.'"

Not surprisingly, there's a palpable sense of trust and of being engaged in a common enterprise, if one of infinite variety. Almost all of the campus buildings are open twenty-four hours a day, including the computer labs. Students swing by the dining hall at all hours to grab tea or coffee and cookies from the beloved cookie drawer. (Yes, a drawer full of cookies.) The campus is clearly students' second home; it's well worn and well loved.

The sense of intimacy on campus is boosted by the college's remote location. The students are self-reliant academically, but they're also in charge of their social lives in a way students on urban campuses aren't. The fun here is more creative, and nobody complains of boredom, though several students point out that it's important for prospective students to know that the campus is relatively isolated. "I think it's pretty awesome to look out my window and see Middle-earth past the edge of campus," says a junior from Santa Cruz, California, gesturing toward the mountains. "But there's no middle ground here, no pun intended. We're in a rural location, so that influences how we live. But we're not dull. This is a stimulating place."

The Outdoor Program—dubbed "the OP"—runs recreational trips that involve nearly any outdoor sport you can imagine: hiking, skiing, sea kayaking, caving, climbing, biking—the works—and several students who weren't "outdoorsy types" when they arrived on campus say they've learned to love spending time outdoors. And if you get an unquenchable hankering for a big city, Boston is a two-and-a-half-hour drive away, or you can take the train from Brattleboro to New York City, a four-hour ride.

As you might expect, students who are attracted to Marlboro come with a sense of adventure. Professor Tim Segar, a visual artist, came to Marlboro in 1999 from Amherst College, a very different place: "The students were much more straight-laced. They were traditional A makers. Teaching there was setting the table, and they would help themselves. I came here and learned to teach for a broader range of people," he says. "[Marlboro students] aren't dutiful executors of a set of prescribed actions, and I like that."

Students describe themselves as curious, engaged, unconventional, and comfortable. A gay student makes a point to add that the campus is a very safe place for GLBTQ students. But they are far more eager to talk about their teachers than about themselves. "Our professors are awesome," a junior says. "They are the best part of the school, no question." A senior laughs: "I took them home to meet my parents." It's true: He and a professor took a road trip to Virginia, where his parents live, to attend a conference. Every student talks about having dinner or tea with professors, inviting teachers to their apartments, or getting to know professors' families over dinner.

This camaraderie is partly a function of Marlboro's size: If you were to open a new liberal arts college today, you couldn't replicate Marlboro's model with two thousand students. It's an intentionally small venture, but you can still be a part of it: The college accepts about 88 percent of its applicants; it's a small, self-selected pool of students who want to be a part of this community. The middle 50 percent of them scored between 1140 and 1320 on their SATs and between 28 and 31 on their ACTs.

"We want the kinds of students who want to think, not focus on tests," said Nicole Curvin, the dean of admissions. To that end, Marlboro is test optional, so you don't have to send your SAT or ACT scores. But you should be able to explain why Marlboro appeals to you and express your sense of intellectual adventure.

That sense of possibility doesn't end at the admissions office. Professors embrace it too. "[A Marlboro education] is less about what you've done in the past and more about how you envision your future," says Martina Lantin, who teaches ceramics.

Case in point: Dr. Edelglass mentions a student he describes as "the best student of my life." She had flunked out of a much larger university and ended up at Marlboro because someone from her hometown had recommended it. "Somehow, in the smaller environment with much higher expectations for her work, more demanding teachers, a culture of taking pleasure in and caring about intellectual pursuits, this student flourished," he says. "In the next several years she went on to do the most sophisticated, high-level, original work in philosophy of any student I have ever had." This is not light praise. Dr. Edelglass says he has had "many excellent students" at Marlboro; at Emory, where he earned his PhD; at Colby; and while running a Tibetan studies program in India, where he taught students from Ivy League schools as well as many of the elite liberal arts colleges. The student became interested in the work of the chair of Dartmouth's philosophy department, who served as the outside examiner for her plan. He has since become an advocate for the student, who is now doing graduate work in philosophy.

Her story is dramatic but not surprising. Marlboro is a transformative place that turns out the essential leaven of democracy: bold, clear thinkers; people of vision and character. Quite simply, the college fulfills the promise of liberal education. President McCulloch-Lovell describes it perfectly: "We're small, but we have something to say to the rest of higher education." And if the rest of higher education would listen, it could learn a lot from this little college on a hill.

Ursinus College

Collegeville, Pennsylvania

"Ursinus is a star of the first magnitude in the small galaxy of colleges that change lives."

—LOREN POPE

Every rankings-obsessed student (and parent) should visit Ursinus College to understand why lists based on arbitrary formulas fall far short of expressing the value of a place.

Such lists can't capture the diversity of stories at a college like this one: Some students say they were very good high-school students who lacked imagination until professors challenged them to cut their own academic trails; others who were borderline in high school have blossomed under professors' care and mentorship. Still others had never been out of the country until they flew to Japan or Costa Rica to spend a semester, and those who were burned-out overachievers in high school fell in love with learning again on this wide-open campus. There are 1,750 students on campus, and each has his or her own tale of transformation.

"We don't attract that cookie-cutter student," says a senior business major. "You could look at our diversity statistics, but I just don't think you can get a sense for all the kinds of people who come here and really love it." Though most of the students come from the Northeast and Mid-Atlantic states, the student body represents thirty-five states and twelve countries; 20 percent are students of color.

The campus has an egalitarian vibe inherited from its forefathers. Members of the German Reformed Church, its founders established in 1869 a college for men who chose to follow the simple, "low church" style of worship. The college was named after Zacharias Ursinus, a sixteenth-century academic and theologian whose work defined this plain worship style. Women enrolled beginning in 1890.

Today the college's denominational ties are very loose, but Ursinus still lacks pomp and circumstance. It does a few things very well: teach the liberal arts; help students hone their independence; ignite passion for learning in those who arrive without it; and show students how their learning and their values connect.

As with many things, the component parts are simple; the implementation is where the magic happens. The college's strong liberal arts core begins with a yearlong, seminar-style course for freshmen called the Common Intellectual Experience (CIE). Sixteen students and a professor from any discipline read and discuss canonical texts, including the Bible and excerpts from works by Plato, Galileo, John Locke, and Karl Marx. The course invites students to use the texts to help answer three questions: What does it mean to be human? How should we live our lives? What is the universe and how do we fit into it?

"It gets heated," says a senior from Florida, who adds that he liked having "real discussion" because in high school there was never room for students to share their views. Other students say it builds intimacy among new students and gives everyone a basis of learning that they refer to during the rest of their time at Ursinus. "I still have professors saying, 'Remember the *Epic of Gilgamesh*?' or 'What would Locke say about this idea?'" says a junior from New Jersey. Because it's a required course, some students grumble, wishing they had more choice, but the vast majority say they are grateful for the intellectual and social benefits.

The faculty are even more enthusiastic. Professors from all departments take turns teaching CIE, and each term, CIE leaders meet once a week to discuss how best to teach. The CIE model makes it inevitable that professors will teach outside of their areas of expertise, giving teachers an excellent venue to model what it means to be a student. "It's hard to give up your mastery; it's exciting but also nerve-wracking," says Dr. Paul Stern, a political philosopher. "We take very seriously that it's an experience for students. We want them to think hard about how intellectual inquiry affects one's life, and the best way to teach that is to do it alongside them."

Japanese professor Dr. Matthew Mizenko, who went to Columbia University as an undergrad, makes this distinction: "At Columbia [which has a legendary core curriculum], the focus was on understanding texts, not what those texts had to say to us. It was a far more passive experience than the one our students have. The true end [here] is what wisdom we can garner from the text."

Ursinus shows a steady commitment to the liberal arts, requiring students to take classes across disciplines, and then it ups the ante. Every student must complete an Independent Learning Experience (ILE): independent research or a creative project, participation in a summer research project, study abroad, an internship, or student teaching. The spirit of the requirement is self-directed learning. A student must find and pursue a path to build confidence and an understanding of self. Socrates would approve.

The value goes beyond beefing up résumés. One senior says she has done two internships. The first, with an attorney practicing family law, was a bust. "I hated it, which answered my question about whether I should go to law school," she says. A year later, she got a summer internship working for Lockheed Martin's finance department; not only did she enjoy her work, but the company hired her to work once a week during the academic year. (The career-services office estimates that as many as a quarter of students get part-time jobs from their internships.)

A premed student interned in the orthopedic department at the University of Pennsylvania Hospital. "It was an incredible experience," he says. "I got to be in the OR pretty often, and I learned a lot not just about medicine but also about doctors' lives. Surgeons don't have a lot of time to spend with their families. It taught me so much about choices."

For students interested in research, Ursinus runs a thriving program called Summer Fellows. As many as one hundred students get stipends to stay on campus and conduct research with a faculty members. This intensive experience plus the richness of mentorship yields life-changing results. It's fairly common for these students to have their names on papers published in academic journals and to travel with their professors to professional conferences to present. With gleams in their eyes, professors mention how their undergrads are often mistaken for graduate students at these conferences.

Professors talk proudly about how dramatically their students grow in skills and in self-confidence in four years, how their aspirations rise, and how their perspectives broaden. The students see themselves in such a different and brighter light than when they arrived on campus that doing an internship abroad or joining in cutting-edge research seems like a logical next step. "If you would have told me the first day I got here that I'd do half of the stuff I've done here, I would have called you crazy," says a senior from New York. "But you grow confidence here. You look around and expect someone to be like, 'Your idea is crazy.' Instead they say, 'That's brilliant! Try it out. See what happens.'" Ursinus students learn to take calculated risks, a skill they'll use the rest of their lives.

Professors use words such as "awakening" and "igniting" to explain what happens to students. Some admit they only planned to stay a few years before moving on to a research university, but then something happened: They got hooked on seeing students blossom under their care. "There's an incredible sense of fulfillment, watching them change over four years," Dr. Mizenko says. How does it happen? Professors develop strong courses, set high expectations, give students tremendous support, and spend a lot of time advising their young scholars.

The dedication to teaching is legendary. Several students laugh when they mention that science professors, especially in the chemistry department, are notorious for sleeping in the labs or their offices if there's a snowstorm, so that they're available for students conducting research. Dr. Erec Smith, an Ursinus alumnus and English professor, knows the value of professors' commitment: "Everything I am as a scholar is due to professors who guided and encouraged me. They shaped my life. I want to give students the kind of experience I had here."

Students are eager for that interaction. They might have different academic and personal backgrounds, but they have a few excellent traits in common: civility, character, and an eagerness to learn. They're a happy band of young people, friendly and open, who give credit to their peers for creating a community where everyone feels comfortable. "Students are all-around great people," says a senior, echoing a common refrain.

They don't strike a visitor as demanding, but perhaps that's because they don't have to shout to be heard. President Bobby Fong, who began his service in 2011, sits in the student center for a few hours a week, and any student who wants to address an issue or ask a question is welcome to chat. Often there are lines of students waiting to speak to him—sometimes about complaints, but more often about ideas they have that might improve their experiences. "It's impressive," says a senior from New Jersey. "If you ask him a question or you have an idea, he follows up within about a week or less. He's actually listening." Without exception, when asked if they feel comfortable approaching a senior administrator about a problem, students, even first-years, say yes.

This egalitarian spirit shows up in subtle ways too. Every student is issued a laptop during freshman orientation and an upgrade at the start of junior year. If a student wants to take an extra credit hour—nineteen instead of eighteen—he won't pay more for it. Students studying abroad on an Ursinus-approved program take their financial aid with them, a policy that is expensive for the college but underscores Ursinus's commitment to making international study possible for all students. (In 2011 students could choose from sixty semester-long programs in forty countries.)

The admissions office embraces wholeheartedly the philosophy that Ursinus is a place for a wide swath of students. "We want people who want to learn; straight-A students might not necessarily be those people," says Richard Floyd, director of admission. "We look more closely for students who have their curiosity intact, and we really value character." The college accepts 60 percent of applicants. The middle 50 percent of admitted students scored between 24 and 29 on the ACT and between 1130 and 1330 on the SAT (critical reading and math), though the college is test optional, so you don't have to submit your scores if you think they're an inaccurate reflection of your ability. Instead of giving weight to standardized test scores, which are tenuous predictors of a student's potential, Ursinus asks every student to submit a second essay or a graded paper—which gives a much clearer view of a person's ability to think and reason. (If you're a strong and creative writer, you should also plan to submit part of your portfolio for the Creative Writing Award, a $30,000-per-year scholarship for "creative writers of outstanding originality and potential." The winner gets to live in the same dorm room once occupied by J. D. Salinger, who attended Ursinus for a short while.)

Even the college's 170-acre campus seems to embrace Ursinus's culture. The college's patchwork of buildings reflects different styles and eras in the college's history, but they all blend beautifully into a handsome landscape. The college's first building, a Romanesque structure built of Pennsylvania blue marble, still stands near the center of campus. Not far from it, the Berman Museum of Art shows off a new contemporary glass facade, a wing dedicated to storage and lecture space, and new galleries. And the college's impressive outdoor sculpture collection makes an enjoyable walk around campus even more pleasant.

It's a busy place: Rigor matters, and students mention that their workloads are significant. "The things I think are easy now would have overwhelmed me in high school," says a senior biology major. A junior on the premed track adds, "I like that it's not easy to get an A. It's good to know when you're performing your best and when your work isn't up to a high standard. I think that places where the grading is easy, the professors have kind of given up on the students. They stop seeing potential in them. That's not happening here."

But it's not all work. Ursinus students report having very good social lives. The calendar of campus activities is rich and varied, and for anyone who needs a big-city fix, Philadelphia is only twenty-five miles away. The college's performing and visual arts programs have grown in strength, reputation, and stature in the last decade or more, and college athletics are healthy here. Competition on the field (or court or pool) is vibrant but not dominant.

The magic that swirls around this place—magic that is actually very hard work performed by people who share a common vision—has garnered a lot of attention. Ursinus has a Phi Beta Kappa chapter, putting it among only 8 percent of colleges and universities that have chapters of the country's most prestigious academic honor society. It is one of forty schools that participate in the Watson Fellowship program, which awards one-year, $25,000 grants to graduating seniors for independent study and travel outside the United States. (Earlham, Hendrix, Lawrence, Reed, Rhodes, University of Puget Sound, and Whitman are also among this esteemed group.) And it's one of twenty-nine member colleges of Project Pericles, a nonprofit organization that works with colleges and universities to foster programs that bolster participatory citizenship and equip graduates to be leaders in a democratic society. The college is also part of the Annapolis Group, a consortium of 130 independent liberal arts colleges that share best practices and celebrate the value of liberal arts education.

The bottom line is that thought leaders in higher education look to Ursinus for examples of excellent work and great ideas. Ursinus doesn't have the resources that some other schools enjoy—its endowment is healthy but not gargantuan—but it has an enviable spirit of focus that is both rare and essential. Money can't buy the kind of devoted campus culture you'll find here.

Students feel it deeply. "I've grown to be the person I wanted to be," says a senior on the premed track. "I developed a ton because of support from my teachers, the tender loving care I've gotten. I don't want my name on anything, but when I become a doctor, I want to invest in this place like it has invested in me."

MID-ATLANTIC

Emory & Henry College

Emory, Virginia

"Emory & Henry is an extended family that uncovers unrealized talents, instills values, and develops the desire and ability to serve. It is a national asset. It has aspects of the parable of the talents since the well-known three [most prestigious and selective institutions in Virginia] turn out pretty much what they take in, whereas Emory & Henry doubles talents."

—LOREN POPE

Virginia has no shortage of familiar schools with robust reputations. But Emory & Henry, in the colorful hills of the state's southwest corner, does the finest job of them all of producing contributors to society.

The college's magic is no secret: Professors are pros at motivating students and developing talent. Classes are rigorous and small. Support is abundant. And the pervasive spirit on campus is generosity—of time, talent, and knowledge.

The result is a campus culture that exudes warmth and care for others. "We don't separate personal transformation from community transformation," says Dr. Rosalind Reichard, the college's president since 2006. "We're unique in that way. Many colleges educate students—very well, I might add—for the students' own benefit, and nothing more. But the culture here is deeply connected to the surrounding community. Students connect their learning with their service and vice versa."

Part of that connection is a function of the campus's geography. On the edge of a tiny village near the small town of Abington, E&H is in the heart of Appalachia. About 45 percent of its students come from within a 120-mile radius, and more than a quarter are the first in their families to go to college. The reality of life beyond this idyllic campus is not a mystery. A sophomore from Atlanta says, "We call Emory home, so even though I didn't grow up here, I care about what happens here. It's an interesting place with some serious challenges and really amazing people. I always want to care this much about the place I'm living."

Professors model the kind of service to others that distinguishes E&H. Dr. Reichard, who came here from Meredith College after years of teaching math at Elon University, sums it up: "I come from institutions where the faculty are really good, but the faculty here are the most dedicated I've ever worked with. The faculty and staff's relationships with students are stronger than anywhere I've been." If that's not endorsement enough, six of the college's professors have been named Virginia or U.S. Professor of the Year by the Carnegie Foundation for the Advancement of Teaching and the Council for Advancement and Support of Education. No other Virginia college or university has been so decorated.

To this top-notch faculty the college recently added a revised core curriculum that nearly guarantees that a student cannot graduate from E&H without being able to write well, think critically, and solve problems. It also helps freshmen understand how to perform well in college classes.

The first course, Transitions, is an introduction to the liberal arts for freshmen in the fall semester. Students choose from a range of courses, each of which focuses on one topic or problem: the global impact of Starbucks, what citizenship means in a scientific age, or what science has to say about paranormal phenomena. The focus is on critical thinking, research, and writing skills. Students describe their Transitions classes as "very cool," "more fun than I thought college would be," and "superhelpful."

The second course, required in the spring of freshman year, is Foundations—an introduction to fundamental questions asked by history's great thinkers. Professors emphasize critical thinking, a skill that often seems in short supply in the world. All students use the same core textbook, a collection of canonical readings with introductions written by E&H faculty. Discussions focus on ethics and knowledge.

During their remaining three years, students complete Great Works in Context, a multidisciplinary study of great works from literature, music, art, theater, and film; and Foundations II, a rollicking study of how people *know*, with a close look at the foundations of modern science and technology.

And finally, the college has launched Emory Across America, a creative way to introduce students to the social, economic, and political influences in great American cities. Students study a place and then travel to that place during the spring semester; a class on immigration policy treks to Philadelphia; a class on justice and leadership goes to D.C.

E&H's retention has jumped about 20 percentage points—to about 85 percent—since the college adopted the curriculum, suggesting that students value these courses and are better equipped for the challenges of upper-level classes.

One early spring morning, students in a Foundations class grapple with Aristotle's Golden Mean, the idea that virtue is found at a point between two polar opposites: gluttony and starvation, for example, or giving all one's money to the poor and hoarding wealth. "Do you have any questions about the reading?" Dr. Jack Wells, a historian, asks. "Yes!" a chorus of students chimes. Nobody seems to feel ashamed at not understanding all of Aristotle's dense writing. Instead, students are eager to sort it out—and before long, they have.

The discussion progresses into how Aristotle's definitions of moral living compare with those of Jesus of Nazareth, as expressed in the Sermon on the Mount. Then Dr. Wells breaks the class into three groups and asks them to evaluate a series of situations based on the Golden Mean. In one scenario, a student gets a check for fifty thousand dollars in the mail on the same day he receives a request for a donation to help the poor. One young man argues that Aristotle would say he shouldn't give any money to charity "because my parents are working themselves to the bone for me to get this education. That money should go to them."

This marriage between intellectual pursuit and real life makes Emory & Henry a vibrant, inspiring place. Students have a real sense that their education is not their own; it's a tool to make their slice of the world better—right now. "It feels like I'm doing something here, you know?" says a senior from Winston-Salem, North Carolina. "Not just checking off boxes and waiting it out. I'm actually learning and getting stronger intellectually, and then I go volunteer at the [on-campus] after-school program, and it's like I'm doing for those kids what my professors do for me."

The students are an empowered group, kind, funny, and thoughtful. "Imagine how awesome the world would be if everyone knew their own power to do good for someone else," a junior from "just down the road" says. The college fosters students' faith in their abilities by inviting students to sit on faculty hiring committees and other decision-making groups.

Of course, not all students arrive with the academic skills or social maturity to be stars on day one. Emory & Henry does a very good job supporting students who haven't hit their stride yet. The Powell Resource Center, the hub of student support on campus, houses Career Services, Counseling Services, and Academic Support Services. Unlike other places, where students barely mention the college's support services, students at E&H are quick to laud the PRC, where all services are free.

The center pairs struggling students with peer tutors who excel in an area. Note-taking help is available, often in the form of photocopies of notes from another student, arranged through the center. (The note taker gets a small fee for her work, but she never knows the identify of the peer who picks up her notes.) Students with learning disabilities work with the PRC to create a plan for accommodations, and workshops help students build study skills.

A sophomore from the D.C. area says the PRC was one reason he came to Emory & Henry. He was diagnosed with dyslexia as a high-school student and bounced between schools, home school, and the local community college, trying to find a good educational fit. "I was reading at a first-grade level in ninth grade. I never thought I'd go to college," the economics major says. "But now I have the resources I need to do well, and it turns out that I'm a pretty good student."

Emory & Henry is a place for all types of students. Academic whizzes will find plenty of challenge here, and late bloomers will find the support they need—and the motivation—to excel. (The middle 50 percent of admitted students have ACT scores between 20 and 26 or SAT scores between 910 and 1100—critical reading and math combined. They have solid B GPAs.) "We have people who come here well prepared and who never stumble. And we have students enroll who haven't yet hit their stride," says Dr. Celeste Gaia, chair of the psychology department. "And isn't that the point of college? To find your talents and develop them? We're very good at helping all kinds of students do that."

Dr. Jack Roper, a beloved history professor, offers two examples: The son of a school janitor came to Emory & Henry, got turned on academically, and headed to Duke Divinity School after graduation. Another, who was "painfully bashful," became the student body president and then enrolled at Princeton Divinity School.

And then there's Michael Lane. An alumnus and chemistry professor, Dr. Lane has a story representative of many students' lives. He grew up in rural Virginia with parents who hadn't finished college. He decided he wanted to study chemistry at E&H but didn't perform well on the placement test. "My professors told me, 'You'll have to work hard to make it through,'" he laughs. He did more than that: After earning his degree at E&H, Lane headed to Stanford, earned a PhD, and then worked in New York for several years. But he wanted to come back to his alma mater, to do for students what his professors (many of them now his colleagues) had done for him. "You're never alone at Emory," he says. "It's teaching, but it's also everything that happens outside of class. I listen to my students in lab; I listen to them in my office; I see them at events across campus. That's how it was for me, and it hasn't changed."

All this support and care propels students into service work—and right through the doors of the college's Appalachian Center for Community Service. The center arranges long- and short-term opportunities for students to give their time and talent to the college's neighbors. It also houses the Bonner Scholars Program: Eighty students spend eight hours a week at a volunteer site and two hours reflecting on their work—a component all of the Bonners laud as "essential" and "fantastic." In exchange, students get financial support that meets 100 percent of their demonstrated need. E&H's program is one of only twenty-seven in the country.

Bonner Scholars insist that they get much more than financial help. "I never knew you could be homeless and have a job," says one, a senior from Nashville. Another adds: "Before, I could say, 'That needs to be fixed.' Now I say, 'What's making that problem happen?'"

And in perhaps the finest summation of Emory & Henry's culture, another senior chimes in: "Seeing kindness in people can really change how you see yourself. Bonner opened my eyes to a nonselfish world."

Given this spirit of selflessness, perhaps it's not surprising that Emory & Henry students seem free from one of the common plights of college life, particularly in rural settings: "the bubble," that invisible force field that students credit for keeping them "stuck" on campus. But here, not a single student uses the term. Instead, students chat about their weekend service trips, their plans to go for a hike in the hills next weekend, or the nearby Barter Theatre, one of the last remaining professional resident repertory theaters in the country. Its support of E&H's theater department is legendary. (Theater majors take master classes and internships and enjoy mentoring from professional actors and directors.)

The campus's relative lack of typical boundaries is most evident in community service, of course, but also in its strong Outdoor

Program. E&H's location makes it a prime spot for anyone interested in "silent sports": hiking, backpacking, canoeing, kayaking, rock climbing, caving, cross-country skiing, and biking. The program is divided into two halves: The Adventure Program is open to any student, regardless of experience; many participants are first-timers. Students who choose to sharpen their hard and soft skills can apply to the Leadership Program, which trains them to lead their peers in outdoor adventures.

The Outdoor Program isn't just a recreational outlet; it's a prime educational tool. A sophomore says she tried out a paddling trip "just to do something I hadn't done before." She fell in love, came out of her shell, and is now a member of the Leadership Program. She is headed to the Amazon for three months in the summer as part of the prestigious National Outdoor Leadership School.

The program is run by Jim Harrison, who also teaches creative writing. "Emory & Henry leaves room for creative vision," Harrison says. "So when a writing professor suggested that the college launch an outdoor program, and that there would be some crossover skills from the academic realm to this world of physical and creative challenges, the college supported it."

Students agree that the program supplements their classroom learning. "We're problem solvers," says a senior. "We have to budget, communicate, think beyond the immediate situation. I can tell any employer exactly how I'll handle a crisis after standing in the middle of a downpour, in the middle of nowhere, with a group of people looking at me for guidance. I know my strengths."

His ability to reflect is indicative of the whole campus: Students here are keenly aware of their personal transformations. A theater and history major from North Carolina says, "I was the smart, quiet girl in high school. I let people walk all over me. Now I'm extroverted. I know that whatever I decide to do, I can do it."

Another student, a senior environmental studies major from Kentucky, says, "Before I got here, I believed in things, but I didn't really stand up for things. I'm from a coal region. I have had huge debates with my friends back home about complicated ideas, and I'm surprised by how much they don't know. We don't have to agree, but I've learned here not to accept ideas at face value. You've got to evaluate and examine things from a lot of angles. Emory taught me that."

E&H's measurable outcomes are impressive too. Within one year of graduating, approximately 40 percent of students are enrolled in graduate programs. They enroll in a wide range of programs; recent grads have gone to med school at the University of Virginia and Vanderbilt, the biochemistry program at Wake Forest, the mathematics program at the University of North Carolina at Chapel Hill, and law school at William & Mary. And these aren't just a handful of virtuosos. They're representative of a significant number of E&H alumni. What's more, the alumni give the college their heartiest endorsement: E&H ranks among the top 5 percent of all American colleges and universities in the percentage of alumni contributing annually.

Emory & Henry graduates future teachers and preachers, doctors and activists, professors and politicians. They go on to lead successful professional and personal lives. But Emory & Henry's real contribution is graduating young adults who go on to help *other people* live successful and happy lives. The college isn't just changing students' lives. It's changing communities' lives too.

Goucher College

Towson, Maryland

For students who are looking for a lively liberal arts college in a city and a campus where there's room for all kinds of people, Goucher is an ideal spot. It's close to Baltimore's northern boundary and within an hour's drive of Washington, D.C. (if the traffic cooperates), but a visitor driving into the campus enters another world: a hilly, idyllic, parklike spread of 287 acres.

It's a place rich with conversations about other places, thanks to Goucher's distinctive requirement that every student go abroad for at least one term. Its 1,500 students can choose from programs all over the world and can go during the three-week January term, in the summer, during a semester, or for a full year. The offerings are so rich—and the opportunities so enticing—that as many as 30 percent of students choose to go twice.

"My feeling is that it's impossible to be a well-educated person if you don't have some international exposure, perspective, context," says President Sandy Ungar, under whose leadership the requirement came to be. "In this era, you cannot really know how to solve problems, you cannot really have the broad perspective you need no matter what you're doing, without some touchstone outside the United States. . . . I just hope every Goucher student will have one idea, big or small, from overseas that might be helpful to American society, culture, government, what have you."

Students may choose from Goucher-sponsored programs, which are short-term options in the summer or January term, or a wide range of semester- or yearlong programs offered by other schools or third-party providers. If a student chooses a Goucher-sponsored program, her financial aid travels too—an enormous benefit—and every student gets a $1,200 voucher to offset expenses such as plane tickets, immunizations, and visas.

Before each Goucher-sponsored trip, students must take the corresponding semester-long course to build context and knowledge; these trips are the opposite of touristy, sightseeing jaunts. For example, one class learns about the history, politics, and science of HIV/AIDS in South Africa and dives into questions of access to health care, social stigma, poverty, and justice. Each student develops a research topic in the class and then conducts interviews with researchers, health professionals, activists, employees of AIDS orphanages, and others in South Africa during the three-week trip in January. Dr. Janet Shope, a sociologist, co-led a program to study HIV/AIDS in South Africa with one of Goucher's political scientists. "It was transformative for the students, but also for me," she says. "It was one of the most significant events in my professional life."

The college is still working on the best ways to integrate this requirement, passed in 2006, into the curriculum. Students are rhapsodic about the ways their individual experiences have influenced them but frequently mention that Goucher could find more ways to help students reflect on their time overseas and then apply their learning to the immediate community.

There's no question that students are wild about their experiences abroad. "I was skeptical about the requirement," says a senior from New York who went to Italy for a semester. "I was panicked a bit, but now I can't imagine not having gone abroad. I'm grateful. You come back a different person; you mature." A senior who went to South Africa on a Goucher program tied to the study of rural education adds, "The kids [I taught in South Africa] are the reason I want to get up and teach every morning for the rest of my life. I saw the reason for education in ways I had never thought about it before. My purpose is to empower kids so they can empower themselves." Students agree that the requirement deepens the culture and community on campus. "It's amazing to sit in a class and hear people talk about the university system in Denmark or the ways people communicate in social settings in China," says a senior majoring in international relations. "We all bring something unique to the discussion, and everyone else is interested."

Goucher is well positioned to make the most of these conversations; it is a liberal arts college of the first magnitude. Students have to fulfill specific distribution requirements so that no one can leave Goucher as a specialized ignoramus. Instead, Goucher graduates get a broad-based education that makes them nimble and creative, confident and capable of carving their own paths to success.

And unlike the prestige-driven schools, where the vast majority of students show up prepped for success, Goucher nurtures A students as well as B and even some late-blooming C students who show curiosity and eagerness to embrace all that Goucher offers. The college invites about 74 percent of applicants to enroll. The middle 50 percent of admitted students earned GPAs between 2.94 and 3.6 in high school. They scored between 1080 and 1310 on the SAT (critical reading and math) and 24 and 29 on the ACT. "We do a terrific job with the students who are a little rough around the edges," says Michael O'Leary, vice president for enrollment management. "We serve a wide range of students really well."

Professors agree. "Many of our students do not come here knowing how to do college. Maybe they don't have the work ethic or study skills or motivation," says Dr. George Greco, a chemist. "But the students we graduate in chemistry get just as good an experience as anyone who went to a top-flight school." (He would know: Dr. Greco earned his PhD at MIT.) "Goucher has excellent teaching at low levels and enrichment at upper levels." Dr. Shope agrees, adding, "The real pleasure is being witness to and participant in a student's new discovery—the discovery of passion. We do that well. There's a lot of room for ideas and connections here, and students respond powerfully to that exploration."

The faculty make the difference. They're concerned about

honing their craft and discovering new ways to teach students effectively. Small groups called "teaching partners" take turns observing each member in the classroom and then give feedback on the teacher's methods. Larger groups of professors—"teaching circles"—get together to share ideas about what works for their students and what doesn't. In the fall of 2011, many of them were engaged in a book-club conversation about *What the Best College Teachers Do*, a look at the ways professors best influence their students' learning. Even President Ungar teaches a Frontiers class, an introductory course for freshmen; having the college's most senior administrator in the classroom underscores the school's dedication to teaching.

Students respond to this devotion. "Here it goes way beyond professors being a voice in the classroom. It's about being a part of each other's lives," says a senior from Palo Alto, California. Another senior, who describes one education professor as "like my mom," adds, "They treat you like you are one of their own." A junior pipes up: "There's an e-mail in my in-box right now from a professor inviting our class to her house for a study break." With characteristic reasoned thinking, several students point out that not every professor is a rock star, but the majority are "gems."

Goucher also offers an array of support services that good students find as useful as do those who are struggling. One is a voluntary writing program to help students improve their skills to meet the writing proficiency requirements or perform better in other courses. More than one-third of the student body makes use of the Academic Center for Excellence (ACE); a lot of bright students discover in college that they don't know how to study effectively. The ACE not only helps those with learning problems but also conducts sessions on test-taking techniques, test anxiety, and time management. Sessions on meditation, yoga, and Reiki, plus a space for quiet contemplation, help students manage stress. You're almost as likely to see an A student at the center as you are a C student.

Another bright idea: Goucher assigns supplemental instructors— students who excel—to the toughest courses. These peer teachers give lectures and lead study sessions outside of class. Research shows that students learn better and more effectively in small groups than by working on their own. What's more, this option boosts the collaborative spirit on campus.

And for students who find inspiration (and perhaps motivation) in beauty, Goucher has one of the country's most impressive spots to study. The Athenaeum, completed in 2009, is an airy, contemporary space open 24-7 that pulses as the heart of campus life. It houses the new high-tech library, also open 24-7; an amphitheater; an art gallery; the student radio station; a café; classrooms and group study spaces; a workout room; and casual places for students to hang out, chat, and study.

The building gets its name from the ancient Greeks, whose Athenaeum attracted Athens's scholars and philosophers. It was the hub of intellectual, political, and cultural life—elements the Greeks might not have considered separate entities, as we tend to do today. And that's the point. "I think that the Athenaeum sets a tone of making it clear that intellectual life is related to cultural life, to social life, to serving the whole person. The library is not a separate destination; the library fits in with the exercise equipment and café," President Ungar says. The Athenaeum is a near-perfect embodiment of the kind of life inspired by the liberal arts.

Goucher students (only 17 percent of whom come from Maryland) strike a visitor as spunky, self-assured, friendly, and fiercely proud of their community. "They still have some verve, some individuality about them," President Ungar says. "They haven't taken on this idea that to succeed in your education or to succeed in life, there's a single set of characteristics that you have to have." Students describe themselves as eccentric, eclectic, open, and liberal. A few suggest that conservative students might not feel like they have a voice on campus, a sentiment echoed by dean of students Gail Edmonds. But everyone agrees that nobody bullies students who are right-leaning; they just won't find a lot of philosophical camaraderie.

To keep the conversation lively and the perspectives broad, Goucher hosts a noteworthy array of speakers and performing artists. Its proximity to Baltimore and D.C. makes it relatively easy to get guests to campus, and President Ungar, who had a long career in journalism before his gig as Goucher's leader, has made it his personal mission to give students first dibs on asking questions during the public forums that follows speakers' presentations. "Goucher has long been a place known for learning to write. I think it ought to also be a place where people learn to ask questions," he says, revealing a journalist's proclivity for smart inquiry. "I want students to be good on their feet."

Already, students feel comfortable in their skin—and on their campus. Their quality of life is great, they report. Classes are rigorous but not impossible. The food is good. Professors and senior administrators, including President Ungar, are available and eager to help. (The president holds several "open hours" sessions each semester, when anyone from the college community can swing by and chat about anything; no topic is off limits.)

A few "extras" add to Goucher's appeal. It is one of a small number of liberal arts colleges with a very strong dance program. For equestrians, the college maintains an on-campus riding facility with two full-care barns, indoor and outdoor riding rings, ten turnout paddocks, several riding fields, and acres of trails. And students are very pleased to point out that Goucher has no fraternities or sororities. As a loose alternative, it has thriving living-learning communities, groups of students who share a common interest—music, a foreign language, green living, or wellness, for example—and live together to explore that interest.

Freshmen get an intro-to-college course, Connections, which meets throughout the first semester to ease the transition to Goucher. The course is peer led—that is, taught by an upper-class student—and it covers such topics as the college's expectations of them, their own responsibilities, time management, study-abroad options, graduation requirements, and on-campus resources. First-years who want to get a jump on meeting their classmates can participate in Early-Immersion Programs. A few days before orientation begins, small groups of freshmen and an upper-class leader participate in adventures near campus to build friendship and foster learning.

All these individual pieces add up to a hopeful, vibrant community. Spend a day at Goucher, and you'll probably hear students and faculty say things like "You can be multiple things here" and "You can have it all at Goucher." The college is a place of possibility, a good spot to discover who you are, where you excel, and what you love to do.

Not all colleges offer Goucher's brand of nurturing—not even the places that the American public imagines to be the gold standards of higher education. Case in point: President Ungar earned his undergraduate degree at Harvard. "The world opened up to me at Harvard," he says. "I loved it. I was dazzled. . . . I got a very good education at Harvard. One of the reasons I did was that I was a pretty aggressive young guy, and if I wasn't getting what I needed, I reached out to people, and I had several faculty members who had a major influence on my intellectual life and my time there. But for those who were less aggressive . . . my wife, for example, who was at Radcliffe; she did not have this kind of ideal experience. She was not so aggressive about what she needed."

The difference at a place like Goucher—and indeed, all of the colleges in this book—is that you don't have to be aggressive to get what the college offers. "We will in many cases be aggressive on your behalf in order to make sure you're exposed to what you need," President Ungar says. Students make the point over and over again, with tales of professors who pulled them aside after class and encouraged them to submit papers to writing contests, apply for internships, consider taking another course in the department because they showed promise, or choose a particular study-abroad location that aligned with their passions.

A Goucher graduate has had a solid liberal education—better than she'd get from a prestigious university in many ways. What are these ways? Richness of experience from being an active participant in independent study or student-faculty research projects, seminars, and tutorials; from living and learning in a foreign country; from enjoying close relationships with teacher-scholars; and from being a contributing member of learning, not just a passive ear earning course credits. All these things add up to the crucial twenty-first-century ability to go ahead on one's own. The Goucher graduate has met the highest standards and has been the beneficiary of a superb faculty whose members love teaching and who take genuine interest in the individual student.

Lynchburg College

Lynchburg, Virginia

Lynchburg College is pretty place of 214 acres in the eastern foot-hills of the Blue Ridge Mountains. The college's buildings, most of them brick, show off the beautiful symmetry of Georgian architecture. ("This is what college is supposed to look like," a student boasts.) Adirondack chairs entice students to a midafternoon break, and the sprawling quad has seen more than a few pickup games of Ultimate Frisbee.

About 2,100 undergraduates and 550 graduate students fill the campus with verve and warmth. They come from thirty-seven states and nine foreign countries. Even though their campus looks like a Hollywood set, Lynchburg's students don't represent the typical private-college population: One-third of undergraduates are Pell eligible, and one in four is a first-generation college student.

What they like best about Lynchburg is the all-for-one-and-one-for-all esprit. "People here are all in," says a junior from Virginia. "If you're at Lynchburg, you're part of the family, and you get the full benefit of people paying attention to you. There's plenty of support to go around." An only child says, "I found the big family I always wanted here." It's no wonder that many students say they chose Lynchburg because they sensed the strength of community when they visited. "It just felt right" is a common sentiment.

If you feel the same way, here's some good news: Lynchburg accepts 89 percent of its applicants. Their average high-school GPA is 3.2—a solid B+—and the middle 50 percent scored between

920 and 1120 on the SAT (critical reading and math). Many students reveal that they were average high-school students who did only what they had to do to keep their parents and teachers off their backs. But they wondered what they were capable of accomplishing, and Lynchburg's nurturing environment has sparked their curiosity and confidence and nudged them toward higher aspirations. "This place taught me to like learning," says a sophomore accounting major. A classmate adds, "I wish high school had been more like Lynchburg because I would have been so much happier and more successful."

Virginia has no shortage of well-known schools. Several students mention that they got into places with more prestige— University of Virginia and Virginia Tech—but they couldn't resist the pull of this small, cheerful place. A few mention that they weren't admitted to the College of William and Mary or the state universities, but a year at Lynchburg persuaded them that the college was the right fit.

Lynchburg has more vocational majors, such as nursing, accounting, and sport management, than more traditional liberal arts colleges, and it lacks the interdisciplinary spirit that pervades other colleges in this book. But it has a solid core curriculum that requires students to study broadly. Specialization is secondary.

Students mention how grateful they are for the core requirements. "I needed someone to tell me that I had to take science, or I would have avoided it," says a senior English major. "But I ended up enjoying my science classes. Courses here are so different from high-school classes, it's worth being exposed to subjects again to see if you find your passion the second or third time around."

Professors express deep satisfaction in helping students discover their interests and talents, especially given how many students are first generation or come from families of modest means. "I enjoy that very few students feel entitled to this education," says Dr. Dan Lang, a political scientist. "They display an openness to learning and possibility, which makes teaching a real thrill. I've stayed [since 1984] because of the students."

These teachers make it clear that they're happy to work with students of varying abilities. No one will write you off if you're not producing brilliant papers or mind-boggling lab results on day one. "In some ways, our students are very ordinary, and yet I see again and again, we and they are very good at fulfilling their potential," says Dr. Richard Burke, an English professor. "This is a patient place. Growth and learning take time, and we stick with students as they grow." All the while, professors are very good at boosting students' aspirations, so that once a student hits one milestone, someone is there to say, "Good job. Now what if you aim higher?"

Professors, especially those who have taught at larger universities, point to the college's flexibility. "If we know something is good for a student, we make it happen," says Dr. Jan Stennette, dean of the School of Education and Human Development. "Other places are like factories, pushing students through the pipeline and pumping out teachers. I like that our education majors are exposed to our educational philosophy. We're nimble for them. We don't hold bureaucracy in high regard, and I think that empowers them to be problem solvers on behalf of their students when they become teachers."

The commitment to student engagement stretches all the way up to the college president's office—as it should. Dr. Kenneth Garren, an energetic former physics and math professor, has a sense of mission born of personal experience. The son of high-school dropouts, he realized that he could get a college education when his older brother earned scholarships. "It was a turning point in my life," President Garren says. "I suddenly saw that education was going to change our lives because schools were willing to invest in students. If I had a shot, I was going to make the most of it. That's the attitude we embrace here."

Students see the president all over campus. "He asks us about class and how we're doing. He wants to know if we're having any problems," says a junior from North Carolina, speaking for many of his classmates. President Garren celebrates students' victories—academic awards, fine-arts performances, and athletic championships alike—by inviting the participants to his home for a steak dinner. And students go wild for the "Hornet Hop," choreographed and performed by President Garren and his wife, both avid ball-room dancers.

The community and professors' commitment to students are sufficient reasons to look at Lynchburg, but the college has even more to offer. Every student has access to hands-on learning oppor-tunities through Experiential Learning Grants (ELGs), which waive the cost of up to three credit hours for internships, faculty-student research, study abroad, or community-based research dur-ing summer and winter programs (not the regular academic year). Best of all, every student can get an ELG each academic year. The college's goal is to see 100 percent of its students participate in activities that encourage learning outside of the classroom.

An excellent complement to the ELGs is the Claytor Nature Study Center, a 470-acre preserve twenty miles from campus. It has two lakes, wetlands, a milelong stretch of the Otter River, as well as grass and woodlands. In 2011, Lynchburg was in the pro-cess of transforming the preserve into an eco-friendly research hub, complete with facilities powered by solar energy. Claytor is already home to an astronomical observatory equipped with a twenty-inch, research-quality telescope whose optical design is identical to that of every major telescope in use today, including the Hubble Space Telescope. The center has spawned dozens of student-faculty re-search projects—all of them related to science and math—but it's also a prime spot for art students to find inspiration. The college continues to find ways to integrate the preserve's resources into other academic disciplines.

Anyone who has spent a lot of time on college campuses will be struck by Lynchburg's commitment to a broad spectrum of stu-dents. "Our job is to help all students grow," says Mari Normyle, assistant dean for academic and career services. That might as well be Lynchburg's motto. Some colleges work very well with specific populations—type-A high achievers or first-generation students or young adults with learning disabilities—but Lynchburg has a big-tent approach.

For high achievers looking for an extra challenge—and entering college with a 3.5 GPA and a 1200 SAT score (critical reading and math)—there's the Westover Honors Program. Westover Fellows take a core of honors courses, which fulfill most of the general-education requirements, and a series of interdisciplinary electives. Each Westover Fellow gets two advisers—one in his academic discipline, the other in the honors program—to expand his view of what's possible during and after college. And during senior year, each fellow conducts original research for a thesis, which he presents publicly.

Lynchburg also gets high marks from student athletes. The college competes at the NCAA Division III level, and it has a long tradition of winning championships. "I really like competing here," says a track athlete, speaking for several student athletes. "I have friends who run track and play ball other places, and they always feel pulled between academics and athletics. Here it's pretty seamless." Each team has a faculty mentor who cheers on the sidelines and serves as a liaison between the faculty and the athletics department. Students, faculty, administrators, and coaches understand sports' value and their proper place in the students' experience. Lynchburg doesn't have football—a common complaint among students—but they say they show up often for lacrosse, baseball, basketball, and soccer games. And there's plenty of room for athletes who don't compete at the varsity level: 70 percent of students play on a team, including intramurals and club sports.

For students with learning disabilities, Lynchburg is worth a look. Like most of the colleges in this book, it doesn't waive requirements for any student, but it makes accommodations that students need to succeed—and they do. Students with LDs return and graduate at rates equal to and sometimes higher than the general student population. "We're not a good fit for students who have not learned how to manage their own disabilities," says Dean Normyle. "But for those students who are resourceful and resilient, Lynchburg can be an excellent choice."

The college is also a good fit for anyone who wants to be involved. Students volunteer more than seventy thousand hours a year—an astounding sum—and the most enthusiastic about their experiences at Lynchburg are committed to service work, clubs, an athletic team, or any combination of extracurricular activities.

The total effect of all these different experiences is increased confidence and independence. Students at all stages in their college careers rave about the personal changes they see in themselves:

"I was always involved but kind of in the background. Now I take on opportunities whenever I see them."

"I was shy in high school. Westover Honors started me looking for ways to be involved. I've gone abroad twice and done National Model UN—things I never would have imagined myself doing. I've gotten more out of college than I've ever wanted."

"Everyone is on a level playing field here. We'll all just trying to do our best, and when a professor tells you that you've done a good job, you feel like you can take on anything."

"The best decision I've ever made was to come here. I'm the person I always wanted to be. I'm confident and excited about my life, and I do believe I can make a difference in one small part of the world."

Data from the Collegiate Learning Assessment (CLA) show that the college really does raise trajectories in the way students describe. The CLA uses open-ended questions to test a random sample of first-year students' and seniors' critical thinking, analytic reasoning, problem solving, and written communication skills to see what happens during the four years students spend at college. The CLA examiners compare results across a variety of four-year colleges to answer the question: Are students really learning anything?

Based on students' standardized test scores (generally from the SAT or ACT), the CLA predicts how well they'll perform on its exam. At Lynchburg between 2005 and 2011, the prediction has been accurate for freshmen. By senior year, on average, students outperformed the prediction by a full 20 percent, showing that Lynchburg's emphasis on teaching and liberal learning boosts students' abilities in the areas that matter significantly to their postcollege success.

Lynchburg also participates in the National Survey of Student Engagement (NSSE), which asks a random sample of freshmen and seniors how often they participate in activities that research shows boost learning. The college participated in the survey six times between 2001 and 2010, and the results show a solid boost in seniors' academic engagement over time—proof that the college is examining itself and striving to build on an already solid academic experience. The college also scored notably higher than its peer institutions on several key measures in the 2010 survey:

- 91 percent of seniors reported having a practicum, internship, or clinical assignment, compared with 75 percent of seniors at similar colleges.
- 88 percent reported doing community service, against 76 percent elsewhere.
- 80 percent said they had a culminating senior experience, compared with 64 percent at peer colleges.
- 42 percent said they worked on a research project with a faculty member, compared with 32 percent elsewhere.

The college is committed to this kind of assessment, even building some of its own measures to see where its curriculum is most effective and where it needs some sharpening. This devotion to constant improvement should hearten families who are looking for a place where faculty and staff take each student's learning seriously. Lynchburg's star will continue to rise—and with it the talents and aspirations of all its students.

McDaniel College

Westminster, Maryland

I f you're looking for a college free from pretense and full of genuine care, put McDaniel at the top of your list.

The college's 1,600 students from thirty-seven states and twenty-seven countries get ample help and inspiration from a team of professors who work together to boost students' talents and aspirations. The sense of camaraderie on campus is extraordinary.

The attractive 160-acre campus, about sixty miles from Washington, D.C., sits atop a prominence overlooking the little town of Westminster, and the second-story lounge area of its handsome library boasts one of the loveliest views on any campus, across a central Maryland farm and woodland vista to the Catoctin Mountains, site of the presidential retreat Camp David.

McDaniel was founded in 1867 to be a "creative and innovative liberal arts college," as the charter claimed. In the late nineteenth century, "radical" would have been more accurate, since it was the first coeducational school south of the Mason-Dixon Line and one of the few anywhere open to all, regardless of sex, color, race, religion, or ethnic origin.

It continues to be a place that serves a wide range of students very well. Teens from public and private schools and those who were home-schooled or educated overseas can find a place at McDaniel, if they're willing to make use of all the college offers in terms of both help and enrichment. The college accepts 79 percent of its applicants. The middle 50 percent of admitted students scored between 1040 and 1250 on the SAT (critical reading and math) and earned high-school GPAs between 3.07 and 3.8. And the college is particularly good at working with first-generation college students: 40 percent of the incoming classes in 2010 and 2011 were the first in their families to enroll in college.

What do they have in common? "Our students are willing to explore, with a little encouragement," says Dr. Gretchen McKay, an art historian. "They're eager but not supercompetitive." Adds Dr. Robert Kachur of the English department, "Our students are unpretentious. They're not posing. There's no one-upmanship. They're lovely people." This is a community of kind, earnest, unassuming students who realize they're getting a first-rate education and who regard their teachers as friends and mentors.

Students follow the McDaniel Plan, a curricular path marked by liberal arts guideposts that emphasize ways of thinking instead of particular disciplines. Students must hone their skills in areas including critical thinking, persuasive public speaking, cogent writing, and analytic reading, but they can choose from an extensive list of courses to build these skills. Chances are that no two McDaniel Plans are the same, and that's the point. Students are encouraged to explore and follow their curiosity, with a few nudges to take courses that the faculty believes are valuable no matter what a student chooses to study.

Freshmen begin with the First-Year Seminar (FYS). They choose from thematic courses taught by professors from all disciplines; these classes help students sharpen their critical-thinking, writing, and analytical skills for college-level work and learn about the kinds of resources McDaniel offers. Freshmen also take Introduction to College Writing, a priceless course that beefs up their writing skills and helps them break free from the formulaic writing patterns that tend to dominate high-school writing curricula.

In the second year, each student must take a Sophomore Interdisciplinary Study (SIS), a course that examines an idea or problem from multiple perspectives. The courses are team-taught by professors from different disciplines. "SIS is one of the places where you can see students really develop because many of them come in having a hard time making connections," says Dr. Debora Johnson-Ross. "At the beginning of the class, a student might not talk at all, but by the end of the course, he's got ideas just bubbling out of him. He's figured out what we're trying to develop in him, and it's exciting to see."

Juniors must complete the Junior Writing Experience in their major. Each department develops its own course to ensure that students understand how to write for that academic discipline. And seniors complete capstone courses in their majors, classes that help them synthesize and reflect on what they've learned.

Sprinkled through a student's four years are "critical inquiry" classes—courses on areas of knowledge that reflect different ways of thinking. These areas stretch across the natural sciences, social sciences, and humanities. Students must also take three classes in "global citizenship," defined as courses with multicultural or international emphases.

The McDaniel Plan is a good framework, but like curricula at other schools, its success hinges on professors' commitment, which is sky-high here. Students unanimously report that their teachers are accessible, creative, encouraging, patient, and dedicated.

And professors speak happily about how little bureaucracy they encounter when they want to try new courses or ideas. "We want our students to explore different things, but faculty get to explore too," says Dr. McKay. Dr. Bryn Upton, a historian, adds, "We have so much flexibility to do what we want to do. Elsewhere, history professors are stuck teaching the same two decades over and over." By comparison, McDaniel invites professors to innovate. When someone donated papers from a local celebrity to the college, Dr. Upton had an idea to create a January-term class that teaches students about archiving historical documents. Senior administrators were enthusiastic, and a class was born. This freedom sparks professors' creativity and curiosity, both invaluable for students.

McDaniel's faculty is also willing to try new techniques that might strengthen students' learning. Consider this example: Three professors created a course whose goal was to write the syllabus for a new class. They invited a small group of students who participated fully in creating the course. "Students really started to take ownership of their learning," says Dr. McKay, one of the participating professors. "They helped us evaluate readings and assignments, and it really made them consider how they learn best."

Dr. Sara Raley, a sociologist and participating professor in this create-a-class experiment, invited a student to participate who was quiet in her FYS. "Now I'm helping her prepare for graduate school. When I had her that first year, I never would have mapped out that future for her, but she has grown tremendously."

Dr. Mohamed Esa, a German professor, offers another illustration: He asks his students to submit questions for their upcoming exams. Each test is roughly half student-submitted questions. "The questions they ask are really tough," he says. "They show me what they've learned by posing the question. It makes them think about the material more carefully." Similarly, Dr. Upton requires his students to submit discussion questions for class ahead of time. "They get better and better at asking questions. That's important for research. You have to find the very best questions to drive your research."

The college is alive with a spirit of collaboration. The departmental turf wars that define faculty culture at other colleges don't happen here. Instead, professors dream up courses together, have impromptu discussions about pedagogy over lunch, and team up to help a student get into grad school or score a competitive internship. Dr. Kachur of the English department gave up a tenure-track job in the University of Massachusetts system to come to McDaniel because he wanted a place where professors all understood that their roles are first and foremost to be teachers and mentors. "People [at my other school] thought it was weird that I wanted to interact with students," he says. "Here, the atmosphere is so much what I yearned for. It's so collegial."

Students are effusive about their academic work and their professors:

"Individualized attention is really strong here."

"Professors take an interest in you, even if you're not the smartest person in class."

"Through relationships with professors and time in extracurriculars, I've gained confidence. I can do anything I want to try to do."

"McDaniel does a good job fostering personal growth of people—academic and social growth. I love that professors say, 'I heard about this great opportunity and you should check it out.'"

"Professors foster your development. They're very honest with you. I'm incredibly grateful. I feel like good things are going to happen for me because of what I've learned here."

"Professors know us well enough to know when something is not right."

"Professors are phenomenal. They want me to share ideas in class. We can debate them and still be friends at the end of class."

"I'm from Denver and couldn't go home for Thanksgiving. A professor I hadn't ever had class with invited me to Thanksgiving with his family. It was really nice."

Not a single student had anything less enthusiastic to say about the academic experience, regardless of background, major, or class year. It seems the professors have found a way to reach everyone.

These students will be delighted to discover, once they leave this attractive campus on a hill, that their education is even better than they had expected. This story from two former chemistry majors, who got engaged at McDaniel and then headed to Yale for PhDs, tells why: "I think the most important thing I learned at McDaniel is that I am capable of so much more than I ever thought I was. That is something you cannot learn just anywhere. The students and teachers helped me discover who I really could become," says the alumna. Once at Yale, she and her fiancé both discovered they were much better prepared than their classmates. At McDaniel, her fiancé says, "The course work is very comprehensive; rather than teaching about their own area of expertise, professors truly work on expanding their knowledge and ours. It definitely made taking the GRE a much easier task." The alums add that they had already been research collaborators with real professors and had published papers at McDaniel, whereas some of their classmates "had only helped green graduate students, and then only around the edges."

An alumna who went to medical school says she used two of the same textbooks there that she'd had at McDaniel. What's more, "I explained a lot of immunology to some of my classmates, and I [was] the chief dissector in our anatomy group. . . . I'm glad I showed up for classes, studied all the time, and did all those annoying problem sets, projects, papers, et cetera [at McDaniel]." The college "prepared me just as well as my peers who came from Harvard, Cornell, NYU, Columbia, et cetera."

The college's focus on students is woven into almost every aspect of campus life. Every first-year student is paired with a peer mentor, an upperclassman who has been hand-selected and trained to help freshmen adjust to college life. Peer mentors answer questions about campus, introduce new students to older students, guide freshmen to resources on campus that might help ease the transition to life away from home, and make students feel welcome.

The innovative New Parent Orientation program, launched in 2011, is another example of McDaniel's commitment to student success. In the summer, the college hosts a two-day session just for parents of incoming students. Parents attend sessions on campus safety, the wellness center, the classroom experience, technology, financial aid, student life—everything their students will encounter at McDaniel. Parents sleep in the dorms and leave with a binder full of information about McDaniel and the surrounding community. "We make sure parents get an education about everything we have to offer because it helps them better support their students," says dean of students Beth Gerl. "We can work together better when we have a shared knowledge base." If a parent can't afford to attend, the college has financial support available.

President Roger Casey, himself once a first-generation college student at a liberal arts college, is fierce about preserving the college's focus on educating and inspiring students. The college's expression of this commitment extends even to where the president works and lives: His home is at one end of the campus's main stretch, and his office is on the other—on the student center's first floor, not tucked away in an administrative building.

Students cite two main reasons for choosing McDaniel: the strong sense of community they felt here and the college's generous financial-aid awards. A football player who came to McDaniel, he says, because no one from his high school would be there, expresses surprise at how irresistible the community is. "If someone looks upset, even if I don't know them, I ask if they're okay. I even surprise myself. That's just how McDaniel works." Another student, a senior philosophy major, gives this powerful testimony: "My mom passed away from cancer last year. The support from this community was so strong that I didn't take a semester off. This is where I needed to be to heal."

Other students were attracted by the college's Honors Program. The top 10 percent of the incoming class is invited to apply, and students who "demonstrate academic promise" in their first semester can apply to join the program for their sophomore year. Honors students take two seminars in great Western works at the start of their college careers and complete several honors electives as part of the McDaniel Plan. Each participating student pursues an honors project in his or her major. Honors students live in suite-style dorms—to create a living-learning community—though some students, in and outside the program, say they feel that the separate housing causes an unnecessary rift in the student population.

The other most common complaint is a poor transportation system around Westminster and to D.C. and Baltimore, though students feel the college is working on a solution.

These hiccups aren't enough to dampen their fervor. Every student says he or she would choose McDaniel again without hesitation. They express hope and excitement about their futures and wonder at the changes they observe in themselves.

Professors think this optimism is right on. McDaniel is a safe place to discover who you are and who you want to be—not just professionally, but personally too. "People can fail here and then they can learn to succeed," says Dr. Herb Smith, a political scientist who has been at the college since 1972. "After they get past sophomore year, I'd measure our students against students anywhere."

SOUTH

Agnes Scott College

Decatur, Georgia

Agnes Scott is a college you have to see to believe.

It's not just a beautiful place—though its beauty will surprise you, no matter how many brick paths and expansive quads you've crossed in your hunt for the right-fit college. Its aura will lure you in, and everything you thought you knew about women's colleges will evaporate in the midst of this powerful and warm community.

All kinds of women come here: bold and timid, rich and poor, liberal and conservative, and especially those who are still figuring out their place in the world. What they all have in common is a passion to learn and the self-awareness to know that a women's college is the place where they will grow most.

It might be easy or tempting to stereotype the women who enroll at a single-sex college, and a few students even admit to supposing all of the women here would be raging feminists or social misfits, mousy nerds or girls who just couldn't get a date and gave up.

What they found instead are more than nine hundred smart,

feisty, kind women who welcome them into a community of sister-hood. Students come from forty-three states and thirty-seven coun-tries; 12 percent of the student body is international. More than a third are minorities, and almost half are Pell eligible. These demo-graphics prove that students at single-sex colleges aren't all the same—not even close. Here, students' most common trait is zeal for the ways their education influences their lives.

"You feel empowered as soon as you get into class," says a senior from Texas. A first-year put it another way: "With no guys here, the girls are really independent." The absence of male students, they say, helps them focus on their academic work, feel more comfort-able talking in class, and take on leadership roles. With uncanny frequency, students say, "I've found my voice here." Some describe themselves as very shy in high school; others say that Agnes Scott has tempered their tendency to talk too much. "I've learned that you can be outspoken and still show restraint," says a junior from Mem-phis. "We have hard discussions here, and we have them well."

A majority of "Scotties" say that they never intended to enroll at a women's college, but their visits swayed them. "I fell in love with everyone being so friendly," says a senior. A soccer player from Geor-gia says, "Everyone I met, I loved. The soccer players were so ambi-tious; it totally changed my perspective on what a college athlete should be." Those who shopped other women's colleges say they didn't find any that matched Agnes Scott's warmth and vibrancy.

Women rave about the freedom they feel to explore ideas and take risks, all in a community that feels safe and shares values. "This is a really open-minded place. If you want someone to tell you what to believe, you'll be disappointed," says a senior from upstate New York. That said, Agnes Scott is not flapping in the wind. It espouses certain values, and it expects students to abide by them.

The most explicit is honor. Agnes Scott's honor code is the foun-dation of its culture. It reads: "As a member of the student body of Agnes Scott College, I consider myself bound by honor to develop and uphold high standards of honesty and behavior; to strive for full intellectual and moral stature; to realize my social and academic responsibility in the community. To attain these ideals, I do therefore accept this Honor System as my way of life." Every student signs the honor code in a ceremony during new-student orientation, and the whole community recites the code at the opening convocation each academic year.

The rewards are sweet: Tests aren't proctored. Students even self-schedule final exams, which means they take them when they're ready within a stretch of several days. Better still, "you feel empowered when people trust you. The level of respect [among students and professors] is unlike anything I've known," says a first-year student. It's no surprise that professors have similar feelings. The honor code frees them from the time-consuming ridiculousness of making multiple versions of a test and policing students while they take their exams. "If you don't have honor inscribed on your heart, life is going to be a long haul," says Dr. Lerita Coleman Brown, a psychologist. Agnes Scott gives young women the chance to reflect on what it means to be honorable and then choose that path.

"This is an aim-high place," says President Elizabeth Kiss, PhD, whose sense of passion and mission is legendary among students and alumnae. "Agnes Scott has always been a place for smart women, for intellectually curious and ambitious women who don't necessarily have perfect SATs. Women who graduate from here know how to make a difference in the world. It's an essential part of what they learn."

Consider the college's mission statement, which President Kiss happily claims is the most beautiful in higher education: "Educating women to think deeply, live honorably, and engage the intellectual and social challenges of their times." The message here is clear: A person's intellect is bound to her values, and her values to her work.

Scotties test this theory all the time. Like Rhodes College in Memphis, Agnes Scott makes the most of its location, six miles from downtown Atlanta. For many years students have interned at the Centers for Disease Control and Prevention, which welcomes young scientists to join in cutting-edge research programs. Economists get opportunities at the Federal Reserve; budding business leaders at

Coca-Cola. Students interested in humanitarian work intern at the Carter Center, and those who want to learn about media and broadcasting get work at CNN. About two-thirds of Agnes Scott women do at least one internship before graduating. Atlanta is like the college's other campus.

Another bonus: Atlanta is teeming with colleges, which have formed a learning consortium called the Atlanta Regional Council for Higher Education (ARCHE) program. It allows cross-registration with any of the nineteen other colleges in the area. A student at Agnes Scott fills out a one-page application—the women are eager to point out how simple it is—and if room allows, she can take any class she likes: Arabic at Emory or a philosophy of technology class at Georgia Tech, for example.

Atlanta is also an ideal setting for a vibrant social life. The nearest subway stop is an easy five-minute walk from campus, and women say they take full advantage of the city and their neighboring colleges. (And men who are good at ratios realize where they ought to visit if they're eager to meet women. There's a running joke about the uncanny number of Agnes Scott–Georgia Tech marriages.) Nobody says she wishes the social scene were better. "We're not in the backwoods somewhere. You can focus on class, but when you're done, you can go have fun if you want it," says a junior from Georgia. "There are women here who are supersocial, and there are women who prefer not to go to parties. And whatever is your thing is fine with everyone else. We respect each other's choices." A senior adds: "I like that it's so serene here. You can go to a Tech or Emory party, but you get to come back here, and you don't have to deal with drunk frat boys."

The college feels both tucked away in a vibrant and charming community and influenced by its place in an urban center. Decatur is paradise for foodies; excellent independent restaurants line the town's central square—a ten-minute walk from campus—and attract diners from all over the metro area. "We like to say that Decatur's unofficial motto is 'There's a festival for that,' because the town is always celebrating something," says a senior. "It's great to walk a few minutes to be part of a festival where you see families and professors and members of the community all together."

While Decatur is attractive and desirable, Agnes Scott's campus is breathtaking. Collegiate Gothic architecture meets southern charm on its one hundred acres, where porch swings hang above wide, broad terraces on some of the residence halls and rocking chairs dot smaller porches. At one end of the library, a huge working fireplace warms the space on winter days and students settle in to an array of cozy study spaces. The new interdenominational chapel, the first in the college's history, has won architectural awards and is a place that practically begs passersby to stop and reflect on big questions.

Students testify to an exceptional quality of life. The college tends to the little things that help make living away from home more comfortable: Parking is cheap. Laundry is free. The food is good. A variety of housing options, including lofts for sophomores and juniors and apartments for seniors, gives students choice in how and where they want to live.

But more than anything, Scotties rave about the academic program, a robust liberal arts curriculum taught by professors who adore students. The feeling is mutual. When asked to describe their professors, a group of students beams—every single one of them. "They know us really well," says a senior. Her roommate adds: "I love how invested they are in us." Every student volunteers examples of ways her teachers have influenced her. They tell stories of how professors remembered work they had done years before, nominated them for awards or internships, invited them to their homes for dinner, and identified talents the women hadn't even seen in themselves. A junior from Idaho says, "High school didn't prepare me for Agnes Scott. My professor in my intro English class coached me through my writing. I couldn't tell you how many hours we spent together, and she never seemed irritated. She just knew I could do it, if someone took the time to teach me. Every professor is like that. I've grown so much as a student here." This woman recently returned from an internship with an NGO in India that served HIV/AIDS populations. "Agnes Scott gave me financial support. A professor recommended me, and it's all thanks to this college that I had the courage to apply. I learned I can change things for people right now."

Professors are equally ebullient. "The happiest day of my career was the day I got the job offer here," says Dr. Lock Rogers, a biologist who taught at the University of Florida, Lewis & Clark College, and Georgia Tech before landing at Agnes Scott. "I'm incredibly proud of the community and students here." Dr. James Diedrick, an English professor and the associate dean of the college, repeats a common refrain: "As a faculty member, you feel the extra energy here. Students are really motivated. The experience in the classroom is enriching and gratifying."

The absence of men has some significant benefits, professors say. "[Women here] don't defer work to someone else; they're staying with the challenge," says Dr. John Pilger, a biologist. Professors laud the collaborative spirit among students and their willingness to take risks. For example, "Being in studio is about being vulnerable and being safe," says Professor Nell Ruby, an artist. "To make mistakes at all can be hard for women between the ages of eighteen and twenty-two, especially when men are present to see them. But here, you get to perform making and fixing mistakes in a way that nurtures and helps you grow. Students here are so respectful of each other."

The college recently added majors in neuroscience, dance, economics and organizational management, and public health—a relative rarity in liberal arts colleges. It also offers several dual-degree, 3:2 programs with local universities, allowing students to earn two degrees in a compressed period of time, usually three years at Agnes Scott and two years at the other college or university: engineering with Georgia Tech, computer science with Emory, or nursing with Emory. In 2011 the college was working on a joint program with Emory's Rollins School of Public Health that would allow majors in public health to earn a BS from Agnes Scott and an MPH at Rollins in five years.

The benefit of these programs is the liberal arts foundation: Students don't specialize too early, so they learn about and solve problems using information and methods from a range of disciplines. (It's a philosophy right in line with Einstein's definition of genius: finding the invisible connections between things.)

On top of it all, Agnes Scott does an excellent job helping students financially. For the three years leading up to the 2011–2012 school year, the college kept increases in fees for tuition, room, and board below 3 percent, below the national average. The college meets 92 percent of demonstrated need, on average, and the average aid award was more than nineteen thousand dollars in 2011.

Given all of Agnes Scott's strengths, it's no wonder that alumnae are rabid devotees of the college. The alumni giving rate is just shy of 50 percent, ranking Agnes Scott in the top twenty or so colleges in the nation in alumni support. But even more valuable to the students is the moral and professional support they get from alumnae. More than at any college in this book—except maybe Wabash, a men's college in Indiana—students bring up how often they see graduates on campus or how often they meet alumnae who offer to answer questions about their fields and help them get internships. "I feel so good about my future because of the women I see walking around this campus five or even twenty-five years after they graduated," a junior says. "They know how hard we work, and they know the quality of education we're getting, and they know that we're honorable. They just want to help us move to the next step."

No doubt this enthusiasm comes from the value alumnae see in their Agnes Scott educations. The Higher Education Data Sharing Consortium, a group of private, four-year colleges that gather and share information to help with strategic planning, recently conducted a survey of Agnes Scott graduates from the 1950s to the 2000s. More than 97 percent of respondents said they were "generally satisfied" or "very satisfied" with the quality of their education. An astounding 99.4 percent said they were "generally satisfied" or "very satisfied" with the quality of teaching, and almost 98 percent with their contact with faculty. Career services scored the lowest— 54 percent said they were satisfied—but Agnes Scott has made strides to beef up its career counseling, and alumnae have played a big role in mentoring new graduates.

And the college keeps racking up accolades, which are especially impressive given its small size. Agnes Scott is ranked second of all American colleges and universities in per-capita production of economist PhDs. In 2009 two students won Goldwater Scholarships, a national award for outstanding math, science, and engineering students; coincidentally, Harvard, which has a student body more than seven times the size of Agnes Scott's, had the same number. And an alumnae survey of graduates from 2011 showed that 91 percent of students who applied to grad school were accepted.

None of the women interviewed seem surprised by their classmates' success. "Agnes is a place that challenges you to keep thinking and growing," says a junior from Georgia. "You're surrounded by people who say, 'Don't settle for that.' They challenge you to open yourself to new things."

That opportunity is available to women with a wide range of abilities. The college accepts 77 percent of applicants. These women have a mean GPA of 3.6, and the middle 50 percent score between 24 and 29 on the ACT and 1090 and 1300 on the SAT (critical reading and math combined). And if you think your test scores don't reflect your ability, you don't have to submit them. Agnes Scott is test optional, so you can interview with an admissions counselor or submit a graded writing sample instead.

If you decide to become a Scottie, you'll get an experience that will change your future. You'll have to be bold, because people perceive women's colleges as nostalgic or strange or single-minded, but don't let them dissuade you: Agnes Scott is a remarkable place, and if it's even on your long list of possible schools, visit. You'll leave a believer too.

Birmingham-Southern College

Birmingham, Alabama

The idea of liberal arts education in Alabama—much like in Texas—is a bit foreign. For a lot of folks here, the choice is either the University of Alabama or Auburn, and the college experience is defined by the craze of Alabama football rivalries.

As a result, Birmingham-Southern feels set apart—gloriously so, according to the people who belong to it. Students from Alabama feel like they've discovered "what college ought to be," as one junior says, "not what you see on TV. I love football, but if that's the highlight of your college years, I'd say that's pretty sad." Instead, she has stumbled from the upper half of a mediocre public high school to BSC, from ideas about being an accountant to the realization that she really wants to be a scientist, from seeing studying as an obligation to finding it thrilling. And she is not an outlier here.

As if in a Greek chorus, students sing the same mantra: BSC has shown them possibilities and boosted their aspirations. "You can't even imagine what you'll find at a college like this," says a sophomore. "You don't take anthropology in high school or photography or ancient religions. This place has totally blown up what I thought school was for. I could literally stay here forever and be happy." His parents might not agree, but at the very least, no doubt they—like the rest of his 1,500 classmates' families—appreciate the enthusiasm the college inspires.

This enthusiasm is even more notable in light of the college's recent history. In 2010 news broke that the college was in financial straits, after several years of overspending and mismanagement of financial-aid dollars. (The college awarded too much aid due to miscalculations.) The college tightened its belt, cutting staff, faculty, and several programs, and its former president resigned just weeks before the 2010–2011 school year started.

A lesser place—a place where people lacked a coherent vision of the college's purpose—would have floundered, grabbing recklessly at the hippest trend or flashiest fix. But the feeling at BSC is that the essence of its mission remains. "Faculty and staff are deeply committed to the learning experience of our students," says Provost Mark Schantz, PhD. "That never changed."

This kind of trial weeds out anyone who's not committed to an organization's mission. The vast majority of faculty and staff stayed on during the tough times—a kind of guarantee that they're devoted to the life of the college.

The morale on campus in the fall of 2011 was high, thanks in large part to the faculty who served as anchors and encouragers for students during a difficult year. "The faculty teamed up and lifted us out of the mess," says a senior economics major. "And now, I'd say the morale is better than it's ever been during my time here." The students sitting around him nod eagerly.

The college's new president probably has something to do with the campus's optimism. A former Marine Corps commandant— the highest-ranking officer in the Marine Corps and a member of the Joint Chiefs of Staff—General Charles C. Krulak is unlike any college president in the country. And that's probably a good thing.

Everyone calls him "the General," except for a few students who feel comfortable enough to call him "Poppy," as his grandchildren do. For his first year at BSC, he and his wife lived in an apartment for upperclassmen on campus. He takes no salary; he has no college-funded car; he has no contract, which is just how he likes it. When he is on campus, he holds office hours daily so students can talk about whatever is on their minds.

The General is just as willing to chat about a student's upcoming exam as he is about geopolitics. He spends hours a day walking around campus—in fact, you probably couldn't find another campus in the country where the president is as visible as the General is at BSC. There's even a new verb on campus: "to be Krulak-ed," a reflection of the frequency with which the General shows up at meetings or asks to join a conversation at lunch. "We like to be Krulak-ed," a student says. "It shows he's paying attention to us."

And his commitment to BSC runs deep. "This is a remarkable place. They just needed structure and financial savvy and to know that they were doing right," he says. The General's first act as president was to restructure the college's debt to reduce its payments, and he has proven to be a very able fund-raiser. "We can fix the financial problems, and we don't have problems of culture or commitment. I wouldn't want to lead a school that does."

He's right: Professors talk about teaching and students in ways that reveal how deeply they reflect on their work. "[A professor's] job is to convince every student that his or her discipline is the best," says Dr. Kathleen Greer Rossmann, an economist who now serves as the vice president for enrollment management. "It's a thrill when someone enjoys an article or idea as much as I do. To see them fall in love with what you love; how could anyone resist that?" Pamela Venz, an art professor, puts it this way: "My son is here, and he's learning to see the world as opportunities. We teach our students to find openings where other people see bricks."

Dr. Mark McClish, a religion professor, sounds much like professors at other colleges in this book: He was teaching at a huge state school and found it "incredibly frustrating," he says. "I couldn't get the students to respond to me. I couldn't get them to engage." At BSC, "the opportunity to be so involved in the lives of students is intoxicating. They expect to be challenged and to be changed by what we're studying. This [experience] is so alive to me."

Professors take pride in the amount of writing they assign and critical thinking they require. "I don't want a little me coming out of my class. I want them to learn to think for themselves," says Professor Venz. Her colleague, Dr. Mark Rupright, a physicist, adds: "In my department, we have to overcome the perception that physics is plugging variables into a formula. We force them to do peer discussion about current topics. They have to think much more widely than I did when I was an undergrad."

During the academic year that followed the news of BSC's financial woes, the faculty banded together to revise the curriculum. "We started with the question: What do we want our graduates to be able to do?" says Dr. Susan Hagen, associate provost and an English professor. The faculty landed on five outcomes that are the hallmarks of a high-quality liberal arts education: effective communication, creative problem solving, ease in engaging the social and political worlds, ability to connect classroom learning with problems and ideas in the wider world, and facility in self-directed teaching and learning. (You might rename this last one "transformation into lifelong learners.")

So instead of requiring students to take courses by discipline— two math classes, an English lit course, and so on—the new curriculum compels students to take courses that are designated by learning outcome. For example, students must take courses that teach quantitative skills—essential to being creative problem solvers—but a student could learn those skills in a statistics class, a math course, or even a social science course that's heavy on computation. "I'd say it's a very brave curriculum," says Dr. Schantz. "It emphasizes the marketplace of ideas. Faculty have to be entrepreneurial and student-focused, instead of assuming that their classes will be full simply because every freshman has to take English 101."

The curriculum emphasizes one of the college's long-standing assets: experiential learning in the form of independent studies, student-faculty research, service learning, and study away.

The clearest example of this commitment to experiential learning is the January Exploration Term, a four-week intensive term when each student takes one course. Professors design classes that include local field trips or take students to foreign countries: In 2012 the offerings included Nonviolence in India, Science and Culture of the Ancient Maya, Service Learning in Ghana, and Berlin and Prague: A Visual Performing Art. Students can intern full time for the month, getting an uninterrupted view of what it's like to work in a particular field, or design their own independent studies. The Student Government Association sets aside money for students who need to travel as part of their independent Exploration projects.

But students are quick to point out that opportunities abound year-round at BSC. There's the Harrison Honors Program, an intellectual adventure that offers interdisciplinary seminars for about twenty-five incoming students each year. Every Harrison Scholar does an interdisciplinary project outside his or her major senior year, funded by a small stipend for travel or other expenses. Best of all, Harrison Scholars don't have to be—and often aren't—perfect high-school students. "They're more the risk takers than the high achievers," says Dr. Hagen, who runs the program. This intel matters if you're interested in applying for the honors program, but it also reveals a little slice of BSC's mentality: You don't have to be the best student to find opportunity here, but when you do find it, you had better be ready to dive in.

A majority of students participate in community service, many of them through the Bunting Center, which coordinates BSC's service-learning program. The center "exists to make sure students don't forget they live in a real world with real-world challenges," says its director (and a BSC alumna), Kristin Harper. For thirty years, since long before service learning was the hot educational tool it is today, BSC has been pairing students with community partners. These nonprofits benefit from student work, but they also enrich students' formal learning—a cycle that pays dividends for everyone.

The college's neighborhood in Birmingham's West End is a perfect classroom for students interested in engaging real problems. It's an area with a higher crime rate than other parts of Birmingham; as a result, a wall surrounds campus and a guard staffs the main entrance.

But like their peers at Clark University in Worcester, Massachusetts, and Rhodes College in Memphis, students here feel strong connections to their neighborhood. A senior on the premed track says he plans to come back to the West End to practice medicine. "It has transformed my life to learn about this community.

They've challenged my perspectives on the world, and I've challenged theirs. I hate the fence around this school because it implies that we need to be protected from something evil out there. It's just the opposite. We need to engage more."

BSC fosters these kinds of reflections, especially about service and leadership. The college's Hess Center sponsors interdisciplinary courses that examine what leadership is and how it works, and the center's summer fellowship program in advocacy pairs students with nonprofits across the country. The fellows come back and run yearlong advocacy projects on campus. "We are always asking, 'How best do you participate in the communities that matter to you?'" says Dr. Kent Andersen, the center's director. "These conversations happen across campus. They're not strictly academic; they're not just coming out of the student development office. They're woven into this community."

With the General on campus, these conversations have reached fever pitch. He has enlisted the help of his friends and former colleagues to establish a leadership program that other colleges would trade their starting quarterbacks to provide. In its inaugural year, the program brought to campus headliners including Andrew Card, George W. Bush's chief of staff; Elisa Massimino, president and CEO of Human Rights First; and Fred Smith, chairman, president, and CEO of FedEx, among others. Speakers spend two days on campus, where they don't just give a keynote address and shake hands with the student-body president. At BSC, they eat every meal with students and teach as many as three classes. The goal: maximum exposure for students to the biggest and brightest thinkers in America.

All of these elements reflect one common theme: BSC's high expectations and hopes for its students. "People saw potential in me that I had never seen in myself," says a sophomore from California. "Faculty back me up when I mention that I might be interested in something. It's amazing to have someone say, 'You can do this.'" Her comment sparks a flurry of similar stories from a dozen students sitting near her. They all have examples of ways faculty, staff, and other students have encouraged them to reach for something that seemed impossible: a spot on a faculty research program, a competitive summer fellowship, the presidency of a fraternity or sorority, or an independent-study project that seemed too wild and risky to pursue. A biology major's favorite professor left for a lab in Helsinki and invited the student to join her during Exploration term. "It was a whole-self growth experience," the student says. The lab was so impressed, she got a stipend to return for the summer and conduct research that turned into her capstone research project.

Best of all, students admit that BSC has confounded their initial ideas about what they would study—a hallmark of a good liberal arts college. A senior student athlete who was at the top of his high-school class arrived at BCS with plans to become a lawyer. His freshman year, he enrolled in an Exploration-term course called Experiments in Intentional Christian Community. The class kindled an interest in Christian communities, which led him to Taizé in France, where, he says, he felt a call to ministry. "It's not overstating it to say BSC changed my life," he says.

A junior from Colorado Springs told about arriving premed, fulfilling the requirements, and interning at an inner-city hospital. An osteopathic surgeon told him to study something he loves, so much to his parents' chagrin, he declared his major in history. "I think it's okay to be unsure about what I want to do right now," he says. "I'm just now figuring out what my options are and what I'm interested in."

These switches are important because they show that liberal learning is alive and well at the college. Self-discovery—intellectual, spiritual, or otherwise—is invaluable and far too rare on college campuses where nobody ever nudges students toward new and unusual opportunities.

Students with a wide range of skills and preparation get access to BSC's opportunities. Unlike schools that define their goals by what others are doing or by how many spots they can jump up the latest rankings list, BSC looks at how to do its job better. And its job is to provide a top-notch, rigorous, nurturing education to all its students. "We're looking for potential," says Dr. Rossmann. "We're looking for future leaders, for academic engagement but not perfection, and for a commitment to the community." Birmingham-Southern accepts about 90 percent of its applicants; admitted students score between 24 and 30 on the ACT, and 1080 and 1300 on the SAT (critical reading and math).

It's clear that students come with a wide range of preparation and skills, and for the vast majority, BSC builds them up from where they begin to places they might never have imagined as eighteen-year-olds. Half of BSC graduates go to graduate or professional school. The college ranks first in Alabama in the number of students accepted to medical, dental, or health-related programs.

Of course, these stats matter because they demonstrate the efficacy of the teaching and learning at BSC, but the General has his own theory about the value of liberal learning that he'll share with you if you happen to get Krulak-ed during a visit: "Training is preparation for the expected. Education is preparation for the unexpected. If you want to do something for the world, get an education that's wide and deep. Get a liberal arts education."

Centre College

Danville, Kentucky

If you were to put do-it-yourself Marlboro at one end of the spectrum of high-quality colleges and life-of-the-mind St. John's with its Great Books and no-electives curriculum at the other, Centre would probably find its position appropriate to its name.

Centre students are bright, wholesome, polite, friendly and personable, eager to do well, and serious about what life holds for them. Intellectually curious, they take many courses outside of their majors, and they are willing to take notoriously tough courses for the sheer joy of satisfying their curiosity, even at the peril of their GPAs. They are neither future pundits nor revolutionaries. For the most part, they might be called the intelligent and responsible (and very engaging) center.

The college's 1,300 students come from forty-four states and nine foreign countries, though about half of the population comes from Kentucky because Centre is the state's leading academic institution. The college has seen growth in its number of students of color, who now make up 16 percent of the population.

Walking around Centre's beautiful campus, whose majestic trees look like they have been there since the college was founded in 1819, you might imagine a community twice the size. At one end of its architectural spectrum are historic landmarks from the 1800s. At the other, more modern end is a lovely structure that Centre claims is the finest arts center in the nation for a college of its size; indeed, a university would be proud to have it. Taliesin

Associated Architects, the firm of Frank Lloyd Wright's students, designed it. In the first decade of the new millennium, Centre invested one hundred million dollars in new and renovated facilities, all to improve resources and the quality of life of students and faculty.

Despite its all-American good looks, Centre is an international hub, thanks to its flourishing study-abroad program: 85 percent of Centre students go abroad at least once, and it's easy to find students who have been twice or three times. The college ranks third in the country in the percentage of students it sends abroad.

Students choose from semester- or yearlong programs in London; Strasbourg, France; Mérida, Mexico; Shanghai; Glasgow, Scotland; Yamaguchi, Japan; and Lleida, Spain. They may also participate in a semester-long internship program in Washington, D.C. The college also offers an ever-changing array of courses designed and led by professors during CentreTerm—the college's January term. And although more than 95 percent of students who go abroad choose one of Centre's offerings, students who want something different can choose from programs organized by third-party providers.

Faculty and students are fanatical about the ways these experiences contribute to the individual and the campus culture. "When they return, they enrich the classroom in different ways. They bring enlightenment back. They bring maturity back," says Dr. Beth Glazier-McDonald, a religion professor and associate dean of the college. "We bring the world on campus to the students in the things we teach and the arts on college. But we also send our students out into the world. That creates a fuller experience." Dr. Peggy Richey, a biologist, points out, "We have buy-in from the whole campus. We tell our premed students, 'Go! Now's the time.' They come back with such deeper perspectives on the world and their work in it that I believe this experience is invaluable." Juniata and Kalamazoo might be the only other places with such a strong commitment to sending science students abroad for a full term.

A senior double majoring in economics and French speaks for his classmates: "Study abroad really gives people the worldly perspective on things. Everyone is trying to reach out to other cultures and see what the rest of the world is like. It makes classes ten, a hundred, times more interesting. We teach each other." Other Centre students offer other paeans "It made me feel like I can do anything. "It was the best four months of my life. "Even though we're in a town of fifteen thousand in central Kentucky, people really do know what's going on in the world."

For all Centre programs, a student's cost is the same as it would be in Danville, except for a round-trip airplane ticket. If that cost is too hefty for a student's family, the college has a special fund that pays for it. Centre even covers the cost of a passport for any student who arrives on campus without one. "No one can look me in the eye and say, 'I didn't study abroad at Centre because I couldn't afford it,'" says Dr. Milton Reigelman, director of the college's Center for Global Citizenship.

Professors aren't just enthusiastic about study abroad because they see changes in their students. Centre actively encourages them to create new CentreTerm courses each year, all over the world. Handsome grants from the Andrew W. Mellon and the Arthur Vining Davis foundations fund faculty visits to new places that might serve as good sites for these short-term trips. Dr. Brian Cusato, a neuroscientist, says, "I was somewhat skeptical until I taught a term abroad. Now, every other year, I lead a class in the study of primate behavior in Barbados. The first couple days we're there, we teach students methods of field research. We collect data on the troupes of monkeys and their movement. The last two weeks, they're doing their own field research. They're just so much more focused on the material. Taking students off campus eliminates distractions. They're great in class; they're even better in the field."

In the country and outside it, Centre's faculty—as can be said of the faculty at other colleges in this book—are earnestly committed to and excel at the art of teaching. It is obvious that they like the students and enjoy working with them. Moreover, there is an unusual sense of community and mutual regard not only among the faculty members but between the faculty and administration as well, which is a rarity. Professors who've been at the most famous universities say they've never experienced the kind of collegiality they enjoy at Centre.

No university faculty compares with Centre's in the impact it has on the growth of young minds and personalities. A full 97 percent of Centre's teachers hold PhDs or terminal degrees in their fields, and they are active scholars. They not only publish, but they also draw students into their research as coauthors and often take them to professional meetings.

A senior who designed his own major in East Asian studies said his Centre career "started off with a bang" when his freshman adviser invited him to collaborate on research about Japanese-African relations in the prewar period. In his sophomore year the student studied in Japan, where he conducted additional research with help from his Centre adviser, and then they coauthored two academic articles. "My relationship with my adviser is not atypical," the student says. "I can think of ten or fifteen people off the top of my head who would tell you similar stories."

Professors are believers in the power of research as an educational tool. When Dr. Glazier-McDonald, a scholar of the Hebrew Bible and biblical literature, got a call from an antiquities collector looking for someone to translate ancient amulets, she welcomed the chance. The college bought three of the amulets—texts written on lead, rolled up, and placed in a casing—and launched an interdisciplinary project: A chemistry professor helped a group of students unroll one of the college's amulets so religion professors and students could translate it with help from a specialist from Yale (which, by the way, has only one of these distinctive amulets to Centre's three).

This bright interdisciplinary spirit is a Centre hallmark. The life-sciences building, expanded and renovated in 2010, houses biology, psychology, biochemistry, and half of the chemistry program to encourage cross-disciplinary brainstorms. "It's really geared toward collaborations among faculty and between professors and students," says Dr. Richey of the biology department. "It's everything we hoped for because faculty and students gave input and feedback on the design." All across campus, faculty offices aren't separated by discipline—political scientists in that corner, literature gurus down that hallway. Instead, most of the social science and humanities professors have their offices together on the fourth floor of the library, which makes impromptu chats easy.

Students give professors high marks. "They're phenomenal," says a junior who designed her own major in Middle Eastern studies. "They've made my Centre experience what it is, helping me analyze all the different options that are available to me, helping me make the best decision." The Student Government Association (SGA) president says he and his adviser went out for ice cream before winter break "and talked for two hours about life and graduate school, jobs I'm applying to, a lot of things that aren't academic." A senior majoring in international studies adds, "I love it because professors get to know you, and they say things very frankly. They're honest with you. Because you have a real relationship and they know you, you don't get offended. The fact that I'm still here shows that professors actually care. They said, 'Change a few things and you can bounce back,' and now I'm one of the top students in my program."

Bouncing back is almost an intramural sport here. Centre attracts very good high-school students: It accepts 67 percent of applicants, and the middle 50 percent of enrolled students scored between 26 and 31 on the ACT and 1140 and 1350 on the SAT (critical reading and math). Their average high-school GPA was about 3.6.

Students quickly learn that the college requires a different kind of work than they did in high school. "I went to an IB [International Baccalaureate] magnet school in high school, and I thought I had gone through the hard school thing," the SGA president says. "I got the worst grades of my life my first semester. I thought a small school in Kentucky would be pretty easy. I was wrong." His story is hardly unique.

From the start, professors ask students to draw on what they've learned in other classes. The emphasis is on examining and integrating information and finding the unanswered questions and developing ways to answer them. "Classes are intense," says a junior, "but people are excited to wake up every day and go to class and learn. At Centre, you don't encounter that feeling of compulsory learning."

Students are delighted to be at a place where nobody is slacking off. So are professors. "They're all going to read the book if you tell them to read the book. That really changes what you can do in class," Dr. Cusato says. "Now you're not teaching the basics of a subject. You can go three steps beyond the textbook. You can get at the bridges they're building from other classes they're taking. That elevates the discourse, and it's much more exciting to be in class. We ask them to do things that perhaps a professor at a large university wouldn't ask them to do."

But it's not all work. Students boast about their high quality of life on a campus full of activities. "I was worried about coming to a small town, but there is more going on [on campus] than you ever have time to do," says a senior. Students frequently describe themselves and their peers as "overcommitted" or "overinvolved." Service is a big deal—more than 80 percent of students volunteer in a single semester—and so is the Greek system, though everyone in a random sampling of affiliated and independent students says there's no social tension between Greek and unaffiliated students.

They express deep appreciation for their classmates. Despite their shared intellectual prowess and eagerness to learn, they're not all alike. An openly gay student says, "Centre is an accepting place. That doesn't mean we all agree. At Centre, you're going to meet people with different values. There's a Queers and Allies meeting, and right next door is a women's Bible study." A senior who had her pick of brand-name colleges says, "There's a real diversity of opinions and beliefs, conservatives to liberals, atheists to the devoutly religious. At some schools I toured, I got the impression that the student body was very privileged. That's not the impression that you get at Centre at all. It's a very loving and open environment."

Another senior pipes up: "Being a minority and considering a small college can be tough. When you look at Centre's price tag, and you look at the brochures and see a white population, you think this is going to be uppity central. It's not. You realize fast that everyone comes from a different background, not everyone has a silver spoon. If you dig into the campus community, you find that everyone has a different story."

It's no wonder 92 percent of freshmen return for sophomore year—beating the national average for four-year private baccalaureate colleges by 23 percentage points—and 85 percent of students graduate in four years, putting Centre squarely in the company of the big-name private colleges. But it has a price tag several thousand dollars below these peers: In 2011, the average freshman got $27,500 in aid (toward a comprehensive cost of $42,500), and 90 percent of students get need-based aid, merit awards, or both.

Alumni are satisfied customers when they leave and for many years after: Centre's alumni giving rate is about 55 percent annually, among the ten highest in the country. What's more, more than half of Centre parents give to the college—beyond their tuition payments.

Why they give is apparent in the results of the National Survey of Student Engagement, which randomly surveys students about high-impact educational practices at colleges across the country. Centre outperforms its peers and benchmark institutions in each of the five categories tested: Level of Academic Challenge, Active and Collaborative Learning, Student-Faculty Interaction, Enriching Educational Experiences, and Supportive Campus Environment. The college publishes all of its results online—a relative rarity—so prospective students and their families can delve into the impressive details.

But if reading spreadsheets isn't your thing, a visit with Centre students will tell you just as much about the college's efficacy. "Centre looks great on paper, but it's even better when you get here," a senior says. "I was skeptical. I thought it looked too good to be true. Everything is here; you just have to take advantage of it."

A laconic philosophy major opened up when asked if Centre has spurred changes in him: "Yes. I'm not really a schmaltzy person, so take that very seriously. In one sense, the change has been what the academic program has done for me. Thinking back to myself graduating from high school, I was a pretty successful student, but I'm much wiser now, I'm much more thoughtful. I know I'm young, but the kind of thinking that Centre professors and classes make you do helps you grow intellectually and personally a lot. I'm very thankful for it."

Centre is a quiet powerhouse, a place that even top administrators find magical. You can find the component parts elsewhere, but you'll have a harder time finding the special alchemy that pulls the pieces together and has such a profound effect on students' lives.

A bubbly junior who has been to Shanghai, Turkey, Vietnam, and Cambodia and who has designed her own major sums it up: "Everyone should know about Centre. Open your minds beyond the stereotype of a small school in the South. The creativity and flexibility and encouragement the school gives you to craft your experience—it's indescribable. It can be as fantastic as you want it to be. I hadn't expected it to be so supportive. Whatever it means to get the most out of your undergrad experience, Centre can make that happen."

Eckerd College

St. Petersburg, Florida

On a sunny, lush plot of land on Florida's Gulf Coast, Eckerd College might seem like the perfect spot for an easy college career, four years marked by sun, surf, and sand. But if you're looking for a vacation, you should enroll elsewhere.

In its short fifty-plus-year life, Eckerd has established itself as a little college that could—a place where a B student in high school could develop his potential as a thinker, problem solver, dreamer, and adventurer under the guidance of a faculty and staff as caring and creative as any in the country.

Eckerd puts a premium on mentorship, so much so that faculty cannot get tenure without an obvious commitment to mentoring students. At the vast majority of American universities, tenure review committees care about research first; teaching comes in a distant second. But at Eckerd, the commitment to student growth is so significant, faculty invest not just in students' academic learning but also in the development of them as whole people. The value of this kind of investment cannot be understated. It is life-changing.

Students call the professors who are academic advisers "mentors," and everyone has stories about mentors and professors going beyond the call of duty to help a student. "My freshman year, I e-mailed a professor at ten p.m. because I had procrastinated, and I realized the night before my paper was due that I needed some help. He called me five minutes later," a senior from Nashville says. A senior from Orlando told of her sudden medical leave because of heart problems sophomore year. "I had just chosen my mentor for my major, and she didn't know me well, but she went to all of my professors and had everyone sign my withdrawal card. She handled all of the college-related stuff so I could focus on getting better." Thanks to her mentor's support, this young woman graduated on time.

Beyond their affection for students, faculty share an obvious fondness for one another, which is good news for students: The more collaborative the faculty, the more innovative they're likely to be when dreaming up cross-curricular learning opportunities, and the more able they are to serve students. "My colleagues are fantastic," says Dr. David Hastings, who teaches marine science and chemistry. Adds Dr. Kelly Debure, professor of computer science, "There's something remarkable about Eckerd, about the level of collaboration among professors and students. I would not want to teach anywhere else."

Perhaps because of its youth, Eckerd hums with a spirit of innovation. It was a pioneer of the 4-1-4 calendar (four classes in the fall, one during a January term, and four in the spring), now used by many colleges. Its 1,800 students have considerable power and responsibility for campus life. "We get to decide almost everything on campus, at least the things related to how we live together," says a junior from Portland, Oregon. "We self-govern in a lot of ways, so we don't have administrators stomping around enforcing a bunch of rules we hate. It's really great to be trusted like that." (A simple example: Students staff the Pet Council, which oversees policies in the college's popular pet-friendly dorms.)

And in a flurry of brilliance, Eckerd long ago dreamed up Autumn Term for freshmen. Three weeks before their upper-class peers come back, freshmen arrive on campus and take a one-course introduction to college-level thinking. A student's Autumn Term professor becomes her first mentor and her professor in the Western Heritage in a Global Context course, a yearlong course that requires students to consider how human beings have known and expressed truth. The class reads a range of Western and non-Western works (from Homer to Dave Eggers's *What Is the What*, about the lost boys of Sudan, for example) to fuel their learning.

The bookend to Western Heritage is the capstone Quest for Meaning, required in the fall of senior year. Through a combination of readings, lectures from various faculty, self-reflective writing, and a forty-hour community-service project, each student thinks about his purpose in life and his responsibilities to himself and his community. Second-semester seniors and alumni talk eagerly about the course's seminal project: an essay and presentation called "This I Believe," in which students have to write and then present their own beliefs in the context of the books and essays they've read in class. "It rocks you," says a senior from Atlanta. "Nobody until that point in my life had asked me to write down precisely what I believe and why. Do you know how hard that is? I hated it, and then I loved it."

A string of other innovations shows off the college's student-centered culture: Professors' offices open onto sidewalks, encouraging students to pop in to chat about academic work or life outside of class. The Freshman Research Associate Program funds about twenty first-year students who want to collaborate with professors on their research. And as students make their way through their college careers, each builds a cocurricular transcript that notes leadership, volunteer work, sports activities, and involvement in clubs. The transcript can supplement applications to grad school, fellowships, and employment to give a broader description of the student.

And then there's the Academy of Senior Professionals at Eckerd College (ASPEC), which gives depth and nuance to this community of young scholars. ASPEC is a group of distinguished retirees with its own intellectual life, rife with forums, speakers, and events. But members of the group also contribute to college classes by participating in lectures and discussions. For students pursuing jobs or internships, ASPEC members conduct mock interviews, review résumés, and put students in touch with former colleagues. One student calls them "surrogate grandparents." Another says,

"I totally owe my internship to a woman from ASPEC who's been mentoring me."

Outside the classroom, Eckerd does just as fine a job focusing on the whole person. The most obvious example is the college's emphasis on studying abroad. As many as 60 percent of students leave the country for a term or more. The 4-1-4 calendar allows students who have particularly tight schedules—like those on the premed track or double majoring—to leave for the monthlong January term. Others, who have looser schedules, tend to go abroad several times. "It's just part of what you do here," says a junior who spent a semester in China and a January term in Eastern Europe. "Everybody's talking about it, and your mentors are asking, 'Where are you going? What's interesting to you?' When you come back [to campus], you just feel so much stronger and interesting—and you're more interested in other people's experiences too."

While they're on campus, students benefit from Eckerd's impressive Waterfront Program, a blend of educational and recreational activities that help Eckerd embrace its beachy locale. The Activities Center is well stocked with wakeboards, water skis, canoes, kayaks, fishing equipment, and a fleet of boats—everything a young adult needs to burn off some stress in the Florida sun. There are twice-daily water-ski and wakeboarding trips—eat your heart out, Syracuse—free to students. The college has a national sailboat team open to any student, and a Coast Guard–affiliated search-and-rescue team.

These resources also support Eckerd's most celebrated academic program: marine science. With a reputation for rigor and an impressive track record of placing students in strong graduate schools, the program offers four areas of specialty: marine biology, marine chemistry, marine geology, and marine geophysics. Students benefit from access to major oceanographic research facilities, including the Fish and Wildlife Research Institute's Marine Mammal Pathobiology Laboratory on campus. Marine science students speak enthusiastically about internship opportunities during the summer, and the program's list of placements is notable. (Eckerd students have won more Hollings Scholarships—awarded by the

National Oceanic and Atmospheric Administration to students interested in oceanic and atmospheric science—than students at any other school in the country.)

Of course, marine science isn't Eckerd's only shining star. Eckerd gets high marks for offering exceptional opportunities across disciplines. Nobel Laureate Elie Wiesel, author of *Night*, among dozens of other books, teaches during the January term. Drs. David Duncan and Joel Thompson got a beefy National Science Foundation (NSF) grant to take six students from any of the natural science or environmental-studies programs to conduct summer research at Xiamen University in China or Hong Kong Baptist University. Dean of faculty Betty Stewart (formerly the chair of the chemistry department at Austin College in Texas) teaches a senior seminar as part of the Ford Apprentice Scholar Program for students interested in careers in academia.

These vast and varied offerings often stem from faculty research interests. Eckerd's strong teachers prove that it's nearly impossible to separate research from teaching at liberal arts colleges—to the students' benefit. For example, computer scientist Dr. Debure earned a hefty NSF grant to fund her work developing and refining computer software that identifies dolphins by their dorsal fins. Marine scientist Dr. Gregg Brooks has a partnership with the U.S. Geological Survey, which has provided nearly one million dollars in funding for his research examining sediment grain size—a key to understanding the earth's geologic past. Dr. Amy Speier, a medical anthropologist, won an NSF grant to study in vitro fertilization in the context of medical tourism.

In every one of these cases—and dozens more like them—students serve as research assistants. The experience is invaluable. "You can really make Eckerd whatever you want," says a woman from Chicago with a double major in theater and human development. She says she "left high school depressed and exhausted," but Eckerd revived her. She has contributed to a theatrical production each spring; she's part of the school's popular improv troupe, "Another Man's Trash," and she works a part-time job on campus. A week at the Sundance Film Festival, three as a volunteer at an orphanage in Malawi, and a four-month stint studying in London have rounded out her experience.

The flipside of Eckerd's flexibility is students' responsibility. The ones who are happiest report participating in the college's unique offerings at much higher rates than students who are less enthusiastic. This phenomenon is hardly unique to Eckerd, but it bears mentioning, especially in a place where it's tempting to spend just a few more minutes basking in the sunshine instead of trekking to the library.

Students describe themselves as happy, accepting, and politically liberal—though a few bemoan the student body's lack of activism. If they have a complaint in common, it is the dorms, which many say are in need of updates. They agree that Eckerd's geographic diversity is a boon: The average student travels more than nine hundred miles to live here. They're trailblazers. (And they look like pure geniuses in February, when their friends up north are trudging to class through piles of gray snow.) Students come from forty-three states and thirty-five foreign countries, so nobody has a home-field advantage. The vast majority show up knowing nobody else and leave four years later with enduring friendships with their peers and professors.

And it's not just the students who benefit. One afternoon during a January term, a group of professors sits around a table and chats about their work at Eckerd. The conversation quickly turns to students and alumni who have amazed them. "We shared a student who loved physics but wanted to be a technical writer," says Dr. George Meese, retired professor of rhetoric, as he points to Dr. Harry Ellis, a physicist. "The student did an incredible thesis on how chaos theory is interpreted by the mass media." He beams. Professor Morris Shapero, who teaches international business, has brought along an e-mail from a graduating senior who is headed to Shanghai for an intensive Mandarin course. The student writes: "[I am] appreciative to you for taking a chance on me during our first class together freshman year. You may not realize how significant taking that class was for me during that period of my life. My relationships with teachers before college were something that had discouraged me. . . . What stands out to me from our initial class together is how you treated me with respect and dignity and valued the work I was doing in class. Thank you for your confidence in me as an individual and awareness to reach out your guiding hand to someone who wasn't really sure how to ask for it." This student, the professor notes, had been a C student in high school.

Shapero, who has an MBA from the University of Southern California and worked for thirty years as a corporate executive with companies expanding their Chinese and Taiwanese offices, sums up the professors' sentiments: "Nothing I did before this was half so rewarding. Being a teacher is my first love."

Perhaps the most emphatic endorsement of what Eckerd has to offer comes from a not-so-surprising place: the president's office. Dr. Donald Eastman came to the college in 2001 from a string of large universities: the University of Tennessee, Cornell University, and most recently the University of Georgia. As he rose through the ranks of administration in academia, his children attended small liberal arts schools—Davidson College and the College of Charleston. And the disparity in undergraduate experiences was significant, President Eastman says. "By the time I was looking at this position, while I loved each of the universities I worked for, I was less and less convinced that they did the kind of job by undergraduates that parents and legislators would want. The modern research university is geared toward the interests of graduate students, faculty, and administrators."

If more high-school students and their parents understood the value and potential in earning a degree from Eckerd, the college would be as selective as the Ivies. But here's the good news: Eckerd accepts between 65 percent and 70 percent of its applicants. "Eckerd is willing to take chances—calculated risks [on borderline students]," says John Sullivan, dean of admission. "It's part of who we are, and often those students are the ones who blossom most." The average GPA for admitted students is about 3.3. Students in the middle 50 percent of the admitted pool earned between 23 and 28 on the ACT, or between 1010 and 1230 on the SAT.

So if you're still figuring out who you are and what you want to do with your life, and even if you haven't hit your academic stride yet, Eckerd might be a good fit. If there's one lesson to learn from current students, it's that what you invest in Eckerd will be rewarded tenfold. Consider this story from a senior marine science major: Because of financial problems at home, she couldn't return to Eckerd in the middle of her college career. She returned to campus, packed up her things, and sat sobbing in dean of students Jim Annarelli's office for her exit interview. When she told him why she was leaving, he asked if she wanted to be there. "I nodded. I was hysterical." The dean made a few phone calls and found the few thousand dollars she needed to stay. "If that doesn't tell you the kind of place this is, I don't know what will," she says. "I will love Eckerd my whole life."

Guilford College

Greensboro, North Carolina

Guilford is a haven for students interested in linking their education with their social concerns. Service and community rank high among students' and professors' values, inspired by the college's Quaker roots.

The pretty and peaceful 340-acre wooded campus is dotted with simple, well-maintained brick buildings and carpeted in broad stretches of grass. It's a perfect backdrop for a place that embraces the Quaker values of simplicity, equality, peace, and integrity. Open spaces seem to emphasize the importance of community, and quiet corners underscore the value of contemplation. "I've never felt more at home anywhere," says a senior majoring in English. "I like that the campus reflects who we are. We're about substance, not anything flashy. You can walk on campus and get a quick read on the type of experience you'll have. It's honest."

It's a friendly place of 1,400 traditional undergraduates and a growing group—about 1,300 in 2011—of nontraditional students, adults who come for day, night, or weekend classes. Students and professors say they appreciate the range of perspectives nontraditional students bring to the classroom, calling this diversity "an interesting reality check" and "a real-world grounding." There's also a small cohort of about one hundred high-school students who enroll in Guilford's "early college" program to get a jump start on earning credits.

Students describe themselves as "liberal," "socially conscious," "opinionated," and "interested in others." They strike a visitor as genuine, kind people who are curious about the world and their place in it.

They come from all manner of backgrounds. Some are Quakers; most are not. Some graduated from high school at the very top of their classes; others admit they just eked out high enough GPAs to earn their diplomas. "I was the bullied kid in high school. I was a C student," says a senior from New Hampshire. "Almost everything has changed: how I present myself, how I argue, network, get involved in my community—everything. People in my hometown keep telling me how proud my parents are of me. They say that my parents can't stop talking about how much I've grown." A junior from Nashville has a different story: "I got all As in high school because that's where I got my self-esteem, but I didn't feel passionate about learning. The biggest change in me is that I have so much confidence and so many passions. I never thought I'd have the confidence to talk to someone I don't know." And a student from Kenya describes herself as "a walking textbook in high school." During her second semester at Guilford, her grades dropped. "I thought my world would end," she says. "I went to talk to one of my professors about it. He told me about the difference between knowledge and intelligence. Knowledge is stuff you know. Intelligence is what you do with the stuff you know. I stopped focusing on just memorizing and started to think about the bigger picture. Now I can quickly apply what I learn to a situation or a question. I'm much sharper."

Given their testimonies, it's no surprise that Guilford meets a lot of students' needs. It accepts 82 percent of its applicants. The middle 50 percent of those who enroll scored between 940 and 1220 on the SAT (critical reading and math) and between 20 and 27 on the ACT. But Guilford is test optional, so if your test scores are weak, you can submit three to five pieces of written work in lieu of your scores. Guilford requires interviews for students who take this route, but don't sweat it: The admissions officers aren't an intimidating bunch. They just want to get to know you and understand how you'll fit in the Guilford community.

Guilford gets high marks for its emphasis on helping first-year students ease into college. In 2008 the college launched its Student Success Program (SSP), which pairs incoming students who might struggle more than the average freshman with student mentors. These freshmen also take a course called Learning Strategies to learn tips and find resources that help boost their academic performance. As a result, the college saw a 13 percent increase in its retention rate from 2009 to 2010.

And like other schools in this book, Guilford understands the value of a comprehensive first-year experience for all new students. Freshmen take a First-Year Experience (FYE) course designed to establish the standards—academic and ethical—the college expects each student to uphold. Courses vary by topic, but they all emphasize critical thinking, clear speaking, and careful listening and integrate tips on how to study in college. A student's FYE professor is his adviser until he declares a major, and the college also offers a First-Year Center, where students can find resources, ask questions, and attend workshops designed specifically for freshmen.

Everyone goes through a core curriculum planned to ensure a liberal education with all its benefits: sharp critical-thinking skills, good communication skills, the ability to see connections where they aren't obvious, and nimbleness to adapt to new ideas and circumstances. Most classes involve discussion and have eighteen or fewer students, which means there's no place to hide. But why would you want to hide? Guilford is such a vibrant, warm place that even students who say they were shrinking violets or bored loafs in high school feel eager to speak up.

The sense of family here makes this participation easy for students. As is Quaker custom, students and teachers are on a first-name basis. Learning here is a "mutual seeking after truth," says Dr. Jim Hood, an English professor and Guilford alumnus. He and his colleagues praise the ways that the Quaker notions of equality and respect for one another's humanity set the tone for relationships with students.

Professors say they came to Guilford because they wanted to be at a place that values professor-student engagement. "I was seduced to come here by the intimacy of the classroom as opposed to the anonymity of a large public university," says Dr. Carolyn Beard Whitlow, an English professor. "There's a sense here of knowing the student as human and individual. This is the institution I wish I had attended." And even though her daughter went to Brown and Johns Hopkins, Dr. Whitlow says she holds out hope that her son will attend Guilford instead of a prestige-driven place.

Professors understand their power in students' lives because of their own academic and personal mentors. "It's not a mistake that I'm here," says Jack Zerbe, chair of the theater studies department. "At each place [in my academic career], a few people took my young, raw, eager self and helped me. They saw potential in me, and I appreciate the impact of those people on my growth. We're here to do the same thing for our students."

There's no doubt the college runs on the power of this committed faculty, who help students make the connection between their in-class learning and the community. The Bonner Center for Community Learning helps professors integrate service-learning components into their classes, an increasingly popular option. The center also matches students who are interested in service with community partner sites. "I get calls all the time from professors saying, 'This student would be great at that particular site,'" says James Shields, the center's director. "Service isn't an add-on. It's an integral part of learning here. It says a lot that professors want their students to have that experience."

Another distinctive offering is the Center for Principled Problem Solving (PPS). (Let's send all of our elected officials there.) The center's goal is to put the college's core values—community, diversity, equality, excellence, integrity, justice, and stewardship—to work in the world. Second- and third-year students can apply to be PPS Scholars and participate in a yearlong program that leads them through academic course work and fieldwork related to ethical problem solving in the community. Each scholar gets a three-thousand-dollar scholarship and three thousand dollars for a summer internship. "We aren't necessarily looking for superstars," says Judy Harvey, a teaching specialist at the center. "We're looking for students who want to find a passion and improve their community."

The center also funds short- and long-term projects proposed by faculty, staff, and students that "address issues in the world through a PPS lens." Faculty members can also apply for fellowships that fund projects related to their fields of interest.

The fantastic Bonner Scholars Program also influences Guilford's culture, as it does at Allegheny, Centre, Earlham, Emory & Henry, and Rhodes (among a couple dozen more colleges). The program provides scholarship money to high-need students who perform ten hours of community service each week and full-time service for two summers. "Bonners are awesome," says a junior from North Carolina. "Everyone knows at least a few Bonners, and they're so committed to their [service] sites and to what they're learning. They make you think, 'How deep is my commitment? How can I make this day better for just a few people?'"

Experiential learning takes other forms too. Students conduct original research and develop their own creative projects, all of which they showcase at the annual Guilford Undergraduate Symposium, an all-day celebration of students' innovation and creativity. And about a third of students study abroad, many of them with the college's programs in China, Germany, Ghana, Guatemala, Italy, the United Kingdom, and Mexico.

Maybe this emphasis on experiential learning is the reason the "bubble" that hovers over many college campuses seems absent—or at least diminished—here. Or perhaps it has been popped by students' concerns about the world and their frequent conversations about significant issues. "We're eighteen to twenty-two years old; we like to have fun," says a senior history major. "But we want to have real conversations too. I feel that difference when I go home. My high-school friends are so satisfied to talk for hours about nothing. I can't do that anymore. It makes me restless." Another senior says, "The culmination of four years at Guilford is knowing how to articulate your thoughts—and how to listen. We're serious about listening."

As is common in families, Guilford has its disagreements too. Students say there's a divide between athletes and nonathletes that they'd like to shrink. Several agree that the college is rife with "great ideas" but that "implementation can be a problem." One astute freshman says, "It's the young-activist problem. We see ways to change the campus, but it takes time and resources, and sometimes we're impatient, or we don't know what the administration is planning."

But students and alumni agree on the bottom line: "This school cares about students, faculty care about what they're doing, and they're very good to us," a senior says. One 2002 graduate, a policy analyst for Business Executives for National Security, a Washington, D.C., nonprofit organization dealing with national defense, gives this version of the same song: "I don't think I could handle this job if Guilford hadn't prepared me so well to be a writer and an analytical thinker. My teachers really pushed me to go one level deeper, one question further." An alumna from Canada who got into veterinary school says Guilford "couldn't have prepared me any better; my professors were amazing, their enthusiasm was contagious."

An alumna who went to Purdue as a PhD candidate in earth and atmospheric sciences had been a double major in biology and English. She says she'd been so well prepared that a professor told her to skip the master's part of the program because "my previous research was more complex and developed than many master's projects." At Guilford, she says, "I felt like all facets of my brain were constantly stimulated, as if my brain were working in overdrive."

The stories all end the same way: Guilford is a warm and accepting community and a mind-opening place of discovery where professors push students—and students push one another—to go beyond what they had thought they could achieve. If you want a piece of paper to get you a job, you can go somewhere less demanding and probably less expensive. But if you want a vocation, a shift in your soul, Guilford is a great choice.

Hendrix College

Conway, Arkansas

"Like some of the faculty members, I was unexpectedly blown away by Hendrix. It is an exemplary college and teenagers of a wide range of abilities and interests would find this a very happy fit socially. . . . There should be at least one college as good as Hendrix in every state."

—LOREN POPE

The living and learning are very good at Hendrix College. It's a place where people smile at strangers, students have resources to explore their ideas, and faculty and staff love to work.

No wonder everyone is so happy: They've discovered a better educational experience than you'd find in many name-brand places. Visit in spring, and you'll wander into an enclave of red and white azaleas, dogwoods, giant willow oaks, and manicured lawns that set off Hendrix's attractive buildings. If you're like most students, you'll be surprised to find this Eden-esque campus in charming Conway, thirty miles north of Little Rock. And inside this lovely setting is a warm community that feels like an extended family.

Don't dismiss it simply because it's in Arkansas (a mistake many out-of-state students say they almost made). Anyone who has visited this stretch of land near the picturesque Ozark Mountains—an outdoorsman's paradise, offering canoeing, white-water rafting, spelunking, rock climbing, horseback riding, hiking, and camping—knows that Arkansas has a lot to offer.

And so does Hendrix.

Not only does it offer a high-quality education in the liberal arts, but it's also dedicated to helping students connect their learning to the larger world. In 2005 Hendrix launched the Odyssey program, which requires each student to complete three cocurricular experiences from any of six categories: artistic creativity, global awareness, professional and leadership development, service to the world, undergraduate research, and special projects (a kind of catchall for anything that doesn't fit neatly into any of the first five options). The goal is to encourage students to apply their liberal arts learning to self-directed experiences—ideal preparation for life after college. "Ideas and book learning should be tested in life," says Dr. Peg Falls-Corbitt, the program's director. "Odyssey gives students a platform for this kind of experimentation, to explore their ideas and who they are—as people and citizens, and as learners." Each student builds an experiential transcript, a brilliant supplement to his academic record.

Odyssey projects are proof positive of what happens when students are electrified by their learning and then turned loose with their inspiration. Students have conducted original research on gender roles in the South, genetic indicators in copperhead snakes in the Arkansas River, and the oral history of the Holocaust. They've composed original organ music and organized dance workshops, volunteered for Heifer International and traveled with doctors in Mongolia, and trekked and meditated along the famed Camino de Santiago in Spain. Every project requires a faculty or staff adviser; Odyssey is a Hendrix family affair.

In the program's first five years, the college awarded $1.5 million in grants for Odyssey projects. The funds don't necessarily go to the "best" students. "It doesn't matter if you just got over the line [of admission] or if you are a Hays Scholar [the top scholarship award]; you have access to funding," says Dr. Falls-Corbitt.

This egalitarian vibe pervades the campus. It's an easygoing, unpretentious, democratic place. A student from Nashville echoes her peers when she gushes: "Everything about my high school was competitive. Hendrix is much more collaborative. The focus on community starts early here," when freshmen arrive a week before their upper-class peers. "Now that I don't have to worry about living up to someone else's standard, I feel like I'm discovering the things that are actually valuable to me."

Students take great care to protect their community, which they (rightly) see as unique. It's why they griped—and alumni chimed in—when the board of trustees approved the addition of Division III football as part of a newly formed conference of eight liberal arts schools, including Rhodes, Birmingham-Southern, Centre, and Millsaps. (The simultaneous approval of women's lacrosse provoked no such response.) "What we have here is so amazing that I don't want to risk it by adding such a culturally powerful force, especially in the South," a junior says. But when pressed, students agree that the open-mindedness they so value in their community could—and should—extend to student athletes who score touchdowns, the same way it extends to those who shoot free throws or clear hurdles in a single bound.

Hendrix lacks another pillar of many southern schools' social scenes: fraternities and sororities. Instead, students say, the school's small size and wide variety of activities give everyone several groups of friends. "And you recognize almost everyone," a junior says. "But not in a claustrophobic way. It's comfortable; it's good. I think that because we have such a range of experiences like study abroad and Odyssey projects that take us other places, Hendrix never feels too small. It's just right."

Also "just right" are the professors, who share a powerful vision of their roles as teachers and advisers; there is one faculty member for every twelve students. "I fell in love with teaching during my doctoral work, much to my surprise," says Dr. Andrea Duina, a biologist. "Hendrix is welcoming of research and teaching. I'm very, very happy here. I'm impressed with our students, and I love the chance to mentor them and get to know them."

Professors are liberal-arts fanatics, either because they had powerful undergraduate experiences at Hendrix-like gems or because they've taught undergraduates at huge, research-driven universities.

"I taught a freshman writing class [while earning my PhD at the University of Michigan], and I was horrified when I realized that I was the only person my students knew in a position of authority to help them solve problems," said Dr. Sasha Pfau, a historian.

Here, the opposite is true. A key medium of the life-changing work done by the colleges in this book is student-professor relationships. At Hendrix, perhaps more than any other place, these relationships seem like friendship (though students are quick to point out that professors are very comfortable giving their "friends" low grades if they're merited). President Tim Cloyd, a political scientist who still teaches a few classes, puts it aptly: "I don't cut students a lot of slack in my class, but there's a lot of warmth."

Almost every student volunteers stories—unprompted—about time they have spent with professors outside of class: mountain biking in the Ozarks, traveling to the annual meeting of the American Chemical Society to present collaborative research, or grabbing a cup of coffee to talk about their favorite political candidates. "My professors come to my theater performances," says a theater major. A senior jokes that his professors are his therapists, counseling him through the impending transition from "this paradise" to "whatever comes next." He gets serious when he says, "My favorite English professor told me, 'You are going to do great things. This is just the beginning for you,' and I believe her."

Hendrix, like other colleges in this book, knows that it must prepare students to live and work in a global context, so students are encouraged to have a term or more abroad. The possibilities are almost paralyzing: Hendrix offers tailored programs in Italy (to study theater arts), Austria (with classes in German and English), London (a dive into British studies), Oxford (with an emphasis on independent study), Shanghai (to study economics and finance), and Harbin, China—the college's newest program—where students study Chinese language and culture. Another new program, in Brussels, gives a cohort of Hendrix students the opportunity to take courses in European history, identity, and security while interning at a nonprofit government agency or think tank and conducting independent research. For students with tighter schedules, such as those on the premed track, Hendrix also offers summer programs in Costa Rica, Italy, Spain, and Turkey.

The college goes a long way toward making its exceptional education affordable for all kinds of families. It meets about 90 percent of demonstrated need and offers a wide and rich array of scholarships, including awards of up to six thousand dollars for students who have had experiences like those offered by Hendrix's Odyssey program in high school; one thousand dollars for students who have received International Baccalaureate diplomas in high school; and the Priddy Scholarship, awarded to students from middle-income families who don't qualify for merit-based awards or federal grants but who show academic promise, leadership, and commitment to service. The Hays Memorial Scholarship provides four students each year with full rides; if you have a 3.6 GPA and either a 1410 SAT (critical reading and math) or a 32 ACT, you're eligible.

And once you're here, you'll find a college that pours resources into the student experience. Its enrollment has grown from about 1,000 in 2005 to 1,500 in 2011, while preserving its exceptional student-professor ratio. With the growth came a boost in retention rate—to about 88 percent. What's more, the student body has never been more diverse: 17 percent are ethnic minorities, and less than half of students come from Arkansas. The rest come from forty-three states and fourteen foreign countries.

Hendrix opened the Wellness and Athletics Center in 2007; its country club–style facility comes complete with a climbing wall, sand volleyball courts, a fitness area, and an aquatics center with retracting roof. The new Student Life & Technology Center, opened in 2010, is a windfall for students: It's the buzzing campus hub with a main floor open 24-7 for late-night study sessions and a (very good) cafeteria on the second floor. Tech support, the office of the dean of students, and other student-centered services are housed here too.

The college has also embarked on an interesting New Urbanism project called "the Village" on formerly undeveloped property across the street from the main campus and near the Wellness Center. With the help of a master planner, Hendrix built two mixed-use buildings. Retail shops—including the campus bookstore and a few restaurant chains—anchor the ground floors, and students live in the apartments above. Nearby, the college built a community of single-family homes and sold them to Conway residents.

While it developed the land, it also rescued the nearby creek with an impressive ecological restoration project. The area now serves as an outdoor classroom for science courses.

You'll find an excellent example of Hendrix's ethos in the underground tunnel connecting the two sides of campus. Dubbed "the Grotto," the tunnel could have become a campus-safety issue—a kind of open invitation for ogres to prey on college kids—but President Cloyd saw potential in the concrete tube. A Boston-based architect and artist designed "Harmonic Fugue," a public art installation that features motion-activated light and sound. The result is a playful destination that reiterates the college's commitment to students.

This kind of creativity is a hallmark of Hendrix. It's everywhere: in the English department's newly developed film-studies and creative-writing programs; in the biweekly, überpopular Word Garden, a literary open-mike night at a local restaurant; in students' desire to build on their Odyssey experiences, even after they've met the projects' requirements.

But perhaps the boldest example of the community's creativity is Campus Kitty, a weeklong fund-raising event organized and produced by students for the benefit of local nonprofits. It's the only time students pay for on-campus activities, which include the Red Light Revue, a student and faculty talent show; a Wiffleball tournament and cookout; a Texas hold 'em tournament; and a concert that brings a headliner to campus. The week culminates in the Miss Hendrix competition, a drag beauty pageant. In 2011 students raised about forty thousand dollars for local charities. "I love seeing my students activate their powers to do good," says Dr. Leslie Templeton, who teaches psychology.

Without exception, students say they'd choose Hendrix if they had to do it again. If you want to choose it too, here's some good news: Hendrix accepts 82 percent of its applicants. The middle 50 percent of admitted students had GPAs between 3.6 and 4.3, ACT scores between 27 and 32, and SAT scores (math and critical reading) between 1180 and 1380. Like their colleagues at the other schools in this book, the admissions staff reviews each application carefully—not to find reasons to keep you out of Hendrix but to discover the unique talents and interests you'll bring to campus.

If you aren't a stellar student yet, fear not: Hendrix identifies at-risk freshmen and transfer students early and gives them advisers who have received extra training to serve this population of students. The college offers a range of support services, including one-on-one tutoring in all subjects and accommodations for students with documented learning disabilities. Students say they feel "totally supported" and "not shy about asking for help." A sophomore says, "It's pretty much guaranteed that you'll have a class that makes you feel overwhelmed, like you wonder if you should be here at all. But help is available from your professor or from the writing center or from tutors, and you make it through. I think you're better off for the struggle."

It should be no surprise that by 2011, Hendrix alumni included six Rhodes Scholars, sixteen Fulbright Scholars, twenty-seven Watson Fellows, and two Truman Scholars. And even if you haven't heard of Hendrix, graduate and professional schools have: More than half of graduates enroll for master's degrees or doctorates. Students' acceptance rate to med school is about 85 percent; to law school, approximately 90 percent.

But Hendrix gives you more than a ticket to the next (exciting) stage of your life. "Students can't earn a degree from here without having to confront the notion of what is meaningful and how they can contribute to that," President Cloyd says. Pair that search for meaning with the benefits of a liberal arts education, the tools to assimilate information and know what's meaningful and true, and you understand why Hendrix turns out thinkers, humanitarians, entrepreneurs, and civic leaders.

In the spring of her senior year, a student from Virginia who designed her own major in international relations and sustainable development—and who was a finalist for the Rhodes—sums up her experience this way: "I'm wrestling with myself. Hendrix calls me to do more and be more than I ever thought I could. It's a challenge, but I'll never get it out of my system. I'll always be thankful for my four years here."

Millsaps College

Jackson, Mississippi

"Every college has dissatisfied students and those who shouldn't be there, but I didn't run into any at Millsaps. The students I queried spoke with one voice, saying the same sorts of things the faculty members did; they liked it here and found it exciting; they talked to and learned from each other; it was so collegial, it was familial and if they had to do it all over again, they wouldn't be anywhere else."

—LOREN POPE

Some liberal arts colleges could do their work just about anywhere. If a meteorological mishap picked them up and plopped them down far from their original spots, they could carry on just as they had been.

Millsaps, with its 1,100 undergrads, is not one of those colleges.

Its identity and history are so closely tied to its place that separating the college from its location is a near impossibility. Millsaps simply wouldn't be Millsaps anywhere else.

When the college was chartered in the late 1800s, its founders declared it a place where even the poorest citizens of Mississippi could get a good education. When Mississippi was oppressive for people of color, and when people of lower classes found little opportunity, Millsaps welcomed anyone who could meet the academic standards for admission. And it was the first institution in the state to have a chapter of Phi Beta Kappa, the prestigious scholastic honor society.

Millsaps still has a mission of accessibility, especially precious in an era when many colleges try to inch up the *U.S. News & World Report* "best colleges" list by boosting their selectivity. The college isn't interested in keeping you out, but once you get in, you had better be ready to work hard and think deeply about your own education and its influence on the world.

The college's location is a challenge: Mississippi is the poorest state in the country; Jackson has a reputation as a rough spot. (There's plenty to like about it too, including a spirited live-music scene and local restaurants to satisfy even the pickiest foodies.) And Millsaps sits at a crossroads: A mile and a half from the capitol building, the hundred-acre campus is flanked by an upper-middle-class community on one side and a low-income community on the other.

"We are owning our Mississippi heritage and the cultural importance of that heritage," says Dr. Keith Dunn, dean of the college. "We're having an impact in our region." Students express their own version of this idea: "The Deep South needs people who can solve big problems and bring people together," and "There's a lot more to being a student than just studying. I can understand what it means to affect someone's life."

All of this matters because it influences students' education in very good ways. Sometimes liberal arts naysayers suggest that liberal learning—studying philosophy and biology and history, even if you're planning to be an architect—is indulgent or impractical. What's the point?

The points are many: Exposure to a broad swath of ideas sharpens the intellect, gives students tools for understanding new concepts, hones problem-solving skills, develops creative thinking, fosters smart risk taking, and enhances a person's ability to communicate well—all essential skills no matter which professional path a student chooses.

But in light of Millsaps in particular, the point is that reflecting on what Plato had to say about a republic gives life to a discussion about voting rights. Learning about biology and physiology and psychology helps students develop educational programs that encourage people to choose healthy lifestyles. Studying history gives context to current events, so students understand what decisions—public and private—led to current problems. Then students work to fix them.

"This is a place where students find their academic passion, but they also find the significance of that academic passion," Dr. Dunn says. "They're trained to make an impact in their communities." To put it another way, there's a real connection between the "what" of students' learning and the "why."

This sense of purpose might be the reason students here are so down-to-earth. Nobody seems cool or self-satisfied. The sense of entitlement that poisons other places is absent.

Students talk eagerly about the community's vibrancy and the ways they have been changed. Many of them are from the Deep South, from communities they describe as "homogenous" or "self-contained." Coming to Millsaps has exposed them to types of people and ideas they had never encountered before. "I'm kind of embarrassed to say it, but for the first time in my life, I had to interact with people who said things that I totally disagree with," says a junior from Mississippi. "I had been brought up to believe that disagreeing is disrespectful, but now I know that if you never meet anyone who challenges you, you never grow. I want to have beliefs and values that have been tested, not just stuff I've absorbed from my surroundings. Millsaps is a really safe place to have those conversations."

Easy exchange is a hallmark of Millsaps. When asked if it's easy to get an A, a group of students laughs. "No way," a junior says. "It's so much more than studying here. Classroom participation is a big deal. You cannot just be the warm body in the room. Your professors will call you out, and if they don't, the people in your class will." But his peers are quick to point out that they push one another because classes are better when everyone participates. "We want to hear what other people think. It's awesome to sit in class and hear somebody have a different interpretation of a reading than I did. I learn so much from other people in class," says a junior from Louisiana.

Dr. James Bowley, a religious studies professor, gave an apt example of the respectful discourse that defines Millsaps: Seniors majoring in religious studies must take a capstone course, an intense, intimate learning environment that serves as a culmination of their studies. "I had two people who were very outspoken in that class. One was a conservative, Pentecostal Christian; the other, a dedicated atheist. I thought, 'What's going to happen here?'" Dr. Bowley says. "But you would have thought they were best friends. They disagreed about everything, but they were so respectful of each other and learned so much from each other."

The other reason Millsaps is such a comfortable and effective learning place is that the faculty members talk to and learn from one another. This culture provides an implicit model for the students; they see professors sharing ideas, reading one another's work, and they do the same. It makes learning collaborative rather than competitive.

One fall afternoon at lunchtime, faculty pack into every available inch of a room off of the cafeteria to listen to a couple of colleagues discuss how students research—how they find sources, what they use, and how that information informs their learning. The spirit is friendly; the sense of mission, shared. Nobody has to attend the session, but it's part of a regular series on best practices in teaching—a topic Millsaps takes very seriously.

This dialogue is lively at Millsaps because professors are entrepreneurial and enthusiastic. They're interested in developing new courses and programs, always with an eye toward what's best for students. An example: The college owns a 4,500-acre biocultural reserve on the Yucatán Peninsula, a biological and archaeological resource where professors from a surprising range of disciplines— business, biology, education, geology, history, literature, archaeology, ecology, and anthropology—teach courses. The value of field study is so apparent that about half of Millsaps faculty teach in the field. Classes travel to Southeast Asia to study the Vietnam War, Paris to examine poetry, Greece to learn about the ancient world, and Albania to study archaeology.

When students return from the Yucatán, they have access to the country's only undergraduate lab focused on biochemical archaeological analysis. The W. M. Keck Center for Instrumental and Biochemical Comparative Archaeology—dubbed "the Keck lab" for obvious reasons—houses state-of-the-art equipment that students and faculty use to discover and analyze the biochemical properties of historical artifacts. "Students are using cutting-edge technology they wouldn't get their hands on elsewhere," says Dr. Michael Galaty, an anthropologist.

The line between faculty research and student learning blurs. "We have high expectations of ourselves, and we want to accomplish things," says Dr. Holly Sypniewski, a professor of classics. "We end up talking to undergrads about what we're doing. Students live in the midst of our intellectual discoveries." Even if a student doesn't want to be a professional scholar, the experience of identifying the right questions, applying smart analytical methods, and examining data for answers is invaluable. Whether you grow up to be a city council member, an accountant, an entrepreneur, or a teacher, you need these skills to be successful.

These faculty-student collaborations spark a student's imagination: Maybe she hadn't considered studying philosophy or ancient Rome or French literature until a professor invited her to see how fascinating it could be. "We have lots of stories about students who have had transformational experiences. They come here and become impassioned about something they didn't expect," says Dr. Galaty. One of his own students took a few anthropology classes and traveled with him on a research trip to Albania that ignited her interest. She earned a Fulbright to go back to Albania and then got a full ride to graduate school. "I wouldn't say she was an exception," Dr. Galaty says. "They don't all get Fulbrights, but we see a disproportionate number of great success stories."

Millsaps makes these opportunities available to every student, and you don't have to have an exceptional high-school record to get in, though you ought to show your commitment to hard work. The college takes 79 percent of its applicants; their average high school GPA was 3.6. The middle 50 percent had ACT scores ranging from 24 to 29 and SAT scores from 1055 to 1300 (critical reading and math). As is fitting for a place committed to accessibility, students who are Pell eligible don't pay tuition or fees.

If you enroll, you'll get the full benefit of a robust liberal arts curriculum that requires students to write well, no matter their major. The college rightly rejects the idea that one freshman English course is sufficient to sharpen students' written communication skills and instead infuses writing instruction through all departments. Each student submits a writing portfolio of work from different classes for evaluation by faculty members; if the student's work isn't up to par, the college either requires or recommends additional instruction.

Students praise Millsaps's distinctive interdisciplinary first-year course, "The Heritage of the West in World Perspective." It fulfills the college's humanities requirements by weaving together "the history of ideas, cultures, religions, creative works, and pivotal problems that have shaped humanity for thousands of years." Each week, participants attend four lectures and three discussion groups—a demanding schedule—but every student who mentions it is over the moon about it. "It's intense but fascinating," says a sophomore from Seattle. A junior adds, "It fills out the pieces you might have learned in high school. You start to see yourself as a part of the whole of human history; it's personal, not just a bunch of stuff you have to memorize. You understand how we are where we are, the good and the bad." The course isn't required, but it's such a fine example of liberal learning that every Millsaps student should take it.

For students who decide they want careers in academia, Millsaps has a distinctive Ford Teaching Fellowship Program (similar to the one at Eckerd College). Each fellow gets a faculty mentor who helps the student hone skills as a researcher and a teacher. Fellows serve as peer tutors, give lectures on independent research, and supervise labs—all under the guidelines of proposals they write with their mentors. The program is a boon for students and good news for higher education: We need more teachers with the talent and devotion of Millsaps's faculty.

A visitor quickly gets the impression that Millsaps is a hopeful place with deep roots and a clear sense of mission. Professors talk of their excitement at seeing in their students so much growth—in intellect, in self-confidence, and in the sharpening of values. And students, as friendly and fun-loving as you could find anywhere, display a layer of seriousness about their education. It's not merely a means to an end. They are probing the human experience, in class and outside it, and they are making informed decisions about how they'll spend their time and talents. Mississippi is lucky to have them; indeed, the whole country needs more colleges like Millsaps.

New College of Florida

Sarasota, Florida

I f ever a school's architecture reflected its culture, it's that of New College. Visiting students and their families meet admissions reps in a large, pink, Spanish-style mansion that once belonged to the Ringling family (of circus fame). One of the students' favorite hangouts is the Four Winds coffee shop—in a converted elephant barn. Social life buzzes around Palm Court, a courtyard of strategically placed palm trees near the modern Pei Dorms, designed by architect I. M. Pei (of Louvre fame). And instead of a grassy quad, the campus showcases a landscape of native plants—part of its commitment to the South Florida environment.

To sum it all up, New College is unorthodox—and that's what makes it a remarkable and refreshing place. Established more than fifty years ago, it's a campus where more than eight hundred bright, curious students come to take responsibility for their own education with guidance from high-caliber, enthusiastic faculty.

Students do not earn grades or accumulate credit hours, and the students and faculty here express an earnest distaste for the idea that an A reflects mastery of a topic. Instead, professors determine whether a student's performance is satisfactory, incomplete, or unsatisfactory, and then provide written evaluations of each student's work that semester. The evaluations reflect a core tenet of the culture here: Learning doesn't stop just because a class is over, so professors often offer suggestions on how a student might improve his research or revise a paper to present it next semester at a professional conference.

And in lieu of registering for a specific number of credit hours, students negotiate contracts with their advisers each semester; each contract outlines a student's courses, short- and long-term goals, extracurricular activities, and "certification criteria"—or what the student must do to satisfy the terms of the contract. A student must satisfy seven contracts as a condition of graduation.

By their nature, these contracts require students to reflect on their lives and their learning and faculty to know students' lives. Short-term goals might be "learn to sail" or "research study-abroad options." Long-term goals often include students' dreams—to write a play or discover a new solution to beach erosion—and more personal reflections of self, like the desire to maintain old friendships from home.

Best of all, students negotiate contracts that leave them room to fail. For example, if the student is taking five and a half courses in a semester, her contract might require her to earn four satisfactory evaluations. "The system makes it all so abstract, it's wonderful to learn," says Molly Robinson, the college's director of recruitment and an alumna (Robinson transferred to New College after a disappointing year at Yale). The emphasis is on student growth and the reality that sometimes growth requires a risk that might not turn out perfectly the first time.

Students talk a lot about taking responsibility for their own education—a notion that's relatively absent from most postsecondary schools, where a prescribed curriculum gives students little choice or little reason to reflect on their own curiosity. If a student here can't find a course on a topic he's desperate to investigate, he can propose a tutorial, a self-designed course he creates with the help of a faculty member. (New College adopted its tutorial system from Oxford's New College—the original New College, now more than seven hundred years old). "Tutorials are the perfect example of what's happening here," a second-year history student says. "They're amazing. Everyone talks about the tutorials they're planning or they're currently doing; [tutorials] are central to our culture here." Recent tutorials include "Theater of the Absurd," "Readings of C. S. Lewis," "Glass Blowing," and "Psychology and Biology of Schizophrenia."

Students fiercely defend the idea of their academic freedom—so much so that they bristle at the idea that any one program is stronger than any other: "We're responsible for our own learning, so if you complain that a program isn't strong, it's kind of your own fault. You're not seeking out the things that really fascinate you," says a fourth-year student. But there's no denying that the school's science programs—particularly in environmental studies and marine biology—are appealing to many aspiring scientists. For example, Dr. Heidi Harley, a cognitive psychologist, studies how dolphins process sensory input. "This is an ideal place for me to do my research—and given our emphasis on student-directed research, I think we do attract strong science students who want the kinds of resources and experiences we provide." Her colleague, Dr. Gordon Bauer, established the Sensory Biology and Behavior Program at nearby Mote Marine Laboratory more than a decade ago; ever since, students have assisted in his research on sensory processes in manatees, dolphins, and marine turtles. Their work has influenced how scientists and policy makers think about conservation.

Clearly, nobody here is taking the easy road, and anyone who thinks that this kind of flexibility sounds painless is mistaken. A fourth-year environmental-studies student from downtown Atlanta says she and her classmates often wish they could "just get grades" for particularly tough courses. It takes real grit and maturity to read a professor's candid and thorough evaluation of your work.

"I feel like I'm becoming a better person here," says a third-year student from Miami, who is concentrating in sociology and gender studies. "I talk to friends back home, and I realize the experience I'm getting is unusual. I feel sorry for them, that they don't get to be here too. They're going to be exactly the same when they leave college. I'm already different."

In addition to her seven contracts, each student must complete three Independent Study Projects (ISPs), each during a four-week

January term. ISPs reflect a core value of a New College education: student-driven research. During the January term, a student delves deeply into a learning experience she designs herself or with a small group of students; a faculty member sponsors the ISP and, with the student, decides how the student's work will be evaluated.

Students are clearly crazy about their ISPs, which give them opportunities to chase their wildest academic interests: One group of students studied the Holocaust as it's represented in films from around the world; another read five works of contemporary litera- ture to decide which would be best for incoming students to read in preparation for their orientation to New College. A third-year student traveled to Europe to study what the collapse of European countries' economies means for the future of the euro. "You really get to . . . indulge," a second-year student said. "I think 'indulge' is the best word for it."

ISPs are a kind of practice for the culminating academic experi- ence at New College: the senior thesis. Each student publishes a hefty thesis and defends it orally—à la graduate school—during "Bac Week." The public is invited to attend the presentations, and each senior e-mails the entire student body an invitation to his bac- calaureate exam. "Everyone gets really excited about Bac Week," one fourth-year student says and adds, laughing, "Everyone at New College is kind of a nerd."

If that's the case, New College is redefining "nerd." Students here seem confident and warm—and introspective without being overly serious. They describe themselves as "diverse"—which, iron- ically, is how students at most colleges describe themselves—and "friendly." The campus leans pretty far left politically, and students admit (with some obvious glee) that New College has a reputation as a "hippy school." But almost every student quickly adds that the student body is wildly accepting, and most guess that even conser- vative kids enjoy it. (Nobody self-identified as one of those mysteri- ous conservatives.)

Nobody under the age of twenty-five wears shoes—signs in the science buildings remind students "No bare feet"—and the vibe is very casual, thanks in part to the 120-acre campus's perch beside

Sarasota Bay. Faculty describe students as "bright" and "surprising," "with a strong drive to learn, even if they don't have all the skills yet" and "prone to cast their lots in unusual ways."

As at other student-focused colleges, classes are small, and the professors here are teachers first, researchers second. That hardly means they're not on the cutting edge; it simply means they don't separate their own learning and research from their students'. "What can I say? I'm a student," says Dr. Sandra Gilchrist, a biologist in the natural sciences department. "I just get paid for it."

Dr. Gilchrist takes a group of students to Honduras each summer as part of her own research. During the spring semester, she teaches courses in coral-reef ecology and animal behavior, and during the summer trip, first-time researchers assist her or more experienced students with their research; the second summer, students develop their own research projects, write grants to support their work, and even file permit requests with the Honduran government.

Professors clearly love the mentoring they do. Dr. Stephen Miles, a music professor, explains it this way: "It's important for faculty to recognize students' talents and gifts and then draw attention to those talents. You can activate students by recognizing what's great in them and then helping them build on that greatness."

New College marries this kind of mentorship with top-notch faculty research. Year after year, professors win major cutting-edge research grants from federal agencies. A physics professor won a whopping $1.7 million grant from the U.S. Army Research Laboratory to study nanotechnology. A biologist with a National Science Foundation grant studies the nutritive tissue in maize and how genetic events in the early stages of its growth can impact nutritional value. Her research has implications for the fight against world hunger. And the fledgling Chinese language and culture program scored grants from the Chinese government to pay for seven students to study abroad in China—at absolutely no cost to the students. In every one of these examples (and dozens more like them) students are serving as research assistants to faculty and conducting their own research—invaluable experiences.

Students describe their professors as "approachable," "so cool," and "as varied as the student population." Professors love that students are in their classes because they choose to be—not because the registrar requires it. "People invest when they have an interest," says math professor Patrick McDonald PhD. "Once students have enrolled in my classes, I can help them do remarkable things. Students' academic freedom makes this place work. Plus, students here learn that the flip side of freedom is responsibility, and that's a lesson that we all should understand."

Dr. Harley adds, "Students here push you really hard. They ask tough questions, and they don't do what you tell them to do just because you tell them to do it. They want to know why."

As you might guess, New College produces big thinkers, ambitious graduates who are wildly capable of achieving their dreams. Graduate schools agree: Among the 153 graduates in the class of 2010, 29 percent went directly to graduate school. And of that group, nineteen of the twenty-two who applied to PhD programs were accepted (86 percent); twenty-two of the twenty-eight who applied to master's programs were accepted (79 percent); and all of the five law-school applicants were accepted. They're small sample sizes, true, but they're indicative of what happens year after year. (About 80 percent of New College grads go on to graduate or professional school within six years of graduating.)

And New College is among the top producers of Fulbright Scholars per capita of any undergraduate college or university in the country, besting Harvard, Yale, Stanford, and other brand-name schools.

If this style of learning sounds exciting to you, here's the good news: The college admits about half of its applicants. But those applicants tend to be strong students—more than 95 percent are in the top half of their high school classes—and they want this kind of community. "If you're the type of student who needs to be spoon-fed, you'll hate it here," says a second-year from Fort Myers, Florida. "As much as you can, you need to figure out if New College suits you before you get here." Another woman adds that it's hard to figure out what it means to be in control of your own education after thirteen years of "filling an educational path someone else set." Every year, the college loses about 14 percent of its first-year students, many of whom don't want the kind of rigor and accountability New College offers. (It's important to note that a college that retains 86 percent of its students is doing a far better job than the vast majority of schools in this country.)

But if New College is for you, you'll get a warm community of smart, eccentric people. Despite all of their intellectual achievements, New College kids also know how to have fun. Every Friday and Saturday night in Palm Court, there is a "wall"—a dance party where the speakers are set up on the wall (not Novo Collegians' most clever moment, but the name has been around since the eighties). Walls are themed. Think Body Art Wall, Jersey Shore Wall, Tacky Christmas Sweater Wall, and Headphones Wall (where everyone wears headphones and dances to his or her own beat—a near-perfect metaphor for the campus).

There aren't any athletics, unless you count a few intramural sports and the occasional pickup Ultimate Frisbee game, and there are no fraternities or sororities. "We're pretty much one big fraternity, without the pretense," a third-year explains. "We just look out for each other."

The college looks out for them too. Students repeatedly bring up professors' exceptional mentoring and availability, and they point out that more formal resources are available to them help them succeed too. The Academic Resource Center houses a Quantitative Resource Center and a Writing Resource Center—both staffed by trained peer tutors—and a Language Resource Center where students can beef up their foreign language skills with the help of software, print resources, and even games.

What's more, the college's buildings are lovely—and designed to foster learning and community. The eleven-million-dollar, LEED-certified Academic Center and Plaza, opened in 2011, adding ten classrooms, forty-five faculty offices, and spaces for faculty-student interaction, including a gorgeous outdoor plaza. The Pritzker Marine Biology Research Center has more than one hundred aquariums, including a 15,000-gallon research and display tank. (Students designed the natural filtration system that draws and recycles water from the Sarasota Bay for use in the tanks.) The Public Archaeology Lab, built in 2010, is a small but mighty space designed to support students and faculty conducting research on local and regional history. The lab doubles as a kind of gallery, where students and faculty launch exhibitions to educate the community about South Florida's cultural heritage.

So there's a lot to love at New College—and students do. Their primary complaint is geographic diversity: 80 percent of students come from Florida. But you can hardly blame them. As a public honors college, New College is a screaming deal for in-state students. It also meets about 94 percent of demonstrated need, so out-of-staters should seriously consider this place of wild intellectual adventures.

If you come, you won't get an Ivy League education. You'll get something better: a sense of your own power to learn and discover and achieve. And unlike the Ivies, where reports of grade inflation are as common as a 3.9 GPA, New College isn't about the gold star. It's about the process. Students who like the pure thrill of learning—of wrestling with tough topics and coming out the other side—will love it.

Rhodes College

Memphis, Tennessee

"First-rate, caring scholar-teachers are the hallmark of the colleges in this book, but I was especially impressed with the ones I talked with at Rhodes. The college awards rich monetary prizes each year for outstanding teaching, for research and creative activity, and for service to the school. It is one of those few colleges that gives what it proclaims in the catalog in full measure to its lucky students."

—LOREN POPE

As you may have noticed if you've been a diligent student of this book, many liberal arts colleges are in small towns or not-quite cities. Rhodes is an exception. In the heart of Memphis, it's an excellent choice for a student who isn't willing to trade the city life for a high-caliber liberal arts education.

Memphis is a city with a lot to offer and a lot of need. "Two miles from here you have a real laboratory for what we have to get right in America," says Dr. William Troutt, the college's beloved president. "We also have booming business and rich cultural events and a community that cares deeply about its future. And in the heart of all this, we have a rigorous liberal arts college that encourages learning and reflection and service. I think it's a near-perfect situation."

In this southern city famous for blues, barbecue, and the mighty Mississippi, Rhodes's campus might surprise you. Its Gothic architecture is heady and enchanting. A community of prospective students raised on Harry Potter will no doubt draw comparisons to Hogwarts; a community of scholars, to Oxford. Every stone from its many buildings comes from the same quarry because a long-ago president accepted the quarry as payment for a debt to the college.

But the real magic happens inside the stone buildings. With an average class size of thirteen students, and more than 97 percent of professors holding terminal degrees in their fields, Rhodes is a community of learners—much thanks to the faculty, who share a vision of themselves as mentors, teachers, and encouragers.

Consider Dr. Mary Miller, a biologist. Dr. Miller came to Rhodes from postdoctoral work at The Rockefeller University, a place renowned for its scientific research, particularly related to human health. "I didn't have an educational background at a liberal arts college, but the day I found out they existed was like nirvana," Dr. Miller says. "Teaching energized me, but at The Rockefeller, the culture wasn't focused on teaching. Here, I get the best of both worlds. Students here work really hard; they want to learn and get better. The pace is slower, but they're thinking at the graduate level after two or three years in the lab. I love it here. Rhodes has a happy faculty."

It also has happy students, about 1,750 of them, who feel like they're getting their money's worth. A junior from Charlotte, North Carolina, puts it this way: "The people here are helping me figure out who I want to be." Her classmate adds: "Once professors find out what you're interested in, they're helping you find your way. I'd say students and professors are always looking for ways to tap into whatever talent you bring to campus, to develop it. Passion runs this place."

A parent—a partner in a large law firm in Memphis—says that after his daughter spent a year at Louisiana State University, she wanted to enroll at Rhodes. "I was worried about whether she could get in and stay in," her father says. "She wasn't very interested in academics in high school or in her first year of college." But she blossomed at Rhodes, he says, "because of her relationships with her teachers. They turned something on in her."

The college's commitment to students is on display virtually everywhere. President Troutt moved his office from the third floor of an administrative building to the first because he wanted to be closer—and more accessible—to the students. "Now I can just open this door"—he demonstrates—"and see who's passing by." He catches sight of a student and calls out his name. The student waves back and hollers hello, the way he might to his fraternity brothers across the quad.

In 2005 the college opened a brand-new library that is one of the most impressive at any college in the country. Inside, a grand staircase, etched glass doors, and arched doorways give an air of earnestness. The library's study spaces—private rooms, cozy corners furnished with English club chairs, and a dome-topped reading room on the second floor—emphasize Rhodes's commitment to student work. "Even when you don't want to study, the library sort of calls to you," says a junior from South Carolina. "You feel so scholarly in there. I'd say it's inspiring." The library is home to two hundred computers, including laptops students can check out, and expansive tech resources. There's even a thirty-two-seat movie theater for film classes and independent study projects. The Middle Ground, a twenty-four-hour coffee shop, fuels late-night study sprees. And if you're in need of some bookish inspiration, head outside to the Southern Literary Garden, home to plants mentioned by renowned southern authors in their books, poems, and essays.

In 2011 Rhodes began two more projects. The first is a whole-scale renovation of the college's main dining hall, the Burrow Refectory—affectionately dubbed "the Rat" by students. The new facility adds a range of eating options for students (a bakery and brick pizza oven among them) and a new fireside lounge and kitchen. The second is the West Village, new dorms that comprise single- and double-room suites, each with its own bathroom and a furnished living room.

Even more exciting is the Rhodes Fellowship Program. The college has taken its many opportunities for experiential learning—internships, fellowships, summer research positions, and service work—and created a structure that helps students tap into these positions. The program gives students access to funding if they need it and, equally important, a process to evaluate their learning as they work. Every fellow must have at least one faculty mentor—providing yet another platform for faculty to know and encourage students—and Rhodes evaluates each fellowship to make sure it meets accepted standards for high-impact practices.

The diversity of fellowships is a sign of their appeal: One student wrote and produced his own short film; a group of aspiring scientists mapped the distribution of lead in Memphis soil; an art history student researched the famous Kress Collection, which has received relatively little scholarly attention, at the nearby Brooks Museum of Art; three young biologists researched the impact of urbanization on snake populations. Other students interned at the Memphis mayor's office—a popular, ongoing relationship between the college and city hall—while a team of talented Rhodes musicians launched a guitar club at an inner-city middle school to help boost attendance. It worked.

"It's not enough to say, 'Our students do research, and our students intern, and our students volunteer.' We want to make sure those experiences are valuable educationally," says Dr. Scott Garner, the director of Rhodes Fellowships. "We've created a model for connecting students to these opportunities, supporting them through the experiences, and then making sure that students are getting what they ought to be getting. We can answer the question, 'Is this stuff working?' And if so, we know how and why. If not, we tweak it."

In the heart of Memphis, Rhodes is uniquely poised to offer these kinds of experiences. After a tumultuous and fascinating half century, Memphis is a raw place full of potential and—for the first time in a while—hope. Rhodes does an excellent job of helping students understand and participate in the political, economic, and systemic forces that influence the city.

For example, the Rhodes Institute of Regional Studies gives more than a dozen students each summer the opportunity to conduct original research related to the mid-South, about a two-hundred-mile radius from Memphis. Each student receives a three-thousand-dollar stipend, plus housing and research expenses; faculty members from multiple disciplines teach a one-week intensive regional-studies seminar and then serve as mentors to student researchers. At the end of six weeks, students present their research; many of them build on their work to create honors theses or articles fit for publication in academic journals.

For many years, Rhodes has also had a relationship with St. Jude's Children's Hospital. Called St. Jude Summer Plus, the program matches Rhodes students with opportunities to work in the labs at the celebrated hospital for two summers and an academic year. "You feel so awesome walking into the lab. You're working with scientists who are literally saving children's lives," says a biochemistry major from Dallas who headed to an MD/PhD program after he graduated from Rhodes. "I wouldn't have had that opportunity anywhere else. It probably sounds clichéd, but I realized that I'm good at science, and I can actually change the world with the skills and knowledge I have. It all happened because a professor noticed I was good with detail in the lab and suggested I apply."

There's more: Rhodes awards stipends to sixteen Summer Service Fellows who spend nine weeks volunteering at nonprofit organizations in Memphis to better understand—and help solve—some of the problems that trouble cities across the country. Another program, Crossroads to Freedom, digitally archives materials that document the civil-rights era in Memphis. Fellows collect and process documents, learn about the civil-rights movement, and promote the archive to the public.

Opportunities to get into Memphis aren't limited to extracurricular or summertime work. Rhodes has recently added an interdisciplinary program called Environmental Studies & Sciences. A student can choose to earn a BA in environmental studies by taking an amalgam of course work in history, anthropology, humanities, science, and social science, or a BS in environmental science with a stronger emphasis on biology and chemistry.

The college's location is a boon for the new program: Nearby Shelby Farms Park Conservancy is the largest urban park in

America—almost six times larger than Central Park—and serves as a living laboratory for students and professors. The Mississippi River is a rich resource. And of course, Memphis gives students an up-close-and-personal look at the messy marriage of public policy and environmental issues.

It's no wonder that students and professors brag about Rhodes's ability to connect liberal arts education with real-world scenarios. "You would have to work really hard not to find something you love here," says a sophomore from New Orleans. "You'd basically have to avoid your professors, quit reading your e-mail, stop attending campus events, and hide from your roommate. People are always offering ideas for how to get involved. Sometimes it can be over-whelming because you think, 'I want to do that and that and that other thing too.' But I'd rather have this many opportunities than wonder how to get into research or how to find an internship."

Her comment hints at another element of Rhodes's personality: Rhodes doesn't have the low-key vibe of Hendrix or the casual aura of Earlham. Students are "extremely social" and "pretty tuned in to what everyone is doing," they say. Social life swirls around Greek life—about half of students belong to Rhodes' fourteen fraternities and sororities—but not a single student feels that nonaffiliated stu-dents have a hard time finding fun. Students frequently volunteer: "We work hard and we play hard."

In some circles, Rhodes is perceived as a school for J.Crew-wearing, iPad-toting students who feel entitled to other people's attention. The reputation is undeserved. Sure, Rhodes has more students who can afford the sticker price of college than many of the schools in this book, but affluence doesn't equal affectation.

"My family is poor," says a senior from Knoxville, a first-generation college student. "Other people's affluence doesn't show here. It doesn't enter into my relationships at all. People are extremely accepting." What's more, he makes this bold proclama-tion in front of a group of his peers. Nobody bats an eye.

Students mention a "changing campus" and a "new sense of community" at Rhodes. In the past, students weren't inclined to bring up topics that would rock the campus, they explain. But in recent years there has been much more open communication about weightier topics, such as how the college community treats gay, lesbian, bisexual, and transgender students. Several seniors bemoan leaving because they say the college community is "entering a new era" and they wish they could be around to see it unfold.

Like all of the schools in this book, Rhodes does the hard work of addressing values—something you won't find much at the diploma machines called state universities. "Some schools don't feel comfortable talking about values, but reflection is an important part of any activity. We build in time and mechanisms for students to consider, 'Who am I? What matters here?'" says Dr. Michael Drompp, dean of the faculty. "Understanding values is an essential part of critical thinking."

To that end, students must complete a series of courses in one of two tracks: "The Search for Values in the Light of Western History and Religion" or "Life: Then and Now." (It's no wonder that students have shortened these titles to "Search" and "Life.") Each is a three-course series, and students take the first two courses during their freshman year. "Search" emphasizes interdisciplinary study of biblical, classical, and Near East traditions, and students use only original texts (translated into English, of course) for their work. "Life" introduces students to the academic study of the Bible as a historical document and then evolves into an interdisciplinary mix of history, philosophy, and religious studies.

Put more simply, one student explains: "'Life' is about religious studies; 'Search' is more about philosophy." So there you have it.

The study of values isn't just cerebral: 80 percent of Rhodes students volunteer consistently, putting Rhodes near the top of the heap of service-minded schools. It's not a political place—Berkeley doesn't have to worry about being outprotested by Rhodes—but students are an integral part of Memphis. "Our students get that Memphis is a place with a lot of need," says Dr. Jeffrey Jackson, a historian and the director of the new environmental-studies programs. "They're doing their quiet work; they're quiet servants, but don't assume that means they're ineffective. They're incredibly effective."

Rhodes is more selective than most of the colleges in this book. It accepts about 60 percent of applicants; the middle 50 percent of them score between 26 and 30 on the ACT and between 1200 and 1360 on the SAT (critical reading and math). Almost 90 percent return for their sophomore year, and more than three-quarters graduate in four years.

Even though accepted students tend to be strong high-school students, they admit that they had to shift their thinking when they arrived at Rhodes. "Just because you were a good high-school student doesn't mean you'll be a good college student, not right away," says a sophomore from Nashville. "[As a freshman], I was surprised by what professors were asking me to do. I didn't really know how to research or how to analyze information to say something original, but now I do. I feel like that's going to be crucial when I leave here. I know that I have my own ideas and how to explain them to people. I know how to advance the discussion to a point where we're talking about new things, not just rehashing what's already been said. I bring something to the table."

Employers and graduate and professional schools agree. The college's surveys of graduates reveal that more than 90 percent of students are employed or earning advanced degrees within a year of graduating. In 2010 two-thirds of respondents said they had been accepted to their first-choice schools; acceptance rates for various programs—MBA, medical, law, and graduate—ranged from 91 percent to 100 percent.

The college ranks in the top 6 percent of American colleges and universities for the percentage of students who earn PhDs in the sciences. And its Postgraduate Scholarship Committee helps students apply for exciting postgraduate awards. Since 2002, Rhodes students have won eight Fulbrights, two National Science Foundation Graduate Research Fellowships, five Watsons, two Trumans, two Luce Scholarships, and one Rhodes Scholarship.

Rhodes is a hopeful place in a city rich with possibility. The continuity between a rich liberal arts curriculum and real-world context is unmatched, and students clearly feel like they're not just preparing to change the world. They're changing it now.

And if you're wise enough join them, you might soon sound like a 1996 graduate, an actor, who describes Rhodes as "a wonderful place that teaches us to be who we dream to be and accepts us for who we are while we are there."

MIDWEST

Beloit College

Beloit, Wisconsin

"[When] one considers that Beloit takes most of its applicants, who represent a fairly wide range of academic ability, and out-produces very selective schools in graduates who make significant contributions and achievements, that testifies to what good teachers have always known: that a mix of abilities produces a good synergy; it also says something good is happening in and out of its classrooms. . . . Many professors I spoke to agreed that a mix of abilities produces a more intellectually stimulating class of students who are much more willing to ask questions."

—LOREN POPE

Beloit (rhymes with "Detroit") College will surprise you. It has long been doing the quiet and important work of producing some of this country's leading thinkers and problem solvers. But it's not a prestige-driven place. Its free-spirited culture embraces learning as an adventure and a thrill, not a means to an end.

What else would draw—and more important, keep—1,350

students from nearly every state and forty countries to this quirky campus on the Wisconsin-Illinois border? Not the winter weather, certainly.

Much of its power comes from a faculty that relishes their roles as mentors and teachers and from a community that gives students incredible power over their education and their campus.

Students repeatedly bring up how much autonomy they have in satisfying their curiosity. One woman gushes about the college's creative writing program. "I'm writing my own play. It'll definitely be performed when I'm done." How does she know? "That's just Beloit. It's a nurturing environment. Nobody tells you no."

A sophomore from Texas who is a first-generation college student can't stop smiling when she says: "I feel like we're some of the luckiest people in the world. Beloit students have a strong sense of efficacy."

A student from San Francisco who transferred from the University of Arizona calls Beloit "the quirkiest place in the world, and absolutely the place for me." Another, a political-science major who guesses she may be one of a handful of politically conservative students on campus, says that she feels her viewpoints are heard in her politics classes but doesn't feel professors in other disciplines are as open about discussing a less liberal worldview. Still, she says she loves the campus because people are kind and interesting, and she feels supported. "Everything you do here opens another door for you," she explains.

The college sets the tone for this cerebral adventure with its Initiatives Program, a progressive program that guides students through their first four semesters. Many colleges require introductory courses for first-year students, with varying degrees of success, but Beloit's program goes beyond introducing freshmen to studying the liberal arts. Its goal is to guide each student gently so she can figure out what electrifies her academically. By the end of her sophomore year, she has designed her own academic path, and she understands its value and purpose.

The program begins with First-Year Initiatives (FYI), an interdisciplinary course that introduces students to Beloit's resources and the ways the college expects them to work and learn. In the summer, each freshman chooses the topic that most interests her, and the professor of that course becomes her adviser for her first two years. The course begins during New Student Days, orientation for first-year and transfer students a week before returning students show up, and continues through the first semester.

Second semester, students meet with advisers during formal and informal sessions, and many FYI classes meet socially—often at professors' houses—to catch up. "We become very fond of each other," says Olga Ogurtsova, a professor of Russian. "I love teaching FYI; it's such fun to get students early and watch them figure out just how much they can do."

Sophomore year, students can opt to take two more Initiatives courses: "Transformational Works" delves into works of literature, art, architecture, music, science, and film that had particular influence on the professors' and others' intellectual and personal development. "Enduring Questions" studies challenges or controversies that have afflicted human communities. Both reveal why and how the study of liberal arts helps solve complex problems.

And after four semesters of intellectual fun, students have solid plans for their learning—and Beloit rewards their diligence with Venture Grants, two-thousand-dollar awards that fund summer projects. Students must propose a project and apply, but the parameters are wide: The college encourages students to relate their learning to the idea of the "local," broadly defined.

Venture Grant winners have studied the birthplaces, museums, and libraries of lesser-known U.S. presidents; researched job satisfaction and conditions in garment factories in Bangladesh to see their impact on communities; and studied a food co-op at another college in order to establish one at Beloit.

The Initiatives Program works because professors are committed to it and to their students. "The most important thing here is how we deal with and communicate with students," Professor Ogurtsova says. "Students are part of my life. They come to my office at all hours; they come to my house; they call me and e-mail me almost nonstop. I know about their moms and their girlfriends and their dogs back home."

Professors are clearly fond of their students. "I feel like I've died and gone to heaven here," says Dr. Steve Wright, an English professor, who came to Beloit from Williams College. "The students here aren't as polished as Williams students, but I like what comes with that. Beloit students as a group aren't as interested in making a lot of money, but they're more interested in doing significant work."

To that end, Beloit emphasizes what it calls "liberal arts in practice," opportunities to test knowledge and solve problems outside the classroom. "Liberal arts in practice" is an organizing principle of the campus and the new curriculum launched in the fall of 2011. Crafted by a committee of professors, staff, and students, the curriculum requires each student to complete an experience beyond the traditional classroom: off-campus study, research-related fieldwork, an internship, or a community-service project. The curriculum also requires three writing courses—hefty but invaluable in a world where professionals' first impressions are often formed via e-mail—a cultural literacy course, a quantitative reasoning course, a capstone experience (likely related to a student's goals after college), and five "breadth" courses, one from each of five loosely organized academic areas. The goal is to promote interdisciplinary thinking, making connections among disparate topics to hone problem-solving and communication skills—and, of course, to connect the liberal arts to the real world.

Beloit has a long tradition of sending students abroad to test their ideas and skills in other cultures. About half go abroad at least once, and the college gets high marks for helping students prepare for their experiences in other countries. If you want to go abroad, you must complete an extensive application that asks you to anticipate the challenges you'll face. "I was much better prepared for my study-abroad experience than other people in my program [who weren't Beloiters]," says a woman who studied in Japan. "I had thought about what I hoped to learn and what my life would be like on the other side of the world. Most other people had just worried about the financial stuff and seemed surprised by and unable to really navigate the cultural differences. Since I had processed stuff earlier, I think I had a richer experience."

But it's not just study-abroad opportunities that prompt chemist Dr. Brock Spencer to call Beloit "rural but cosmopolitan." A notable 10 percent of students come from foreign countries, and the college also hosts an annual International Symposium at which students present their learning experiences, particularly as they relate to internships, volunteer work, field research, and personal reflection. And as part of the Weissberg Program in Human Rights, the Weissberg Chair in International Studies brings to campus a leader in international understanding. The residency lasts about a week, during which the guest gives a public talk and meets with students in formal and informal settings. For the 2010–2011 year, the Weissberg Chair was Iraqi minister of defense Ali Allawi.

In the spring of 2011, Beloit earned well-deserved recognition for its work equipping students to understand complex global issues: NAFSA, a nonprofit organization dedicated to international education, gave the college the Paul Simon Award for Campus Internationalization—one of five such honors bestowed on American colleges and universities. The award is the organization's top honor.

The shared spirit of inquiry at Beloit fuels more than an interest in global issues. "Learning here is collaborative," says Dr. Kristin Bonnie, a psychologist. "I'm learning along with my students. They ask questions I've never considered. We're feeding off each other." Dr. Spencer agrees: "The collegiality here is the reason I've stayed, and when I say 'collegiality,' I mean with other professors and with my students."

Perhaps no event represents this spirit better than the annual Student Symposium, an academic fair where about fifty selected students showcase their original research. Classes are canceled, and most of the college shows up to listen to students' presentations. "I love Symposium Day. It's exciting to learn what everyone is doing," says a junior anthropology major. "I feel like I came to Beloit a half sponge, and I've absorbed so much. I look at people at Symposium Day, and I just feel so proud to be part of this community."

It doesn't hurt that the community is a very pretty one. New Englanders (Yale alumni, to be exact) founded Beloit in the mid-1800s, and the campus is reminiscent of the Northeast, with big, brick buildings, winding pathways, and mature trees. (Lucky for students here, the surrounding community is far lovelier than New Haven.) In 2009 the college opened the Center for the Sciences, a LEED-platinum-rated building that houses the psychology, biology, chemistry, geology, and physics departments. The building's atrium and bright, airy classrooms are a boon for students and faculty, and its study spaces are designed to promote collaborative learning.

In 2010, Beloit unveiled the impressive Hendricks Center for the Arts, a renovated city library in downtown Beloit that houses the theater, music, and dance departments. The building's facilities are a vast improvement over the former spaces, and its location helps connect the college with the town, something students say is important to them.

More important than its aesthetic is the campus's vibe: President Scott Bierman says, "I was struck [when I visited during the interview process] by how wholeheartedly the college turns the campus over to students." It's true: The college relies less on policies and procedures than on a shared set of values. Administrators don't hide in ivory towers, and students mention that it's easy to get a meeting with senior administrators, including President Bierman. "He's everywhere. He's always asking students for their opinions," a junior from Chicago says. "If you run into him, you could have a fifteen-minute conversation about diversity issues or about when we're going to get new furniture in the Java Joint. He's totally here for the students." Not a single student in a dozen different conversations disagrees.

Prestige matters little at Beloit College, which is rather ironic because its graduates are an impressive bunch. For decades, the college has ranked among the top fifty colleges producing the highest percentage of the nation's future scientists and scholars. The

Higher Education Data Sharing Consortium ranks it in the top 10 percent of schools producing future PhDs. And Beloit is eleventh among the nation's most selective liberal arts colleges in the proportion of alumni who earn doctorates. The bottom line: If you want to go to graduate school and become an expert in your field, Beloit is an ideal first step.

What's more impressive is that Beloit achieves these tremendous results with a wide range of incoming students. The college accepts more than 70 percent of its applicants; the middle 50 percent of admitted students have SAT scores between 1120 and 1380 (critical reading and math) or ACT scores between 25 and 30. Their average high-school GPA was 3.5, and 94 percent of admitted students ranked in the top 50 percent of their high-school classes.

Here's more good news: If you have weak standardized test scores, don't fret: The admissions committee is far more interested in the classes you've taken in high school, your writing skills, and your interest in the kind of education Beloit offers. Test scores tend to be poor indicators of a student's aptitude for college work, and Beloit knows it.

Not a single professor complains about this mix of incoming students. Instead, they all express excitement at the chemistry created by students who aren't uniformly perfect—at least when you measure them against the false standards of test scores and high school ranks. "Not all our students are academic rock stars, but there's a symbiotic relationship among all kinds of students on campus. Even those kids who aren't rock stars know they have something to contribute," says Dr. Charles Westerberg, the associate dean of the college and a sociologist.

"We have good students—excellent students—and not-so-good students here, but we don't have boring students," Dr. Ogurtsova adds. "We believe in student growth. Where you start at Beloit is not where you will finish."

The campus is a generous place, a haven where people give their time and energy to help their peers, colleagues, and students hone their talents and pursue their interests, no matter how unusual. So it's fitting that the college has a tremendous financial aid policy. It meets 96 percent of demonstrated need, and loans make up only 10 percent of the average award—far more generous than colleges that have more resources and less educational impact. Beloit is a value.

Its scholarship programs reward strong academic performances in high school, but there are also awards for leadership, music, and National Merit Finalists, plus scholarships for students who are typically underrepresented on college campuses—first-generation students, ethnic minorities, and students from low-income families—and for students who studied abroad in high school. That the college invests in such a range of students shows its interest in creating a community of people with different talents, experiences, and interests.

Even a short visit will reveal that Beloit knows the recipe for a happy campus. Students say their confidence levels have skyrocketed since Beloit's professors helped cultivate their talents and taught them to trust their hunches. "Every semester, I get happier and happier," says a junior chemistry and French double major. "People are genuinely nice to each other here, even if they're not in your group of friends. Beloit isn't a place where you feel like, 'Okay, I've gotten everything I'm going to get here.' It's like reading a good book that just keeps going and going."

A couple of students complain that even though the college has a strong international-student population, its ethnic diversity is weak. Others wish they were a little closer to a major metropolitan area. (Chicago is about ninety miles away; Madison and Milwaukee are each about an hour's drive from Beloit.) More common are complaints about public transportation—"almost nonexistent"— and the food. (One student wonders: "How is it that Beloit can do hard things really well, like get international leaders to campus, but it can't do anything about our food?" His friends laugh.)

But the vast majority have only positive things to say about their experiences, and even those with complaints say they'd choose Beloit again if given the chance.

One alumna, an English PhD candidate at the University of California at Davis, sums it up perfectly (a skill she likely sharpened in her four years at Beloit): "Beloit alums don't settle for lives they don't have to live. They choose the lives they want to live." And there's no better endorsement for a liberal arts education than the freedom to choose your own adventure—not just for four years but for the rest of your life.

Cornell College

Mount Vernon, Iowa

"Speaking at a Midwest counselors' convention many years ago, I said, 'Cornell College will give your advisees a better education than Cornell University. The college's students will be actively engaged in their own education, not passive ears. Its able professors are there because they love to teach, and their research keeps them on the cutting edge. In the university the reverse is true; teaching undergraduates is a nuisance chore that helps fund research and the professors do little or none of it.' Seated next to me was Cornell University's admissions director. He treated it as a joke. But it was true then, is true now, and will always be unless there is an earth-shaking change."

—LOREN POPE

Take note: Cornell College, population 1,200, was the *first* Cornell, founded twelve years earlier than the university in Ithaca. It has a pioneering spirit: Its first student, in 1853, was a woman. Cornell was also the first college or university in Iowa to grant a degree to a woman and the first west of the Mississippi to give a woman a full professorship with a salary equal to that of her male colleagues. And in 1870 the college declared, "Color and race shall not be considered as a basis of qualification in the admission of students."

So it's fitting that Cornell College has a revolutionary calendar to match its spirit. Generally called the Block Plan, the Cornell version is dubbed OCAAT (pronounced "o-cat"), which stands for "one course at a time." The academic year is divided into eight blocks, each of which lasts for three and a half weeks. A student takes one course per block, has a four-day break, and then begins her next course. Similarly, professors teach only one course at a time. At a place where the average class size is seventeen students, that means the professor is focusing on a very small cohort of students. You'd be hard-pressed to find this kind of attention anywhere else.

A student spends three to five hours in class each day, Monday through Friday. A day might be divided however the professor sees fit: discussion and lecture, lab and fieldwork, independent research and group work. There are no artificial boundaries to cut off a class if it's hot on the trail of a new discovery or deep in a heated debate.

Cornell adopted OCAAT in 1978, when colleges were competing for fewer freshmen and the college's leadership realized Cornell needed something to distinguish it from the other very good liberal arts colleges around the country. A few professors suggested the college study the unique calendar offered by Colorado College. After a lot of research and study, the faculty voted to adopt it.

Make no mistake: OCAAT was not a marketing venture. It was a pedagogical one. "It seemed like a good idea, but only with experience have I come to realize how good an idea it is," says Dr. Craig Allin, a political scientist who was a junior faculty member during the late 1970s.

The advantages are many: Each professor can build the class schedule best suited to teaching the content instead of molding the content to fit the schedule. That means that professors infuse experiential learning opportunities into class frequently because they have the time to do it. A professor might lecture in the morning, and after lunch a guest speaker will visit, students will present a review of relevant literature, or teams will debate the relative merits of two divergent theories. And professors can dream up and offer off-campus courses because, of course, their students don't have to be anywhere else.

There are subtler benefits too. Students on strict schedules—those on the premed track, for example—can study abroad for a block, expanding their perspective on the world without losing pace with their prerequisites for professional school. Because classes all happen simultaneously, students in the sciences don't have to share lab space with another class, so they can conduct open-ended experiments, not the canned, three-hour labs so common in introductory college classes. Art students don't have to move easels or pack up their materials before another group moves in.

Professors are fanatical about OCAAT. Scientists love the time to work in the lab—to learn science by actually *doing* science. Linguists love the language immersion OCAAT offers. Artists love that the clock doesn't trump the muse. Over and over again, professors say they couldn't go back to the semester system because of the freedom the Block Plan offers them and their students.

Dr. Melinda Green, a psychologist, gave up a tenure-track job at another small college to come to Cornell for a two-year position. It was a risky move, but she eventually moved into a tenure-track position at Cornell. "[At my previous job] I was having to lecture a lot to be sure the students understood the content. I would try to include experiential activities and time for discussion, but the time was so compressed; we had three fifty-minute sessions a week. It just wasn't conducive to the kind of teaching I wanted to do," she says. "Here, we use so many different strategies and activities, I find that retention [of information] is dramatically improved."

Dr. Allin, who knew Cornell before the Block Plan, sums up the feelings of many of his colleagues: "For people who love to teach, OCAAT is like dying and going to heaven because the pedagogical possibilities are limited by your own imagination. Ever since we adopted it, Cornell has been attracting a very specific cohort of teachers, people who are excited by that degree of freedom."

Part of the attraction is what the calendar does for students. "On a typical semester system, students are taking four or maybe five courses. The student has a hierarchy of courses; something gets shirked," Dr. Allin adds. "Here, every student in every term is in the most important course. The level of involvement we get from our students went up dramatically when we made this change."

Professor Tony Plaut, an art professor, agrees: "Under the semester system, art might be of secondary value if a student isn't overly committed to art. Here, when they're in my class, making artwork is students' highest academic priority. I think that's not a small thing. Students who are taking my art class to fulfill a gen-ed requirement find themselves immersed in it. Rather than it being something they have to slog through, art becomes something that gets under their skin."

The intensity means professors have to be on their game, so the Block Plan is a kind of fail-safe against lazy teachers. It demands innovation and runs on intimacy, so professors who aren't interested in being creative and spending hours a day with the same small group of students rarely apply. And if they do, they don't get hired.

Professors must also be very, very prepared. "If I were teaching a new course on the semester plan, I could be a few steps ahead of my students. But here, I spend my time outside of class giving feedback on papers and labs. I can't be putting the finishing touches on my course," says Dr. Craig Tepper, a biologist. This idea should encourage families who wonder what they're getting for their investment in college: At Cornell, students get top-notch instruction from experts who love to teach and who turn their full attention to the content and the pedagogy that best suits that content. No flash, all substance.

And rigor. Students use the word "intense" to describe their academic lives, but they uniformly profess loving OCAAT. "You're getting the richness of the material all at once," says a senior from Los Angeles. A senior English major says, "We'll read three or four books during a block, and I can make so many connections in my mind since I'm not studying anything else." Another senior spent a semester in Greece on a traditional semester calendar. "The first three months felt so slow. It wasn't until the fourth month when I felt like we really got into it. Here, you jump in and start learning right away." They also feel that Cornell has sharpened their writing and ability to discuss and analyze—and cured them of any tendency to procrastinate.

Like professors at all of the schools in this book, Cornell's are devoted to students. "As a bunch, they're the most caring people I've run into," says a junior from Albuquerque. "I've never had a professor not give me his or her home phone number so I can call at night, at a reasonable hour, if I need help." A senior from Southern California has an illustrative story: "Last year, I was diagnosed with chicken pox. I was in my stats class, and I thought I would have to drop it because I needed to be in class to learn the material and ask questions. But my professor encouraged me not to give up. She met me on the weekends after I got better to help me catch up. She gave me her cell number and told me I could call her anytime. I made it through the course. Here's the thing: What she did was remarkable, but it's not unusual for Cornell. You could talk to anybody on campus, and you'd hear stories just like mine."

Cornell is a highly supportive place, but it's not for everyone: The Block Plan—coupled with professors' high standards—means that Cornell is not an ideal place for students with some types of learning disabilities, particularly if those LDs are related to reading. The pace here is fast. Some students benefit from the opportunity to focus, but if you need additional time to process information, Cornell might not be for you. Ask your admissions counselor to put you in touch with the college's director of student advising, who can help you determine if Cornell would be a good fit for you.

The college accepts about 64 percent of its applicants. The middle 50 percent of admitted students have GPAs between 3.2 and 3.8, SAT scores (critical reading and math) between 1140 and 1350, and ACT scores between 24 and 30. These are impressive numbers, but don't be intimidated if your transcript isn't quite so strong. Every year, Cornell accepts students whose records aren't perfect. Admissions staff members look closely at the level of academic preparation, motivation, and performance but they also have room for students who are able to demonstrate their intellectual curiosity, a sense of adventure that would make them achievers and contributors to campus.

Cornell's progressive history and unorthodox calendar set the tone for its campus culture. Only about a third of students come from Iowa; the rest come from forty-eight states and twenty-four foreign countries, and the campus embraces them all. Students frequently mention how comfortable they feel. "There's room for everyone at Cornell; you don't have to conform to anybody else's idea of a Cornell student," says a senior from Pennsylvania. Adds a senior from northern Virginia: "People are really friendly and open-minded." Professors often mention how impressed they are with their students. "They're serious and devoted and earnest," Professor Plaut says. "Cornell students are at college for the right reasons, not to escape something else or because their moms and dads made them come."

Some teachers muse that Cornell attracts a student who likes the unconventional. It takes some guts to come to a small town in Iowa where a school with the same name as an Ivy League university performs its primary task—teaching undergrads—differently from the vast majority of colleges in this country. But the statistics suggest that many of them love it: The college retains about 85 percent of its students from freshman to sophomore year—besting the national average for four-year private baccalaureate colleges by more than 16 percentage points—and 70 percent graduate in four years, more than 23 percentage points better than the national average for its peers.

Students are split on how they feel about Cornell's home, little Mount Vernon, which looks like it was plucked from a Norman Rockwell painting. Between Cedar Rapids and Iowa City (home of the University of Iowa), Mount Vernon is only 200 miles west of Chicago and 320 miles from the Twin Cities. But it feels set apart. Pretty Victorian homes, many of them inhabited by faculty and staff, surround the hilltop campus, and boutiques, coffee shops, and restaurants line First Avenue, the main street. A junior from Chicago says he loved it because he feels like the town adopts the students, making it easy to feel at home. A senior from Los Angeles says her adjustment to small-town living was hard. "Do I see myself living there after graduation? Absolutely not. Do I appreciate its charm? Yes, I really do. I think college students need to challenge themselves and put themselves in a new environment. That's what

I did, and I learned a lot about community that was different from my upbringing." Other students say that when they yearn for big-city amenities, they drive to Chicago or Minneapolis on their four-day breaks between blocks. And nobody complains of boredom.

Like many liberal arts colleges, Cornell has beefed up opportunities for students to apply their learning to the world beyond Mount Vernon. In 2009 the college reengineered its career-services center to marry career advising and experiential learning. Today the Career Engagement Center provides students innovative opportunities to test their ideas in the world of work and fire up their imaginations about what's possible with their liberal arts degrees.

Fortunately, Cornell's alumni network is vast and enthusiastic. "Alumni host interns [at their companies and organizations], do mock interviews, speak on campus, invite us to their companies," says R. J. Holmes-Leopold, the CEC's director. "We have alumni who are working in industries that seem to have little to do with their majors, but they're applying what they learned here in very different ways. The benefit of being liberally educated is that you have lots of options. Cornell couples this education with hands-on experience to make students even more competitive and help them clarify what they want to do."

One of the most exciting opportunities is Cornell Fellows, a high-level summer internship program. Students apply for thirty spots at organizations across the country where Cornell maintains partnerships: Baylor College of Medicine, the U.S. Holocaust Memorial Museum, the U.S. Conference of Mayors, the Mayo Clinic, Orchestra Iowa, the Translational Genomics Research Institute, elected representatives' offices, and many more. There are even posts abroad: The International Law and Society fellows travel to Budapest or Beijing.

The college provides $3,000 to each student interning in the United States, and international fellows get $4,100 to help cover costs. In exchange, students spend eight weeks on-site and must complete a tangible project—no fetching coffee. An on-site mentor gives guidance and helps develop the student's learning assessment. Students submit weekly activity reports reflecting on their experiences, complete a postfellowship report, and give a presentation at the annual Fellows Showcase.

These aren't the only internships available to Cornellians. Thanks again to the Block Plan, students can intern full time for a block, and many students earn credit for their work. And faculty hire students, particularly in the sciences and social sciences, to work on their established research programs each year. "Fundamentally, it's about helping our students build competencies they need and giving them opportunities to practice those competencies, so that by the time they need to put those skills into place, they have the ability to execute," Holmes-Leopold says. "When it comes down to it, it's going to be that student in front of an interviewer, and she's going to have to explain the value of her liberal arts education."

It's a safe bet that she won't have any trouble. Alumni frequently mention how effectively Cornell revealed to them what they could do and taught them how to jump in with both feet. It's enough to remind a liberal arts geek of Aristotle's famous description of excellence: "We are what we repeatedly do. Excellence, then, is not an act, but a habit."

And if you want more assurance of the college's power, consider these outcomes: Cornell ranks in the top seventy schools in production of future PhDs—that's the top 2.5 percent of the country's 2,700 four-year colleges and universities. Two-thirds of its graduates go on to earn advanced degrees. It ranks in the top fifteen colleges in the nation for NCAA Postgraduate Scholars, an award that recognizes academic and athletic achievement.

The marketplace of higher education is noisy. Institutions are losing their sense of mission, and rankings are distorting the purpose and promise of learning at the college level. Amid this rancor, Cornell is refreshing. Professors, students, administrators, and staff work for a common purpose: to educate and equip Cornell graduates for lives of work, leadership, and fulfillment. You won't find even a hint of Ivy envy, and people here are absolutely sure that *this* Cornell sets the standard for learning and teaching. They're right.

Denison University

Granville, Ohio

Denison is as beautiful a college campus as you'll find anywhere. On a hill above the charming New England–esque town of Granville, the university's grand brick buildings, winding pathways, and wide-open quad feel like a campus dreamed up by Hollywood set designers. In reality, renowned nineteenth-century landscape designer Frederick Law Olmsted planned the campus. Olmsted also designed Central Park, as well as the campuses at Stanford, Yale, and Wellesley.

Denison's pretty setting is home to about 2,200 undergraduates who know that the university has substance to match its style, thanks to several transformative decades.

The university has a long history of producing distinguished citizens, scientists, and scholars, but in the late seventies it had the reputation of being a backup school for easterners. Fraternities and sororities ruled the social scene, and the atmosphere was exclusive and cliquish.

In the late eighties, Dr. Michele Tolela Myers became president, and in ten years she significantly changed the ethos. Scholarships for outstanding students and bright new academic programs attracted serious and idealistic students, crowding out the less serious and less engaged. President Myers also boosted diversity and, in the mid-2000s, closed fraternities' houses (sororities had never had them), forcing all students to live in the dorms together. There was a significant uproar on campus (and from some alumni), but the result is a campus that feels scholarly and welcoming.

The change didn't stop there. In the fall of 2007, Denison students closed down the campus for a few days because they wanted to talk seriously about race, ethnicity, and GLBTQ issues on campus. The university had boosted its diversity in the early years of the new millennium, but it hadn't planned well to support its changing population. "Denison didn't think about what it means to have a multicultural campus, and students were upset," says provost Brad Bateman, PhD. Eighteen hundred students attended an all-campus forum, and after seven hours of conversation, more than half of the faculty stayed on campus all night, listening to students in their dorms.

Denison responded quickly to students' concerns—an indication of the type of care you'll find from professors and administrators if you enroll. The curriculum committee reviewed the university's course offerings and thought about how advising worked (or didn't). Based on the committee's recommendations, Denison made some changes: In 2008–2009, it piloted a one-credit First-Year Studies course that meets once a week in a dorm lounge or study area. One professor leads a group of ten students through a close examination of the college's mission statement and statement on diversity. The goal: to help students become more actively engaged in their learning and the college community, and to give them room to examine how they might respond to people and ideas they've never met.

At the same time the committee made its recommendations, Denison received a grant from the Mellon Foundation that funded three summers of faculty workshops on advising. Part of the training coaches professors on how to engage students in discussions about how they can select courses to learn about unfamiliar cultures and ideas.

Then in the fall of 2010, after more than two years of careful planning, Denison added a "power and justice" graduation requirement. A course that satisfies this requirement looks at how issues of power and justice are adjudicated in society.

On top of all these changes, Denison also found new ways to integrate faculty into students' lives outside of class. A new program brings faculty members into the dining halls for dinner several times a year, and professors from the modern languages department serve as advisers at a new Language House for first-year students majoring in languages. The university has reduced its student body slightly—by about one hundred students—and boosted faculty positions, leading to a ten-to-one student-faculty ratio. Every faculty member has a terminal degree in his or her field.

"There's no question we are a college in change," says Dr. Laurel Kennedy, vice president of student affairs. "There's been a contest for which students control the culture of the college. Increasingly, it's the students who are deeply involved and who are trying to get more from their experiences. We're doing everything we can to support that swing, and I think we're doing a good job—a very, very good job—of it."

Dr. Kennedy also lauds the university's model of sustained dialogue. "If you're looking for a place where administrators and teachers care about what you say, that's Denison. The whole community has learned to listen well." For her part, Dr. Kennedy has office hours each week in the student union. "I just sit at a table and students stop by to tell me what they're thinking about."

As if to signal the changes in the community, Denison has revamped many of its facilities in recent years, investing about $280 million in its spaces and infrastructure. In 2009 it transformed the former men's gym into the Bryant Arts Center, a stunning home for the studio art and art history departments, where natural light and raw materials inspire even the most hesitant student. The university opened the renovated Ebaugh Laboratories in 2011; the space includes flexible labs, immersive learning technology, and cooperative spaces to foster student-faculty research.

Denison also takes its students' quality of life seriously. It requires students to live on campus all four years—a key to its strong sense of community—and new residence halls mean that every senior lives in an apartment-style dorm. And in the fall of 2010, the university broke ground on a $38.5 million renovation and expansion of its Mitchell Recreation and Athletics Center, which includes a new Olympic-size pool.

Denison's good looks would be enough to persuade some students to enroll, but the real reasons you should go there are the opportunities for genuine learning. Students at Denison do not float through their four years, checking off required courses and finding the path of least resistance. "It would be so weird for someone to phone it in," says a junior from Pennsylvania. "There's a culture of participation here, in class and in the community. Even if you weren't very involved in high school, you'll find something— more like four or five things—that make you happy and fulfilled."

Faculty support—and expect—that involvement. Across disciplines, there is a spirit of possibility. "Give me your attention, invest your talents, and dare to try something that feels a little uncomfortable—and I can almost guarantee you'll uncover skills and passion that surprise you," says art professor and printmaker Ronald Abram.

Professor Abram came to Denison "because the smallness of my own college community is the reason I am who I am." He loves the liberal arts college, he says, because the arts allow students to express ideas they've discovered in their other classes—but not if those classes aren't engaging. "I think art in a liberal arts context is powerful stuff," he adds. "I can teach you techniques, but you must be the dreamer, the idea generator. That only happens when you're wrestling with new information, ideas you haven't encountered before."

Denison students are willing to work hard for this kind of payoff. Professors describe them as "earnest," "eager," "involved," and "ambitious"—nearly identical to the ways students depict themselves. (Students add that they know how to have fun too. "It's a work-hard-play-hard place," a senior explains. They're also more polished and preppy than students at most of the other schools in this book.)

Dr. Tom Schultz, a biologist, did his postdoctoral work at Yale, where, he says, "students were very motivated and bright, but they were self-satisfied. If you gave them a C—because they earned that C—they protested. Here, students know less about what they want to do, but they're doers. I find it tremendously fun to help students mesh their passion and their careers." Biologists often think they must go to med school, but Dr. Schultz has stories of alumni who teach, consult, lobby, and research.

One of Denison's distinguishing features is professors' interest in the power and art of teaching. "We're restless, never satisfied with our teaching," Dr. Schultz says. "We watch each other teach. In the bio department, we have pods made up of young, midcareer, and older teachers, and we observe each other, share ideas, and give feedback." Other departments have similar programs, all of them initiated by the professors themselves.

An excellent example of professors' commitment to teaching is the Summer Scholars Program, a ten-week session in the summer that gives about 140 students real-life research experience, either as independent researchers with faculty guidance or as assistants to professors. Each student gets a $3,700 stipend and on-campus housing. The program crosses disciplines, so "you have a group of students who are artists and scientists and literary theorists all working on ideas that interest them with faculty mentorship," says Dr. James Pletcher, a political scientist. "Talk about transformative. This is training ground for graduate school."

He would know: Dr. Pletcher is the director of the Gilpatrick Center for Student Fellowships and Research, Denison's clearing-house for scholarship, internship, and research opportunities during and after college. One example of its impact is the number of Fulbright Scholarships Denison's students have won, ranking it among the top twenty liberal arts colleges in the country for Fulbright winners.

The university is also proud—justifiably so—of its arts program. In addition to the BA in studio art, the university offers a BFA degree, a more intensive arts curriculum with emphasis on studio time. It's an unusual offering for a small school. So is the dance major, a course of study that engages the mind as much as the body. The cinema major emphasizes the aesthetic, historical, philosophical, and technical elements of filmmaking, and the theater department has been the launching point for many careers on Broadway and in Hollywood. A dance major explains: "When I came, I was crazy about dance, so I knew I wanted to major in it, but I didn't realize how much our professors would make us connect our art to our other classes and to scholarly thoughts. Arts majors are legitimate scholars too, and nobody here would deny that."

This breadth of experience, combined with professors' passion, makes for satisfied students. "Professors have treated me like their own daughter," says a senior from Southern California. Students from across the country and at every point in their Denison experiences say they'd do it again "in a heartbeat" and "without hesitation." Most say that even though Denison was at or near the top of their lists of prospective schools, the university has exceeded their expectations. The most common complaint is the flip side of a virtue that many laud: the small size. "People know you here. That's awesome when you're in class and your professor can help you get better or you need some one-on-one help. That's not as awesome when you realize people know everything about you," a sophomore says.

Denison retains 90 percent of its students from freshman to sophomore year, and 82 percent graduate in four years; on average, only 48 percent of students at private colleges and universities in the United States graduate in four years.

Denison's list of notable alumni is long, given its size. It includes actors Steve Carell and Jennifer Garner; Disney CEO Michael Eisner; writer James Frey (of the faux memoir *A Million Little Pieces*); Charles Henry, former chairman of the board of Amnesty International; Terry Jones, founder of Travelocity.com and chairman of Kayak.com; and a significant number of politicians, business execs, and researchers.

If you'd like to join their ranks, you'll be glad to know that Denison accepts about half of its applicants. The average admitted student scored between 1090 and 1380 on the SAT (critical reading and math) and between 27 and 30 on the ACT. But if your scores are weak, you don't have to submit them: Denison is test optional, a decision made by an almost-unanimous vote of the faculty.

"We're interested in interesting people," says Perry Robinson, vice president and director of admissions. "There's always been a question about the validity of the SAT and ACT to predict a student's ability to succeed the first year of college, and when we looked at our own students, we found that those who had the advantage of test-prep courses either in their high schools or from outside sources did better." Instead of looking at test scores, Denison looks first and most closely at a student's day-to-day performance in high school courses—a much more reliable predictor of college success.

Denison has a very healthy endowment—about $580 million in 2010—and unlike some schools that have plenty of wealth, the university shares it. The university has boosted its financial-aid funds in recent years. Half of the student body gets need-based financial aid, and 95 percent of students get need-based aid, merit-based aid, or both. "We can really make it possible for students who want to be here to come to Denison," says President Dale Knobel. The average student who borrows money for her Denison education owes a little more than $16,000 when she graduates, one-third less than the national average of about $25,000 (based on data from 2010).

What you'll learn at Denison is well worth the investment. Dr. David Woodyard, an alumnus who has been teaching religion at Denison since 1959—and a patriarch of Denison—has seen his alma mater resist the trends that water down the undergraduate experience at the majority of American colleges and universities. His daughter went to Ohio State and "never even sat down with a faculty member to arrange her schedule," he says. "When it came time for graduate school, she had nobody to write a recommendation." What he has witnessed at Denison in more than fifty years is just the opposite: a community strengthened over time by its unflagging commitment to students and to rigorous education for all who enter. "The academic process is life changing. We hold up for examination what students believe and give them time and resource to reflect. Good teaching changes consciousness, and that changes lives."

Earlham College

Richmond, Indiana

"If every college and university sharpened young minds and consciences as effectively as Earlham does, this country would approach utopia. People would tend to live by reason and the Golden Rule, they would vote by their convictions rather than by their pocketbooks, and our capitalist society would be a model. But by itself Earlham has made great contributions and it quietly sets the standard."

—LOREN POPE

If you're looking for a place that takes you seriously and helps you create a vision for your life—not just your career but your *whole* life—Earlham might be the place for you.

Founded by Quakers, the college has a mission in line with the Friends' perspectives on the world. It emphasizes the pursuit of truth, lack of coercion, respect for others' ideas and values, and a responsibility to use truth to improve the world. The result? A community as caring and sincere as you'll find anywhere.

Its 1,200 students are a passionate, earnest group. They believe in their power and responsibility to change the world; they have a sense of stewardship about their lives.

In the spring of her senior year, a woman from Michigan reflects on her Earlham experience: "I feel like I get the questions asked of me all the time here: Who are you? What will you do? I came here wanting to find out who I was, and I feel like I've developed my talents and I have a sense of what to do with them and why. I'm excited to go into the world and do good work for others. I don't need status symbols to confirm that my work and life are valuable."

A senior from Brooklyn adds: "Earlham gives you time and space to reflect. If I had gone anywhere else, I would be heading to law school because that's what my eighteen-year-old self thought I should do; I was on a path to make money. Now I know that I want to teach. I have asked myself, 'What will make you happiest? Most creative? What's my greatest good?' The answer is teaching."

Students and professors talk frequently about "discovering the teacher within"—a poetic description pulled from the college's mission statement. (Where else do students actually quote the college's mission statement?) It refers to Earlham's power to turn a student into a lifelong learner.

So it's no wonder that 15 percent to 17 percent of Earlham students are children of college and university professors and administrators. Many more are children of K–12 educators. The moral is clear: People who know what a top-notch education should look like send their children to Earlham.

What's more, graduate and professional-school admissions committees know about Earlham. About 10 percent of Earlham graduates go on to receive PhDs, putting it in the ninety-eighth percentile of 1,533 colleges and universities in the country in PhD production. (Those 1,533 schools include such places as Stanford, Indiana University, the University of Michigan, and the University of North Carolina.) Earlham has near-perfect acceptance rates to graduate and professional programs, particularly in the sciences and medicine.

Earlham's eight-hundred-acre campus is handsome and well maintained. The front two hundred acres house the academic buildings, residence halls, and playing fields. Adirondack chairs clumped loosely in the center of this area are called "the heart" of campus. On the back six hundred acres, appropriately called "back campus," you'll find an impressive equestrian center complete with indoor and outdoor riding arenas, plus a natural laboratory of woods, creek, and meadows cut by jogging and cross-country paths.

The community's governance structure depends on the Quaker model of consensus: Instead of merely voting and letting the majority make a choice that the whole group must abide, or giving the highest-ranking member the power, the consensus process emphasizes bringing unity to the group.

Here's (loosely) how it works: A group gathers to discuss a matter. One person serves as the convener or clerk. People share their opinions but never state direct opposition to another person's ideas. (In fact, it's important to address the whole group, not a single person.) The clerk listens and presents a statement that reflects the attitudes of the group. When the participants believe the clerk's statement reflects the opinion of the whole group, they agree to it.

Students use consensus for decisions across campus. For example, in each residential hall, students gather shortly after move-in to decide, by consensus, if the bathrooms will be coed or single sex. The college's new coffee shop is managed by students who use consensus to make all decisions.

A large majority of Earlham's students aren't Quakers, and they admit that at first, the consensus process is "exhausting" or "strange." "You feel like, 'Okay, already. Can we just vote? I have homework to do,'" a senior says. But over time, they say, consensus helps them learn to listen.

Indeed, that's part of its value, says president emeritus Douglas Bennett. "New students can easily think, 'If I don't agree with something, it must not be legitimate,' but we hope that they develop a deep habit of listening to other people." Even Earlham's board of trustees uses consensus to make decisions.

Another of Earlham's crowning achievements is its emphasis on study abroad. As many as 80 percent of students go abroad, putting Earlham among the top schools for international learning experiences. The college runs fifteen programs across the globe and partners with the Great Lakes College Association to offer another half dozen. Earlham also offers a May term, a four-week session at the end of the year, when students often go abroad with professors. Recent courses during this term included "Language, Art, and Religion in Senegal," "Bahamas Iguanas," "Temple and Shrine Pilgrimage in Kyoto, Japan," and "Geology in the American West."

Earlham's curriculum reflects both the interrelatedness of world issues and the fact that international education is not just for the few specializing in international studies, not just for those studying off campus, but for every citizen who wishes to be educated in the broadest sense for life in the twenty-first century. The college's popular Peace and Global Studies Program sends students to Northern Ireland or the U.S-Mexico border to see firsthand the strategies they've studied in class. Earlham has long been an excellent place to learn to speak Japanese and prepare for a career involving Japanese culture. And now the college is expanding its Asian studies with an initiative in China led by a philosophy professor. In the spring of 2010, fourteen professors from different disciplines traveled through China to learn about its history, culture, language, and politics. The goal was to help professors infuse material about China into their regular courses and inspire them to develop new courses that help Earlhamites understand China.

Students (and professors) constantly coming and going in such programs give the Earlham community a cosmopolitan awareness and sophistication. The effect is to make one sensitive to the fact that no man is an island and to the Quaker belief that everyone deserves respect.

As you might guess, the campus is an egalitarian, casual place. Students and professors address one another by first name, and students bubble with obvious affection for their teachers. "You feel like hugging your professors when you see them," says a sophomore from Mexico City. (Notably, this student is a man; it's not just women who gush over their professors.) "My French teacher is one of my best friends," says a senior majoring in comparative languages and linguistics.

The feeling is mutual. Professors emphasize two things: first, their genuine fondness for their students. Students "push you. Their expectations are high, and I don't want to disappoint them," says Dr. John Iverson, a biologist. "They are colleagues." Adds Dr. Kathy Milar, a psychologist: "They're quite fantastic. Even the ones who aren't the top students in my class are engaged. I'm glad to be a part of their lives, every one of them."

Second, professors repeatedly mention how easily Earlham can respond to professors' and students' interests. "Here, we can say, 'This is what I care about,' and the people around us say, 'Yes, we care about it too.' Then it's just a matter of figuring out the details," says Dr. Joann Quinones, an English professor. Dr. Milar gives this example: "I wanted to develop a class for nonscience students who wanted to learn more about the brain. I mentioned [this] to a few other faculty members, and within a very short amount of time, we had a new course called 'Narratives and Neuroscience.'" Professors say that kind of collaboration is one of the reasons they've stayed.

Collaborative learning is elemental to an Earlham education. About twenty years ago, grants from the Ford and Knight foundations established the Ford/Knight Program, which funds fifteen to twenty student-faculty research projects each year. Each professor works with four or five students on a project, which culminates in a public presentation. The topics come from all academic disciplines.

Students call their community a "safe space" to be yourself. "We respect everyone's voice," says a senior English major. A junior adds: "It has messed with the way I think. I see other viewpoints when I come across a conflict."

Notably, when political scientist Charles Murray, author of the controversial *The Bell Curve*, came to campus in the spring of 2011, a student pulled the fire alarm to stop his speech—twice. (A few years earlier, neoconservative Fox News commentator William Kristol took a pie in the face during a speech on campus.) The college community began a long discussion about racial relations on campus; Murray's book argues, among other things, that genetics play a significant role in intelligence and that those factors might be unevenly distributed among ethnicities. The conversation also addressed how a community of learners—who pride themselves on tolerance—responds to a person who represents viewpoints very different from their own.

It's important to note that students who are politically conservative "might not be comfortable" at Earlham and would "definitely be challenged" by their classmates and teachers, students say. "I think Earlham wears its leftist attitudes as a badge of honor.

Conservatives have a hard time here. 'Republican' is kind of an insult," a senior says.

But the college is working to mitigate that attitude. Wendy Seligmann, the associate dean for student success, says there is an "ongoing discussion about how to make conservative students comfortable here. It's definitely a conversation among students and staff."

If you're a liberal eager for a home or a conservative ready to rock the boat, you'll be glad to know that the college accepts more than 70 percent of its applicants; the middle 50 percent of these students have GPAs between 3.2 and 3.9, ACT scores between 24 and 30, and SAT scores (critical reading and math) between 1080 and 1360. About 55 percent of students are in the top 25 percent of their high-school classes. But the admissions office looks far beyond test scores to the whole person. "We're looking for curiosity and a streak of independence in [students'] learning," says Nancy Sinex, director of admissions.

On average, Earlham meets about 86 percent of a student's demonstrated need, and the average package in the fall of 2010 was $32,000, 10 percent of which was made up of loans (the cost of attendance was almost $46,000 that year). Ninety percent of students received financial aid. The college invests a significant amount of its own money in student aid.

Earlham's scholarship programs include Bonner Scholars, a four-year leadership program rooted in community service. Select campuses around the country (including several in this book) were chosen by the Bonner Foundation to participate in this excellent program. The Bonner Scholarship provides tuition and summer support for fifteen Earlham students in each class who demonstrate a commitment to community service. Students with high financial need and passion for community service should apply.

Earlham also participates in the Davis United World College Scholars program, awarding scholarships to international students who graduate from any of the United World Colleges, a network of thirteen schools on five continents that enroll students from all over the world. Earlham has one of the highest percentages of Davis

Scholars of any participating college in the country. (That's one of the contributing factors to its impressive international student population, which makes up 16 percent of its student body and represents eighty-one countries.)

Earlham's own scholarship programs invest in a range of students: Presidential Honors Scholars are students who meet certain GPA, test-score, and high-school-curricular requirements; the award is worth $10,500 a year. The Cunningham Scholarship, also worth $10,500, goes to African American and Hispanic/Latino students with strong academic records, and the Wilkinson Award goes to students who are members of or active in the Society of Friends (Quakers). And new to the roster of awards is the Quaker Fellows scholarship, awarded to twenty-five students who qualify for the Wilkinson and commit to six hours a week of community service and reflection (similar to the Bonner Scholars program).

But the college's support of new students extends well beyond financial aid. To welcome freshmen to their community, a team of upperclassmen serve as mentors during New Student Orientation. Each mentor has a group of ten to twelve new students to help in the transition to college. Mentors reach out during the school year too.

Freshmen take two required courses to ease them through the transition to college-level thinking. In the Earlham Seminar, a group of no more than sixteen students studies a topic with a professor who helps deepen their ability to inquire—to ask analytical questions and approach texts and other sources of information. Professors dream up topics so fascinating, it's a wonder a student can narrow down his choice to one; recent Earlham Seminars have tackled the definition of "true art," asked how different cultures define heroes (and looked closely at such heroes as Beowulf, Batman, and England's King Richard III), and studied literature about the terror attacks of September 11, 2001.

The Earlham Seminar's sister course, Interpretive Practices (IP), emphasizes critical reading and writing. Each IP course is limited to sixteen students, who investigate such topics as war and gender, how our surroundings influence our identity, and the 1804 Haitian Revolution and its afterlives. By choosing topics of such weight, professors proclaim their faith in students' ability to think about issues that matter and prepare them for four years of earnest conversation.

This level of engagement is a hallmark of an Earlham education. Provost emeritus and former philosophy professor Len Clark explains what happens: "From the first day, their responsibility to learn from and with other students is stressed. That is a Quaker tenet and a part of the mission of the college. It takes new students by surprise but then liberates them. It takes some practice to listen to and learn from other students and to build on ideas the other people have. That's a central focus of the humanities program for the first year. They talk about the text and then they talk about one another's analysis of the text. There are lots of exercises throughout the curriculum doing that, and that's of central importance to making students successful later because almost nobody works by himself, in the college or in this new world."

And when graduates get out into the brave new world, they're prepared for lives of learning, service, and satisfying work. A National Public Radio congressional reporter says, "It is the focus and attention of the teaching staff and a ruling sense of social responsibility that makes the school truly change lives." And a 1992 graduate summarizes the thoughts of many others when he says, "Academics, global travel, local community volunteerism, principled community life on campus, individual student-teacher relationships— it all seemed seamless at Earlham, which is why so many alums refer to our 'Earlham experience,' rather than to our 'Earlham education.'"

Hillsdale College

Hillsdale, Michigan

Outside of Lane Hall, one of little Hillsdale College's main academic buildings, is a block of concrete inscribed with two words: "Prove it." In spirit and philosophy, it's a near-perfect representation of this college of 1,400 students in rural south-central Michigan.

Hillsdale is one of very few colleges in the country that doesn't accept any federal or state subsidies. Its keepers are highly skeptical of the constitutionality of the federal government's role in higher education, and by refusing taxpayer dollars the college frees itself from the regulations of the Higher Education Act's Title IV, which requires, among other things, that colleges count students by race.

Hillsdale's objection springs from its founding in 1844. In its charter, the college prohibits discrimination by race, sex, or religion, making it a pioneer in admitting students by ability, not demographics. About 130 years after its founding, the college got into a scuffle with the federal government over this issue of quantifying students by race; the college took on the bureaucrats, and in 1984 the U.S. Supreme Court ruled against the college. So Hillsdale decided it could do its work without federal aid.

Because of this independent spirit—and its nose thumbing in the general direction of D.C.—the college has long been thought of as a bastion of political conservatism. This reputation is, as reputations tend to be, half true. The majority of its 1,400 students lean right politically, but they're not wandering campus quoting Margaret Thatcher to one another or wishing aloud they had been born to live through Ronald Reagan's presidency. As a whole, they're far less interested in politics than they are in the classical liberal arts. So are professors.

"This isn't the headquarters of the Republican army," says a senior English major with a wry smile. "Most of us are conservative, but we don't agree on everything. The expression of our political and personal views is pretty diverse, just like I think liberals' expressions are. Come to class. You'll see much more disagreement and discussion than you will nodding heads." A senior triple-majoring in French, politics, and philosophy says he hasn't thought much about the college's politics since he arrived as a freshman. "Most people are more interested in discussing ideas. The conservative nature of things comes from our belief that there's value in the classical tradition. We want to conserve that."

He's referring to Hillsdale's robust core curriculum, which fills about half of students' credit hours. They study a survey of great books, physical and biological sciences, literature, fine arts, history of the Western world, social sciences, and philosophy and religion. The college also requires a course in the U.S. Constitution. And much like St. John's, Hillsdale relies on primary sources, not textbooks, so students must wrestle with what one student calls "the real thing, not some guy's interpretation of the real thing."

The college has high ambitions for its core courses. People here believe that by examining the biggest, most powerful ideas in history, a student can learn not just how to think critically and solve problems but also to discover truth and, in that discovery, find and embrace virtue. Students talk about "the permanent things"—what has endured over time—and they're generally eager to figure out why those things have lasted.

"The value of the core is twofold," says Dr. David Whalen, the provost. "On the one hand, there's very much of a kind of intellectual cultural patrimony or inheritance that a student receives from the core curriculum. It is one of the primary functions of higher education, to give the students their culture in its many expressions.

In many cases, that's done away with. It's a pot of gold just left to lie on the roadside, and we're very busy getting those treasures into the students' hands.

"Second, a liberal college education is not just about receiving the higher reaches of your own civilization. It's also about perfecting the intellect. Judgment and taste need to be sharpened and elevated. We do that well." Not everyone ends up with the same tastes or opinions, but they do end up with a strong desire for discourse rooted in truth, not fanciful rhetoric.

Students love and struggle with the core. "I was taken aback by the core curriculum. I didn't like the idea that someone else was going to tell me what to study," says a senior politics major. "Now I see that I'm going into the world with the ability to think about a variety of topics in a critical manner. I know how to write. I can spot faulty reasoning. I'm really grateful Hillsdale forced me to learn these things." A philosophy major planned to study psychology when he arrived at Hillsdale: "I took my first philosophy course only because the core required it. The professors said, 'Prove you exist.' I thought, 'I should be able to answer that, but I can't.' It began to shift how I thought about things. It forced me to look at my views and opinions, instead of just accepting them because they came from a high-school teacher."

Hillsdale's rigor is legendary. (The "Prove It" message was a gift from the class of 1875, who probably had red-inked notes to that effect on their papers.) Several students mention the jolt of their fall semester freshman year. The reading load is heavy; writing is central to all disciplines. A senior remembers his first two weeks with a mixture of pain and awe: "I did horribly in some of my classes. I got a paper back and it didn't even have a grade on it. My professor said, 'Please come see me. You'll have to start over.' I went to the guy in the room next to mine and said, 'This is crazy.' But I saw in the upperclassmen such wisdom and excitement. I wanted that too, so I stayed. The academic challenge at Hillsdale made me grow more than any other experience in my life. There's a common thread here that nobody can quite explain, but we talk about how much the academic program has influenced us."

Students are earnest, friendly, and thoughtful. They aren't interested in the easy road or small talk, unless it's about who will win the Ultimate Frisbee tournament. Many of them mention building close friendships at Hillsdale: "I could walk twenty-five steps from my [dorm] room and have deep conversations with any one of five or six guys about life, faith, and existence," says a freshman. A junior beams, "I have found my best friends for life here." Students come from forty-six states and eight foreign countries; 62 percent grew up outside of Michigan. "We're not all the same, but we definitely share an interest in pursuing the truth and defending it," says a senior. "We're sharing this experience, which builds a bond among students. It's awesome to be in class with people who take learning seriously. It's exciting."

The college accepts 54 percent of its applicants. The middle 50 percent scored between 26 and 31 on the ACT and between 1210 and 1440 on the SAT (critical reading and math). They earned GPAs between 3.6 and 4.0. Hillsdale has a retention rate among the highest in the country: 96 percent of freshmen return for sophomore year, and 67 percent graduate in four years, besting the national average for four-year private schools by 20 percentage points.

Students live by an honor code that embodies the spirit of the place: "A Hillsdale College student is honorable in conduct, honest in word and deed, dutiful in study and service and respectful of the rights of others. Through education, the student rises to self-government." Any student you meet can quote it to you. It's distinctive because among liberal arts colleges with great traditions of honor-bound living, Hillsdale's doesn't merely prohibit lying, cheating, and stealing; it explains why honor matters: The honorable learn how to self-govern, which leads, according to the college, to "liberty of soul."

Students leave backpacks in the student union and laptops in the library. Theft is very rare; so is cheating. A senior mentions that when she was a freshman, she lost her cell phone. "I thought I'd never see it again," she says. A fellow student found the phone on the sidewalk, called the owner's mom, and asked for the student's name. He tracked her down in her dorm and returned the phone. "That's the kind of place this is."

Professors respect and enjoy their students, and the feeling is mutual. Students describe the faculty as "amazing," "brilliant," "genuinely kind," and "dedicated to us and to the college's mission." Professors say they love seeing teenagers arrive as high-school students who got rewarded for repeating whatever the textbook said and watching them transform into independent thinkers.

Dr. Justin Jackson, an English professor, speaks for his colleagues: "Students will do what you ask them to do. It is still very surprising to me. You can keep setting the standards higher and higher and they will try to achieve, and not simply for the grades. They're engaged in an intellectual pursuit, and eventually, almost all of them let the pursuit, not the grade, be the prize. My colleagues at other schools long for this type of teaching experience."

Art professor Barbara Bushey says, "I love when students come to my office and say, 'This doesn't pertain to class, but I have a question.' They're connecting ideas from their other courses, and we get to participate in their journeys. I have the best job in the world."

Some professors, especially those who aren't particularly passionate about politics, say they were skeptical at first of Hillsdale. Would they have to walk a particular political line? Would the students be ideologues? The answers are no and no. Professors say they have found a range of political opinions among their colleagues and students, and if students come with political opinions, they learn how to examine, defend, and sometimes revise them. "You might think people here would love Henry Ford, but if you put Henry Ford up against Marx in their visions of the worker as a human being, the students would embrace Marx every time," Dr. Jackson says. "I find that very interesting and refreshing."

Students are dinner guests at their professors' homes and babysit their children. During homecoming weekend, many faculty members host dinner parties for alumni. "I am still in contact with most of the students who have passed through this department in twenty-eight years," says Professor George Angell, chair of the theater and speech department. "I go to their weddings, and I meet their kids. I'm having my first wave of the children of my alums coming back to the college to visit."

Students and professors laud the sense of community at the college, which matters because the town of Hillsdale is almost a blink-and-you'll-miss-it kind of place. Some students admit that the town nearly dissuaded them from enrolling, but they trusted the upper-classmen's promise that the campus was active, so they wouldn't need much from the town. Without exception, dozens of students testify to their busy schedules and to broad campus offerings. And if you're desperate for a change of venue, beautiful Ann Arbor, home of the un-Hillsdalian University of Michigan, is a short seventy-five-minute drive away.

For a real change of pace, Hillsdale offers a satellite program in Washington, D.C., at the Allan P. Kirby Center, which pairs juniors and seniors with semester-long internships at sites including the U.S. House, the U.S. Senate, the White House, news outlets, think tanks, lobbying firms, national-security agencies, and private companies. Students also take two courses while living and working in D.C.: one in public policy and the other in national security studies. The college also offers an intensive program in statesmanship and constitutionalism called the George Washington Fellowship Program. High-achieving sophomores with an interest in public policy and public service apply for the program, which integrates the D.C. internship with a larger set of required courses and additional research and writing related to constitutionalism. Each fellow gets a half-tuition scholarship as well.

Because of Hillsdale's policy on government aid, the college provides all scholarship and need-based financial support by itself. It has a strong endowment for a school its size (almost three hundred million dollars in 2011) and a very reasonable price tag: In an era when good private colleges cost upward of fifty thousand dollars a year, Hillsdale's total costs for 2011 were less than thirty thousand dollars. Its average aid award was twelve thousand dollars—making the average student's net cost lower than that at most of the colleges in this book.

The investment is worthwhile. In the college's own surveys of the classes of 2008, 2009, and 2010—when the economy was deep in the tank—97 percent of graduates were fully employed or in graduate school within six months of earning their degrees. About 20 percent go straight into graduate study, while 45 percent get advanced degrees within three years of leaving Hillsdale.

The effects of a college education are both qualitative and quantitative, and President Larry Arnn, PhD, is perhaps more interested in the qualitative aspects of his students' learning. "We set students' sights on the highest things in this world," he says. "The good, the true, the beautiful. Are we conservative? In the classical sense, yes. The majority of what we teach our students is older than the United States, and it certainly predates the modern conservative movement."

President Arnn is prone to quoting Winston Churchill, the Declaration of Independence, and Aristotle, particularly *Nicomachean Ethics*, the Greek philosopher's views on how human beings should best live. It's a fitting document for Hillsdale's spirit.

The irony of Hillsdale is that in embracing its independence and teaching a classical curriculum, it looks like a renegade in higher education. Its status perhaps has more to say about higher education in general than about Hillsdale in particular: In an era when many colleges and universities don't ask much of their undergraduates, letting them pass off half-baked ideas as college-level work, little Hillsdale stands out. It asks students to examine the biggest ideas in human history, and when they cultivate their own opinions and ideas, their teachers smile and say, "Okay. Now prove it." And they can.

Hope College

Holland, Michigan

Hope College raises higher education's moral and intellectual levels. It is a place where parents can send children of a wide range of abilities in the full expectation that their talents will be increased, their vision broadened, and their ethical acuity sharpened. The result: graduates who have an expansive view of the world and their place in it and who want to put their talents to good use.

"Students graduate from this place with their priorities in order and deep knowledge of themselves," says Dr. Richard Ray, the provost. "We get you ready for real life—to be a professional, a spouse, a parent, a voter, a parishioner. We're concerned with the whole person."

Founded by Dutch settlers in the mid-1800s, Hope is affiliated with, but independent of, the Reformed Church in America. It has students of many religious faiths, including some who do not practice at all. The college's approach to Christianity is not prescriptive— that is, if you don't wish to participate in the college's vibrant spiritual life, you don't have to. Some students have absolutely no faith commitment at all.

But many students come for Hope's distinctive blend of academic rigor and religious life. The majority of students are pursuing their faith in some way, and to get a job at Hope, professors must be practicing Christians. Because Hope embraces a "big tent" approach to Christianity, students and faculty come from a wide range of denominations and traditions.

"I think [spiritual life] is richer because it's a choice, not a requirement," says a senior from Michigan. "I have a lot of friends from very different backgrounds. That doesn't define our relationships"—and it means Hope students know how to talk about significant topics with candor and respect. Nobody here believes that polite company never discusses religion or politics.

Some students feel that Hope is still working out what it means to be a Christian college with a strong academic program. "I think we could do a better job integrating faith and learning," says a senior headed to Princeton Theological Seminary after graduation. A few of his classmates agree, but a senior business major says she feels that Hope has taught her a lot about how to maintain her values in the corporate world. "My years here have grounded me. We talk a lot about values," she says.

Other students come for Hope's tremendous undergraduate research program. Student-faculty research projects are common among the colleges in this book, but Hope sets the standard. The faculty encourage undergraduate research to get students involved in their own education and to promote collaborative learning.

In the summer of 2011, a Hope-record-breaking 180 students in the natural and applied sciences, and forty in the arts, humanities, and social sciences stayed on campus to research alongside faculty. The program costs about three million dollars, so it's a good thing that Hope gets more grant money from the National Science Foundation than any other liberal arts college. Hope also has more chemistry majors than almost any school in the country—including such places as MIT and Stanford.

"Learning by doing is very important; the ultimate currency in sciences is producing new knowledge," says Dr. Moses Lee, dean of natural sciences. "Our students join our professors' research programs, and our professors are on the cutting edge." For example, in the fall of 2011, professors at Hope were developing new materials that can absorb bomb blasts on airplanes; identifying unknown radioactive elements that could have exciting implications for the practice of medicine; collaborating with the National Cancer Institute to discover anticancer drugs; and developing a new vaccine for malaria with collaborators across the globe.

Students learn more than science in the lab. "You learn about the ethics of science, how the funding works, how to know if an idea has been done before," Dr. Lee says. He and his colleagues take students to conferences to introduce them to the broader community of researchers. "We go to meetings at the National Cancer Institute, and they are floored by our students," Dr. Lee says. "I feel so proud." These experiences are among the top reasons why a third of science majors go to graduate school and another third go to professional school.

Research opportunities aren't just reserved for the best and brightest students. "There are very average students involved in research," says Dr. Richard Ray, the provost. "We see students blossom in the lab." Unlike schools that reserve these opportunities for stars in the classroom, Hope knows that students learn in different ways, so it makes sense to give all types of students chances to shine.

Every school in this book runs on the power of student-professor relationships; there's simply no other way for a college to do the life-changing work of mentoring and teaching students. But at Hope, more than anywhere else, students mention how much their professors care about them as people, not just as mini academics. A student mentions getting a note from a professor during a particularly tough time in her life; he wrote that he was praying for her. In dozens of interviews, students volunteer that they eat dinner at professors' homes, meet for coffee to chat about what's happening in their lives, and feel very comfortable relying on professors for advice on issues that don't pertain to class. "It's a game changer," says a senior who speaks for many of his peers. "Every professor I've had cares about me. It has had a huge impact on my ideas about leadership and relationships."

It also means that when professors deliver tough feedback, students feel supported, not attacked. A senior says, "Professors are cheering us on, but they push us. I should say, 'and they push us.' I turned in a paper last year, and the professor e-mailed me and said, 'I don't think this is your best work.' She gave me some guidelines, an extra month to work on it, and her home phone number. I was disappointed because I had worked hard on it, but after I did the revision, I was really glad that she saw better work in me, and she took the time to draw it out of me."

The students aren't the only ones affected. One professor after another talks with feeling about the atmosphere of mutual respect and care among faculty and students. "[Since I began teaching here], I have had 121 students in my undergraduate research program," says Dr. Graham Peaslee, a chemist. "I know where every single one of them is right now. We're really boring to talk to outside of class because we talk about our students all the time." His colleague, Dr. Deirdre Johnston, who teaches communications, adds, "At other places [I've taught], professors talked about the vacuum of antiintellectualism. Not here. Everyone is so enthralled."

Professors also speak passionately about the power of Hope's spiritual life. "I don't think I would have been won over to a liberal arts college without the Christian piece," says Dr. Charlotte Witvliet, a psychologist, who sums up the comments of several colleagues. "It's part of the richness of how we come to know the world and each other. It deepens and widens the inquiry rather than clamping it down."

That spirit of inquiry is one of Hope's most distinguishing features. Students get a lot of opportunities, formal and informal, to reflect on what they are learning and what it means to them and to the world. Like students at many schools in this book, freshmen take a topical First Year Seminar that hones their critical-reading, writing, research, and presentation skills. Hope's spin on these seminars is the reflection piece: Students must think about who they are, who they want to be, and what they value, and one of the course's seminal writing assignments asks them to capture their thoughts in a well-crafted essay.

At the other end of the academic journey is Senior Seminar, the college's required capstone course on faith and values. Each student receives his freshman essay back; it's a tangible reminder of who he was when he arrived and how far he has come. And because all liberal arts colleges know that good writing is mostly clear thinking, each senior must write a Lifeview Paper, which compels him to consider his philosophy for life. Even alumni who do not profess any religious adherence say Senior Seminar was a "very worthwhile" course. An alumna, now a doctor, explains: "A few years pass [after graduation], and your life gets more complex: You have a career and maybe a family. Thanks to Hope, you've learned how to pause and identify what's most important to you, evaluate your path, and make good choices. Those are skills well worth honing when you're young."

You might notice that the basis of these bookend courses is the assumption that students grow and change at Hope. (How dull it would be to teach these classes otherwise!) The emphasis is on development, not perfection, and professors are eager to work with students of all ability levels. "We can take students from wherever they are to places they don't think they can go," says Dr. Kirk Brumels, an alumnus who now teaches kinesiology. Dr. Peaslee agrees: "We have students who struggle, and we also steal the very top students. Everyone gets our attention." And if a student arrives too fixated on a career, professors "pollute their minds with new ideas," he adds with glee.

The academic profile of enrolled students proves this point: The middle 50 percent scored between 24 and 29 on the ACT and between 1080 and 1310 on the SAT (critical reading and math). Hope accepts 80 percent of its applicants, and it has room for B and some C students who are eager to work hard and participate in the college community.

The college does a fine job of helping families pay for this education. Compared to the price tag at most private liberal arts schools in the United States, Hope is a screaming bargain that's ten to fifteen thousand dollars less than most good private colleges and a few thousand dollars less than the cost of attending the University of Michigan if you're an out-of-state student. The college only meets about 82 percent of demonstrated need, but its smaller price tag means that depending on your financial need, even a more modest financial aid package could make Hope more affordable than other private colleges.

And thanks to a strong stewardship program that was in place years before the bottom fell out of the economy, Hope has been able to mitigate the effects of the recession and adhere to slight tuition increases. For the 2011–2012 school year, for example, the college increased tuition by 1.9 percent, compared to an average of 4.7 percent for private, nonprofit, four-year colleges in the United States.

Two-thirds of Hope's students come from Michigan, and the rest from forty-two states and twenty-nine foreign countries. They live together on a seventy-seven-acre campus in pretty Holland, just a fifteen-minute drive from the shores of Lake Michigan. Hope sits on the edge of the town's center, blocks and blocks of boutiques, art galleries, restaurants, coffee shops, and candy stores. "Charming" doesn't begin to describe it.

The campus is a coherent blend of beautiful buildings that show off a range of architectural styles. A Frisbee golf course runs through it, and on pretty days, students lounge in the Pine Grove, an expanse of trees and grass near the heart of campus. Hope's library has long been the envy of its peer schools and has garnered attention from the Association of College and Research Libraries. The chapel is both gorgeous and functional, hosting the college's thrice-weekly thirty-minute chapel sessions and the Gathering, the Sunday-evening ecumenical worship service. Students pack the house at all four services each week.

In the fall of 2011, Hope launched a capital campaign to raise funds for a few new significant buildings: an impressive student center, an art museum, and a concert hall and music building. Hope is one of the only liberal arts colleges in the United States to be accredited in music, art, dance, and theater, a fact that underscores the college's commitment to the arts.

In this idyllic setting, students wrestle with big ideas and real challenges. The college's Center for Faithful Leadership, for example, pairs student consultants with local organizations that need help solving problems. Students collaborate with subject-area experts at the college; the client pays the college for the work, and students earn money and real-world expertise. One team helped a local food bank respond to a 30 percent boost in requests for food; another created a long-term fund-raising plan for a children's museum. Another example: Each fall, the college sponsors a Critical Issues Symposium. All members of the campus community trade their regular schedules to attend lectures and workshops about issues and ideas the college deems important. In recent years, symposia have covered Islam, global health, feminism and faith, and genocide.

Such events align with Hope's expertise in helping students hone their skills while contemplating what some call their calling; others, their purpose. These conversations happen in class and outside of it, in the residence halls and on the twenty mission trips sponsored each year by the Campus Ministries Office. (Hundreds of Hope students forego typical spring-break adventures for a chance to serve and learn from communities in need across the world.) "It can be easy to make everything bland enough to make everyone comfortable. We're not doing that here," says a jazz performance major from Wisconsin. "You have to engage, but people are committed to bettering you as a person. People want to know why you think what you think and why you believe what you believe. And if you need help, I can guarantee that Hope will step up."

Professors too give an important message of assurance that you ought not to miss. "Hope provides a lot of opportunities. At large universities, you have to stake your claim in the department early," says Dr. Johnston of the communications department. "Here, it's just the opposite. We want our students to explore." Dr. Brumels, who teaches anatomy and physiology, is proud to add that students go to medical school having done prosections (dissections of a human cadaver). Dr. Brian Coyle, director of jazz studies, was quick to point out that students conduct ensembles as undergraduates—a notable difference from most large universities. And not to be outdone by his colleagues, Dr. Peaslee of the chemistry department adds, "We have instrumentation that parallels that at major universities. We don't separate our instruments into 'teaching instruments' and 'student instruments.' We all research together. My colleagues at other schools think we're nuts, but we think that's the best way to teach."

Any account of the college would be incomplete without a little attention to the ways students talk about the college community. It is the most common theme. Most students say they came because a beloved teacher, family friend, pastor, or other important adult persuaded them to visit. And when they came, they felt "it"—that sense of belonging that is so important at small colleges. "You feel love at Hope," a junior says. Another woman, who sings in one of the college's two praise bands, adds, "I've never had friends like this. We help each other grow; we challenge each other." And a senior from Wisconsin sums up several students' comments: "You learn how to listen and when to speak up"—essential skills in a healthy community.

Socrates would have loved Hope for its emphasis on the examined life. The college is ideal for students who want to learn, work hard, and live in a community of people who will help them find their places in the world. They leave the college happy with themselves because they know how to lead the examined and productive life.

Kalamazoo College

Kalamazoo, Michigan

"A few years ago, a client sent me a commencement invitation with this message on the envelope: 'Loren. Kalamazoo really did change my life.'"

—LOREN POPE

If you were to build your own liberal arts college, you'd look closely at Kalamazoo College for ideas about how to do it. That's because other colleges offer some of the same distinctive features you'll find at Kalamazoo, but few integrate all of them so thoughtfully to create life-changing experiences.

Kalamazoo's curriculum and its mission are two sides of the same coin. The college professes its aim is "to prepare graduates to better understand, live successfully within, and provide enlightened leadership to a richly diverse and increasingly complex world." Kalamazoo has just the means to accomplish its noble objective: the K-Plan, the college's term for its multilayered academic program.

The K-Plan comprises a solid liberal arts curriculum, robust opportunities to study abroad, an array of experiential learning opportunities—such as service learning or leadership development—and a Senior Individualized Project (SIP), which each student must complete. Participating in all of these opportunities is the norm here, making earning a degree at Kalamazoo a rich (and intense) experience.

"The K-Plan makes so much sense," says Dr. Binney Girdler, a biologist. "The first two years are the students' foundation. The third year, they go far. The fourth year, they go deep. They arrive here, and they don't know how to study or write. By the end of their time here, we're willing to coauthor papers with them. That transformation—I'll never get tired of it."

With guidance from attentive professors, Kalamazoo's 1,200 students have a lot of autonomy in how they knit together these components. "We talk a lot about self-authorship of education," says Dr. Mickey McDonald, the provost. "We want graduates who can navigate the world by themselves." Advisers encourage students to reflect on their talents, weaknesses, and goals, but students get to choose their own paths.

That's because Kalamazoo has a relatively open curriculum, which means that you won't find typical distribution requirements across disciplines. Each student must fulfill his or her major requirements, achieve proficiency in a foreign language, and complete the Shared Passages seminars, which happen freshman, sophomore, and senior year. The seminar series helps students reflect on where they are in their college careers, what they're learning about cross-cultural ideas, and how they're integrating their respective K-Plan elements.

Everyone at "K" touts the advantages of the K-Plan. Science majors, who tend to have more prescriptive paths to graduation, can go abroad. Everyone does a senior project—not just the academic rock stars. Best of all, students don't compartmentalize their lives. "In high school, you have school and maybe work and clubs and sports and community service. They're all little chunks that you bite off and chew one piece at a time," says a senior from Chicago. "It's not like that here. It's more mixed up. You find that everything is connected, and it feels more realistic that way. K students are really into learning, so you take that attitude to everything you do. You're open to what you could learn from any situation."

Kalamazoo's program appeals to the inquiring mind and adventurous spirit, and the timid learn by example—and the occasional nudge from a professor—to become risk takers.

The adventure begins before freshmen even arrive on campus, when the college asks them to engage in a common reading as part of the exceptional First-Year Program. Kalamazoo's savvy approach to welcoming first-years has won kudos from the John Templeton Foundation, and the college was named one of thirteen "Institutions of Excellence in the First College Year" by the Policy Center on the First Year in College and is featured in the book *Portraits of First-Year Excellence in American Colleges and Universities*. Like the curriculum, the First-Year Program has component parts you'll find at other colleges, but its uniqueness is found in how the college weaves these parts together.

Many colleges have common reading programs, but at Kalamazoo, the author always speaks during orientation. It's a good indicator of how seriously the college takes discourse: Kalamazoo won't choose a book if the author can't come speak on campus. You can count on a lively discussion.

All freshmen take a First-Year Seminar. Professors from all departments develop courses about a variety of topics but with the same goals: establish students' writing skills, give them intellectual grounding, introduce them to the library, and hone their discussion and critical-thinking skills. "We try to shake them up and catch them," says Dr. Zaide Pixley, the program's director and a music professor. "It takes students out of their comfort zone, but they know that the classroom is a safe place. They have to learn to trust themselves and their minds, and we set them up for success."

To help, the college employs and trains Peer Leaders, upperclass students assigned to First-Year Seminars. Peer Leaders help first-years adjust to college life academically and socially by organizing events, mentoring students, and giving advice about classes and resources on campus.

First-Year Forums round out the experience. These information sessions are held throughout the first semester, giving students access to important information about the college's expectations, policies on drugs and alcohol, and resources for personal and academic help, among other topics.

Without exception, students say they appreciate the First-Year Program, but they still find Kalamazoo's rigor to be jolting. "I was used to getting As and high Bs [in high school]," says a senior from

New Mexico. "I got my first D here, and it was shocking. But the support I get is really good." Other students say things like "This place is challenging academically and socially" and "K pushes you out of your comfort zone." These aren't complaints: Students say that they appreciate the intensity, even if they don't always love it. A sophomore offers: "It's like boot camp for nerds."

For many students, studying abroad is the most formative part of their college experience, so it's important to understand what's distinctive about Kalamazoo in this regard. After all, most liberal arts colleges offer study abroad—that is, you can find a program, apply, get your college's permission, make sure your courses transfer back, deal with the financial-aid components, and jet off to a foreign land. But at Kalamazoo, the program is thoughtfully and carefully designed so students have experiences that connect to their on-campus learning. The college does a fine job with continuity.

Kalamazoo maintains about fifty programs of its own in twenty-five countries on six continents, and about 80 percent of Kalamazoo juniors study abroad for three, six, or nine months. While they're abroad, many students do Integrative Cultural Research Projects, designed to help students immerse themselves in the local culture. Projects could be internships, community service, or creative works. As students return to campus—a transition that could be very difficult—the college offers events to help them talk about and reflect on what they've learned.

As a result, the college is alive with conversations about other countries' cultures, forms of government, foods, languages, and ideas. The faculty, who might be expected to deplore interruptions, find their students born again, full of a new interest and zest; their courses gain new relevancy. As one student says, "Almost everybody here is in one of two conversations: where you're going abroad or what happened to you during study abroad. It's kind of awesome." Students also report that study abroad "changes who your friends are. You have these amazing and hard experiences abroad, and you tend to bond with the people who are with you. That can make the adjustment back to K a little rough," explains a senior from Baltimore.

Similar to study abroad, lots of colleges offer service learning, a model of education that integrates community service, instruction, and reflection to help students knit together their real-world and in-class experiences. But Kalamazoo has made service learning an integral part of students' academic lives. "It's totally part of the conversation here," says a junior from Chicago. "Those of us who participate are really into it because it changes you."

At Kalamazoo, service learning is an endowed program, which means the college has a sincere financial commitment to it. Dozens of community partners, leaders of local nonprofits, guide students through their work and serve as teachers. Between a third and half of the student body participates in long-term service learning each year, and for a swath of students, service-learning hours are paid as part of the work-study program.

The foundation of the program is its peer-to-peer leadership model: About thirty Civic Engagement Scholars (CESs) oversee as many programs in the community. Each leader is responsible for logistics, schedules, problem solving, and leading her group at a particular site. Also important, these students lead their peers in reflecting on their experiences three times each quarter. The goal: help students put what they've learned into greater context.

Students shouldn't overlook the social impact of the K-Plan. Because about 80 percent of the junior class is abroad any given year and seniors are immersed in their SIPs, sophomores tend to be the campus leaders. It's a different progression to leadership than at most places, and sophomores say they enjoy the responsibility.

The K-Plan has a cultural effect too. Students are quick to mention how hard they work. This intensity is also fueled by the college's quarter system. Instead of two fifteen-week semesters, the calendar comprises three ten-week quarters, plus a summer term when students can go abroad or work on their SIPs, so the schedule feels a little tighter. But the intensity is also born of Kalamazoo's rigor and of students' interest in participating in everything the college offers. "There's an air of competition on campus," says a senior from Portland, Oregon. "It's like, 'Who has the busiest schedule?'"

But Kalamazoo is prepared to support students when and how

they need it. Unlike schools that focus on weeding out struggling students, Kalamazoo embraces them. Students unanimously report that professors are available and willing to help. "Our teachers are awesome," says a senior from New Mexico. Another senior says he's "good friends" with a lot of his professors. Over and over again, students rave about their teachers, even as they complain about the amount of work. That's a sign of good teaching.

And professors speak with a powerful combination of pride and affection when they talk about their relationships with students. "At first, I was surprised by how we talk about students—about the whole person, strengths and weaknesses, how to build capacities for individuals. We see where they need to go and how to help them get there," says Dr. Bruce Mills, an English professor.

"We bring out who they are," says Jeanne Hess, a professor in the physical education department and the women's volleyball coach. "K opens up worlds to them."

Professors say they enjoy the students at Kalamazoo, who come with a span of skills and ideas. Kalamazoo accepts 75 percent of students; it's not hanging its hat on selectivity. The middle 50 percent of admitted students scored between 1130 and 1370 on the SAT (critical reading and math) and between 24 and 30 on the ACT. Their high-school GPAs range between 3.4 and 3.9. "We're looking for more than the student who joined fifty clubs in high school. We want students looking for adventure, risk, and challenge," says dean of admission Eric Staab.

What happens to students here is remarkable. The Collegiate Learning Assessment (CLA) says so. The CLA uses open-ended questions to test first-year students' and seniors' critical thinking, analytic-reasoning, problem-solving, and written communication skills to see what happens during the four years students spend at college. The CLA examiners compare results across a variety of four-year colleges to answer the question: Are students really learning anything?

At Kalamazoo they are. In the most recent CLA study of Kalamazoo students, freshmen scored at the lower end of the "at expected" range—fine, but nothing exceptional—even though their SAT scores were in the ninety-second percentile compared with students at other schools in the CLA pool that year. Seniors, on the other hand, scored at the upper end of "above expected" on the CLA tests; they too had SAT scores in the ninety-second percentile in the CLA pool. Based on predictive factors, the CLA formula estimates how students at each college should score. The seniors at Kalamazoo beat the prediction significantly, so CLA said the students performed "well above expected."

Another measure of Kalamazoo's success is how many of its alumni go on to be scholars and scientists. The college ranks twenty-second among all four-year colleges and universities in the United States and fourteenth among liberal arts colleges in the percentage of graduates who earn doctoral degrees in all fields. Kalamazoo is sixth in foreign-language PhDs, seventh in life science, ninth in chemistry, and sixteenth in English.

None of this surprises professors or students. "During my interview, the students blew me away. At my research presentation [part of the interview process], a student asked a question harder than my dissertation committee had asked," says Dr. Girdler of the biology department. "That's what got me here. What's kept me here is the part I get to play in helping thirteenth-graders mature into people I consider my colleagues."

How does this transformation happen? "You're forced to ask, 'What's the big picture?'" says a senior from New York. His friend adds, "Nobody lets you get away with your first thought. It's like you're constantly having to answer, 'So what does that mean?' And it's your friends who are saying that to you just as often as your professors are." Other students say they have been changed by the increased responsibility for their learning, the almost limitless opportunities to try new things, the trust they feel from professors who invite students to research or travel with them, and the frequent conversations about social justice.

Two-thirds of students come from out of state, and about 8 percent are international. They describe themselves as quirky, liberal, involved, and hardworking. "K students are quirky in the best possible way," says dean of students Sarah Westfall. "We have a student body of individuals. There's very little herd mentality. They display tolerance at the least, but more likely appreciation for people who are different. They feel a call to activism and learning, but they're also garden-variety kids—some from small towns, working-class families, and a good number are first-generation college kids."

They're also enthusiastic about their learning and thoughtful about their responsibilities to their community. A few conversations with current students will convince you that Kalamazoo's component parts are remarkable, but if ever there were a place where the effect is greater than the sum of its parts, that place is Kalamazoo College.

Knox College

Galesburg, Illinois

"On my first visit to Knox . . . I thought, 'What a wonderful, charming place to spend four such important years of a young person's life.' I was impressed by the faculty, the students, and the cloistered tranquility of a campus of large lawns and great trees."

—LOREN POPE

Knox is a place that will take you seriously, no matter where you grew up or what kind of high school you attended. Nobody cares if you want to dye your hair green, wear a cape to class, or dress in a suit every day. Instead, the focus is on cultivating your potential, stretching your limits, and sharpening your values so that when you leave, you are captain of your fate and master of your soul.

Social reformers established Knox in 1837 on the belief that an elite education ought to be available to anyone who could handle it, making the college one of the first in the country to admit women, students of color, and students without financial means. Its founders opposed slavery vehemently, and one of its first trustees was active in the Underground Railroad for more than a decade.

In 1858, Abraham Lincoln debated Stephen Douglas here. Campus legend maintains that Lincoln had to crawl through a window in the main academic building, Old Main, to get to the debate because the speaker's stand had been built too close to the door. Lincoln then announced that he had been *through* college.

More than 150 years later, Knox still delivers an elite education to a diverse group of students, about 1,400 of them. They represent forty-eight states and U.S. territories and forty-six countries. The student body is 21 percent students of color, 7 percent international, and 59 percent women (not uncommon in four-year colleges these days).

As is fitting in a place committed to access, Knox accepts 77 percent of its applicants. The middle 50 percent scored between 26 and 29 on the ACT and between 1180 and 1420 on the SAT (critical reading and math), but the college is test optional, so if you don't want to submit your scores, you don't have to. While 75 percent of admitted students were in the top quartile of their high school classes, class rank matters far less than curiosity and motivation. "We're looking for the personal qualities and characteristics that show promise," says dean of admission Paul Steenis. "I'm looking for students who are intellectually curious and eager to learn, happy to think about ideas and issues, active participants in the classroom."

When you arrive, be ready to chart your own course. There's no set path through the Knox curriculum. Instead, the college emphasizes students' responsibility—with faculty input—to fulfill the curricular requirements in ways that satisfy their curiosity.

A student gets a broad foundation in the liberal arts and experiential learning such as off-campus study, independent research, and major creative projects. He must also be able to speak and write clearly and persuasively, understand and use mathematical concepts, have a working knowledge of a second language, and hone his skills in information literacy—the ability to find and discern worthwhile sources of information.

Each freshman must take a First-Year Preceptorial, a small seminar course based on an interdisciplinary topic such as "Love," "War," "The Social Life of Food," or "Learning to See Water." The class teaches the fundamental skills of liberal learning: framing viewpoints, disagreeing, identifying good sources of information, communicating intelligently, and participating honestly in scholarly conversation. In the spirit of interdisciplinary studies, professors from almost all academic departments teach First-Year Preceptorials.

Then a student is free to explore, as long as she takes at least one course each in humanities, social sciences, arts, and sciences. She must land on a major by the end of her sophomore year, and she must find a second area of emphasis, either a major or a minor.

But these aren't cursory decisions. Knox requires each student to write an Educational Plan by the end of sophomore year. Students reflect on their first two years, what they've learned, what talents they've discovered, which areas still need work, whether they want to study off campus, and where they'd like to focus their energy in class and on campus. Academic advisers must approve all Educational Plans.

This built-in time to reflect ranks high among the things that surprise and delight students about Knox. "For some people, [the Educational Plan is] just a thing to get done, but if you take it seriously, it's a good exercise in knowing yourself," says a junior from Chicago. "I think not many high schools ask students these questions, so you're not used to evaluating your own life. But if you don't practice examining yourself and your goals, you'll just continue down the same boring path forever, maybe a path you didn't even choose for yourself." Other students say they appreciate how invested their advisers are in helping them craft Educational Plans that suit and challenge them. "Nobody here lets you get away with the minimum. You're always pushed to do more, but not in a rough way. Professors just see a lot in us, and they're trying to strengthen us," says a senior majoring in creative writing.

He's right: Knox's sense of mission and its focus on student development are remarkable. "What struck me about Knox [when I was interviewing for this job] was a real sense of the college as a whole," says Dr. Larry Breitborde, the dean of the college. "People had a strong sense of being part of the larger enterprise. It led to them being concerned about how the whole college was working, asking questions about the full experience students are having."

Faculty's comments about their work and their students substantiate this claim. "I tell anyone who applies for a job here, 'The Knox community is a common circulatory system.' You give and take at the rate you need to. We support each other to support the students," says Dr. Judy Thorn, a biologist. "Most of us are addicted to being around students, and we'll do whatever it takes to make sure they're getting what they need, even if they don't know what that is right away.'

Professor John Spittell, a retired executive who teaches in the business and management program (a minor), adds, "I was immediately taken aback by the level of engagement that runs between the professors and students. The excitement among professors to go to class and interact with students—I wish every prospective student could see it. This is my third career, but it's my true love."

And in yet another version of the same tune, Dr. James Thrall of the religious studies department says, "Students in high school who haven't fit into the standard achieving mode, whether it's testing well or working within expected parameters, will find that Knox faculty are pretty accommodating in terms of finding different ways of approaching material. I have been struck with the commitment of faculty to make their subjects interesting and engaging."

Knox is a place where "going to class" means far more than listening to lectures or repeating facts. Students praise their professors for leaving plenty of room for questions and discussion, even in the sciences, where the curriculum tends to be more regimented. And for students who discover topics they want to examine in depth, professors frequently sponsor independent studies.

A couple of interesting immersion programs give further proof of the college's intellectual metabolism—and its willingness to break the mold of typical college classes. Knox has developed an off-campus residential study term at its Green Oaks Biological Field Station, seven hundred acres of Illinois prairie a half hour's drive from campus. Professors from several disciplines study the ecological, historical, and aesthetic qualities of the landscape with students.

For aspiring thespians, the theater department produces a Repertory Theatre Term, when a small group of students transforms into a repertory company and puts on two shows. Students learn the business of a repertory company, study the historical and literary history of the plays, and perform in and produce the shows. "There is something very Knox about it," says Dr. Neil Blackadder, a theater professor. "It's this intensive experience devoted to producing the end product, but a lot of what we do is more about the process. It's the thrill of working in this small group of people. I believe the value of that learning is tremendous."

Such programs are made possible by the college's calendar: One academic year comprises three ten-week terms. The trimester system encourages—and sometimes forces—professors to innovate. "At first, it didn't seem like enough time to teach them everything I wanted them to know," says Dr. Katie Adelsberger, a geologist. "But it got me away from content-based teaching, just trying to squeeze facts into lectures. I had to ask, 'What's a better way to teach this? How can I get them involved?' Classes with fieldwork tend to be most successful because students learn to analyze and apply information, not just swallow it."

Learning by doing is important at Knox. Students who want to conduct their own research or take on creative projects can apply for a share of $250,000 to fund their work. Art majors spend a full term in the studio, creating art for their senior shows and experiencing life as full-time artists. Biology students can't leave without doing research.

"Here, everybody gets a shot, not just the top kids," says Dr. Thorn of the biology department. Such opportunities aren't available everywhere—especially not at large universities, where graduate students take up most of the available spots in professors' research programs. Knox students don't just get the experience; they also get a lot of quality time with their professors. "We chat. I get to know what they're interested in, what they're good at," Dr. Thorn says. "Then I try to get everyone who works with me experience at larger universities. They see what it's like to be a graduate student or a postdoc. I can do that in part because I know what they're capable of and where they'll fit in best."

Like the other colleges in this book, Knox emphasizes the connection between teaching and research. Professors' first commitment is to teaching, but they must find ways to knit student learning into their research programs. "They're not trying to clone students to be academics, but it's important for students to be involved in research because creating new knowledge and mastering problems is going to help them in whatever they do," Dr. Breitborde says.

Students rave about the learning opportunities on campus and about their classes, but they are most enthusiastic about the community. An American student who grew up in Germany chose Knox over Northwestern University. "What persuaded me was the close-knit atmosphere on campus; I got the feeling that people would really care about me here," he says. A Romanian student traveled to Knox all by himself his freshman year. "I got to my dorm, and four people randomly showed up and asked if I wanted to hang out. From that second, I've been interacting with people. They're very keen on helping you regardless of whether you're a close friend or a random person." A junior who attended a competitive science-and-math high school outside of Chicago says her old friends are at places like Stanford and Princeton. "When I compare experiences with them, I think I'm getting just as good an education, but in a place where I'm building relationships."

In the context of this community, students say, they appreciate the college's diversity. "There's no one Knox student. We don't look alike. We don't necessarily act alike, unless you count 'quirky,' which we act out in about 1,400 different ways," says a junior from Chicago. A few students used the phrase "culture shock" to describe their transition to campus. "The things you took for granted, you realize they're not universal experiences," says a senior from Carthage, Illinois. "It causes you to question things, or it makes you believe in things more strongly. You definitely get a more balanced view of what's out there." And Knox's culture makes the college a safe place to talk about differences, students say. "I think you come to appreciate the richness in people that lies beyond or beneath the person you see, the nationality or ethnicity or whatever," says the American student from Germany. "There's always something you can't define or grasp that lies beneath people, and Knox gives you a chance to get to know people deeply. It's part of what we do."

The fact that Knox operates under an honor code that demands integrity in all academic work seems to these students a most natural thing. How could it be otherwise? "It's based on the same principle as the curriculum: We take our students seriously," Dr. Breitborde says. "We assume they're honorable people and want to do things honestly. They have individual responsibility for their learning—both the path and the truth of it."

The proof of Knox's power isn't just in student and professor testimonies; it's evident in the statistics too: 90 percent of freshmen return for sophomore year, compared to about 67 percent at all American colleges and universities and 69 percent at private, four-year baccalaureate schools. The college ranks in the top 3 percent of all U.S. institutions in the production of men and women who go on to earn PhDs, and 65 percent of Knox graduates do postgraduate study within five years of finishing their bachelor's degrees.

Why such success? The college is explicit about its aspirations for students. Everyone gets opportunities to grow and learn. The spotlight doesn't shine on a chosen few—the ones with the best SAT scores or the students who speak up most in class. Instead, the shoe gazers, the ones who haven't yet dared to dream big, raise their eyes to find professors and staff members eager to help them hone their talents and develop their goals.

"There is an esprit here," says President Teresa Amott, PhD, a veteran of liberal arts colleges. "I think its origins lie in Knox's size, the diversity comprehended within that scale, and the intensity of the interactions that are driven by discovery in the classroom. Not intensity like you find at Wesleyan or MIT; you're not going to be chewed up and spit out. I mean an intensity that's an asset, a warmth that I haven't found anywhere else."

Lawrence University

Appleton, Wisconsin

"The Ivies take fast-track kids and turn out fast-track graduates who are not much changed. . . . Lawrence is a place that helps young people find themselves and then make the best of what they find."

—LOREN POPE

This news might surprise you: One of the country's richest cultural and academic environments is on a bluff overlooking the Fox River in east-central Wisconsin. With a lively liberal arts college and a superb music conservatory—and not a graduate student to be found—Lawrence University is a vibrant community unlike any in the country.

A former Japanese ambassador to the United States says of his experience at Lawrence that "it remains in my heart as the most rewarding. It made a deep and lasting imprint on my life. . . . It shaped my outlook. . . . Without it I would not be where I am today. I am very grateful for the education I received at Lawrence; it is one of best colleges in the United States." (He also spent a year at Amherst.)

If you're curious about what you can do intellectually and creatively, take a close look at Lawrence. Unanimously students echo the ambassador's words and say the university gives them room to explore and develop their own paths. In a dozen conversations with small groups of students, the mantra is the same, summed up by a junior from New York City: "Lawrence has shown me what I can do. The biggest change in me is my sense of possibility."

Professors and students revel in a respectful mutual-admiration society. The students give credit to faculty for their commitment to teaching and supporting them; professors, in turn, insist that their students are teachable and eager to learn. "They don't take this education for granted. That makes it a pleasure to think about what they should read and how they should learn," says Dr. Tim Spurgin, an English professor who earned his PhD at the University of Virginia. "We expect a lot; we offer a lot. At bigger places, it's conversely true: 'Don't expect much of me, and I won't expect much of you.'"

In addition to teaching their regular course loads, professors sponsor tutorials—very small classes about topics proposed by students. Tutorials tend to emphasize independent study, so a student in a tutorial meets with her sponsoring professor for about an hour each week. Tutorials are a hallmark of a Lawrence education: Of the 1,800 courses the university offers in a year, 800 of them have only one student. You cannot overestimate the amount of additional work tutorials generate for faculty, and yet not a single student has a story about a faculty member refusing to sponsor a tutorial she dreamed up. What's more, faculty profess loving them.

"The first thing that struck me [when I began my work at Lawrence] was how much time the faculty spends on campus," says Dr. Jill Beck, the college's president, who came to Lawrence in 2004 from her post as dean of the School of the Arts at the University of California at Irvine. "The amount of accessibility is, in my experience, unrivaled. There's no excuse for a student not understanding something, because professors are always there when students need them." Always? "Yes, without exception."

Professors attribute their eagerness to the campus's collegiality. "I love talking to economists and psychologists," says Dr. Beth DeStasio, a biologist. "Plus, my students here are much better than most of my graduate students were. Anytime I go anywhere else [for a conference or meeting], I'm so thankful for Lawrence."

Lawrence's incoming students tend to be quite good high-school students. The middle 50 percent of admitted students have SAT critical reading scores between 580 and 710 and math scores between 590 and 700. Their average high-school GPA is 3.7, and on average they rank in the top 15 percent of their graduating classes. But if you fall below these averages, take heart: Lawrence accepts about 65 percent of its applicants. "We don't have GPA cutoffs; we don't have rank cutoffs," says Ken Anselment, dean of admissions. Instead, the college is looking for curious, eager students who will blossom in dynamic classrooms and an active extracurricular realm.

Students describe Lawrence as a welcome change from high school. Several who say they were at the top of their high-school classes admit that Lawrence surprised them with its rigor. "One of my professors freshman year told me to stop repeating and start analyzing," says a senior from the Chicago suburbs. "I was shocked. Nobody [in high school] challenged me like that, but once I started thinking, it became clear to me why I thought high school was kind of dull. Lawrence is way more exciting and totally fulfilling."

First-year students get a swift proverbial kick from the much-acclaimed two-term Freshman Studies course, designed by former President Nathan Pusey (who left Lawrence in the 1950s to head up a little place called Harvard). It's a kind of intellectual culture shock created to introduce students to the fundamental character of liberal learning. The syllabus is a multimedia celebration of canonical and contemporary works from literature, art, and—of course—music.

Professors from all departments teach Freshman Studies, and they love it. "It's everyone's favorite course," says Dr. De Stasio. "We actually have faculty come here to teach because of Freshman Studies. It's that significant."

Students are similarly enthusiastic. A senior from Milwaukee says, "I was shocked into being a good writer. Freshman Studies strips you down to build you back up, and if you don't love it while you do it, you'll love it afterward." Students say they appreciated seeing a physics professor work through a Stravinsky piece with them or hearing a music professor's take on Jorge Luis Borges's *Collected Fictions*.

It's hard to identify what, exactly, gives Lawrence its vibe, but some students suggest that Freshman Studies sets the tone for the whole campus. "It operates on two levels, right? First, you're introduced to a way of thinking that's kind of risky and fun and pretty hard. And if you're a real Lawrence student, that turns something on in you. Then you take that experience into your dorms and your other classes, and you're just eager for whatever else you can think about in this new way," says a sophomore majoring in geology.

Other students suggest that the unique combination of college and conservatory is a prime reason for the campus's liveliness. Indeed, it's hard to overestimate the "con's" influence on the whole community. It's a power that inspires a deep appreciation for the arts, even among the most nonmusical students. "This thing happens to you at Lawrence," says a senior majoring in political science. "You start going to performances because your friends are in them, or the people on your hall, and after a year or so, you start going to performances because you don't want to miss them, even if you have no connection to the people performing." A group of his peers nod in agreement. "It's so awesome, and something I totally didn't expect when I came here," a junior studying mathematics adds.

And of course, if you love music and want to continue learning without majoring in music, the conservatory is an excellent resource. There are ten jazz ensembles, an orchestra, two bands, three choirs, dozens of student ensembles, private lessons with top-notch faculty—plus three theater performances each year, including an opera. (As many as a third of Lawrence's 1,500 students participate in music making.)

The conservatory's dean, Brian Pertl, is a Lawrence alumnus whose story reveals the university's power to influence students' and alumni's lives. Dean Pertl, a trombonist, didn't get into the conservatory when he auditioned as a high-school student, but he was admitted during his freshman year. "Few places would allow a student to audition again, but that's Lawrence's culture; we give students opportunities to succeed over and over again," he says. His professor, Dr. Fred Sturm, mentored him "with great patience and honesty."

Dean Pertl earned a Watson Fellowship, traveled to Australia, and discovered the Aboriginal didgeridoo, a wind instrument. He went on to earn an advanced degree in ethnomusicology—the study of music's social and cultural aspects—and went to work for Microsoft, where he led a team that chose and acquired the music and other media for Microsoft's digital reference materials.

Then Lawrence came calling. Dr. Sturm, still teaching at the conservatory, nominated Pertl for the dean's position. "It was a no-brainer to come back to a place that had changed me so much," he says. "I never would have had this great professional life without my Lawrence experience."

Dean Pertl and the fifty music conservatory professors are almost fanatical about the value of studying music in the context of the liberal arts. "I am convinced that you can't reach full potential as a musician if you don't have a breadth of experience elsewhere. This is something you won't get at Juilliard or Eastman, and if you're interested in this other element—challenging yourself intellectually in other fields—you'll be happy here." Dr. Sturm agrees: "I see balance in my students here. They bring more to composing and performing from their liberal arts classes. Their inspiration is deep and wide." It's an element he takes seriously: He taught at the famed Eastman School of Music before returning to his alma mater.

The conservatory has worked diligently to widen students' exposure to other musical cultures. For more than twenty-five years, it's had Brazilian samba drumming, and for more than fifteen, Ghanaian ewe drumming and dancing. More recently it has added Cuban drumming and singing, a Balinese gamelan, and of course, Dean Pertl's beloved Australian didgeridoo.

The campus's multiculturalism doesn't stop there. Its students come from forty-three states and fifty countries; 12 percent of students are international. The university's commitment to financial aid is significant for both international and domestic students. It meets between 90 percent and 100 percent of demonstrated need for domestic students, and its scholarship programs don't just honor academic accomplishment; there are awards for music, community involvement, and environmental leadership, too.

Lawrence also invests in the student experience. Its beautiful LEED-Gold-certified campus center, opened in 2009, is a boon for student life, with floor-to-ceiling windows that overlook the river, airy spaces for socializing, quiet nooks for studying, a cinema, an art gallery, and four new dining options (where, students say, the food is "pretty good"—an enthusiastic endorsement from the collegiate crowd).

And then there's Björklunden, a 425-acre campus on Lake Michigan in Door County. Every weekend during the academic year, a different group of Lawrence students and faculty escape to this wooded paradise for a kind of juiced-up, toned-down learning experience. There are language-immersion programs, field-research sessions, music-making extravaganzas, and writing workshops. Professors and students testify to the power of Björklunden. "It removes some of the formality of a classroom and gives us a different way to connect with students," says provost Dave Burrows, PhD. "We're scholars together, and often the conversation turns from the superficial to significant questions about the human condition, students' vocations, their beliefs and ideas about the world."

It's clear that for many years, Lawrence has been a jewel of the liberal arts. It ranks thirty-seventh among undergraduate U.S. institutions in producing future PhDs in the sciences. It has seen a flurry of Fulbright Scholars in recent years, earning four in the 2009–2010 academic year alone—and seen an influx of grant money from such organizations as the National Institutes of Health and NASA.

In recent years it has begun building on the strength of its teaching to add curricular and extracurricular programs to connect students to life after Lawrence. Guided by President Beck's vision, the college is innovating in ways that soundly answer the question, "So what do you *do* with a degree from a liberal arts college?"

Supported by a $350,000 grant from the Mellon Foundation, it recently launched Senior Experience, a required capstone project that gives each senior an opportunity to demonstrate proficiency in her major. Project requirements vary by department, but they all leave room for students to innovate and launch themselves into the next stages of their lives.

A new program, LU-R1, pairs Lawrence students with alumni who are faculty at research universities across the country. Yet another, called Lawrence Scholars, brings alumni from different professions to campus to mentor students, present career options, and advise on internships. Lawrence Scholars in Business awards scholarships to promising students.

Given all this excitement, it's not hard to understand why students are so happy here. A majority use the words "like home" and "supportive" to describe Lawrence. "I felt like I was a part of things here when I visited," says a sophomore from Chicago. "People want to know what you're all about."

A few small decisions make a big impact on the campus community: The university requires students to live on campus all four years, and students from all classes live together. "We have our most sophisticated learners just across the hall from first-year students," says Nancy Truesdell, vice president of student affairs. Lawrence's student government also has much more power than student leaders in most places: Students create and uphold the rules for how they live in dorms, and they manage the housing lottery.

Students believe they've discovered the country's best college, and you should not underestimate the energy produced by a group of enthusiastic, talented, supported college students. Twelve students interested in the Fox River's history and biology initiated the university's new quarter-mile Riverwalk and wrote the interpretative signs along the path. Another student's research on wind power led the university to purchase a wind turbine for the campus.

They are a witty, confident, and kind group—the look-you-in-the-eye kind of young adults whose earnestness is surprising. When asked what makes them so sincere, a sophomore geologist says, "It's all about personal passion here. We're all excited about our own work, what we're learning, what we're involved in outside of class. You just know that everyone has something driving them."

They're not an activist bunch, and some students say they wish the campus were more engaged in political issues. "This is an academically and intellectually intense community, but sometimes I think that cripples our ability to get into our community," a sophomore says. But in their own quiet ways, students respond to the world around them. SLUG, the Sustainable Lawrence University Gardens, grows organic produce on a quarter acre behind the student center. Students designed and hosted a two-day conference on sustainable agriculture in 2011. They also petitioned the Appleton city council to change an ordinance to allow the university to keep bees. And when Wisconsin leaped into the national spotlight over right-to-work laws, a group of Lawrence University students trekked to Madison to support the unions.

At Lawrence, you'll find room to discover what matters to you—and if that sounds hackneyed, consider the words of a 1992 graduate, now a professor: "It would be difficult to overstate the influence that my years at Lawrence have had on the shaping of my life. The impact extends to my academic, professional, and personal development to the person I am today. The academic rigor taught me persistence, critical thinking, and love of knowledge. I developed relationships with faculty that continue today."

Another 1992 alumnus says: "I was empowered to confidently reflect on what it is that mattered most to me. And it is this self-awareness that allowed me to pursue a life of my own choosing rather than something prescribed by societal pressures."

And as only an accomplished writer could, alumna and novelist Susan Engberg wrote in the university's alumni magazine: "These are the people who help us turn into ourselves." And in turning you into yourself, this little school on a river bluff will give you the power to lead a life you love.

Ohio Wesleyan University

Delaware, Ohio

At large universities, professors are frequently isolated, holed up in their respective departments with little opportunity to learn from and collaborate with one another. It's the nature of the beast. And only the very best students get to team up with their professors on research—if any do at all.

Universities would do well to look closely at Ohio Wesleyan. The small university of 1,850 students thirty miles north of Columbus is a shining beacon of what happens when a campus embraces collaboration in the context of liberal learning: All types of students are engaged. Professors are invigorated. As one student says, "We're all about the exchange of ideas here. You come here, and you start having all these ideas, and then you can actually act on them and people listen. It's an amazing place."

OWU (pronounced "oh-WOO") approved a new curricular plan in 2010 that formalizes this spirit of collaboration and adds a shot of adventure. The goal: teach students how to connect theory—everything they're learning in class—to practice, also known as the real world.

One element of the new plan is Course Connections, networks of courses that give students multiple perspectives on one topic of global importance. Imaginative faculty across departments put their heads together to develop six networks, which launched in the 2011–2012 year. Among these first Course Connections are "Crime, Responsibility, and Punishment"—with classes in politics and government, sociology, history, philosophy, psychology, microbiology, and neuroscience—and "Food: How Production and Consumption Shape Our Bodies and Our Culture." Students choose from courses in botany, microbiology, English, physical education, psychology, and zoology.

The spring before Course Connections' launch, professors were almost giddy about the possibilities—another rarity on college campuses. Professors tend to be accomplished skeptics, but at Ohio Wesleyan they believe they've come upon an idea that delivers the best kind of liberal arts education. "The problems in the world are going to be solved by people looking at them from a variety of perspectives," says Dr. Laurie Anderson, a botanist and microbiologist. "It's exciting to be able to help students practice and refine those ways of thinking. I absolutely believe it will have an impact not just on the student but also on our world. And that's not overstating anything."

Dr. Rock Jones, OWU's president, puts it this way: "Never has the world had more need for liberal arts education. The world is more polarized than ever; people are tempted to be narrow-minded, to embrace ideology instead of considering possibility and seeking solutions. Citizens educated in liberal arts colleges know how to listen to and analyze different viewpoints, identify sound reasoning, problem-solve, and then communicate those solutions. Our world needs desperately the benefit of citizens who can do these things." Clearly, the plan is more like a mission, built on OWU's best resources: talented professors and visionary administrators.

That spirit of innovation has also led to a surge of new travel-learning courses, each of which includes a short off-campus experience. For example, a class studying the history of the 1960s traveled to Vietnam for two weeks at the end of the spring course. The group's tour guide had served in the South Vietnamese air force during the Vietnam War and had spent time in a reeducation camp; the students stayed with former Viet Cong members for a few nights. "No matter how talented the teacher, you cannot inspire the depth of learning that happened on our trip," says Dr. Joan McLean, a professor of politics. "The cross-fertilization of ideas amazed me."

Students and professors in other travel-learning courses trekked to Bangladesh to examine how microfinance addresses issues of extreme poverty; to the Galapagos Islands to study island biology; to Brazil to explore the Amazon's ecology; to Japan to follow up on their study of how literature and film depict war; and, in an act of selfless scholarship, to Italy to study the connection between food and behavior. Donations from alumni cover about 50 percent of expenses, putting these opportunities within reach for students who need financial support.

And OWU even has a plan for sowing the seeds of curiosity planted by any of its classes. New Theory into Practice into Theory (TiPiT) grants support students and professors as they delve deeply into academic interests, often in the summer and almost always in far-flung places. TiPiT grants are for work outside of class, underscoring a tenet that all colleges should uphold: The purpose of education is to learn, even if nobody is going to give you a grade or credit. Learning is the means *and* the end.

In that spirit, music professor Jason Hiester took seven students to Salzburg, Austria, for one of the world's premier classical music festivals, where students attended performances and took master classes. TiPiT grants have paid for students to study remnants of the Holocaust in Europe, learn about Minoan culture in Crete, and study how Pakistanis perceived the Americans in Afghanistan during the Afghan war.

As you might expect, the campus buzzes with excitement. Everyone is dreaming big, and the college has the structure to support those dreams. "You can make this school whatever you want," says a senior zoology major from Boston who is heading to Michigan State to earn his PhD. "I've given oral presentations, attended academic conferences, copublished [in academic journals] with the ornithologist on campus. I'm going to the Bahamas in a few weeks to study birds there. I feel like I came here with an interest in birds and I'm leaving with experience and book knowledge that have turned me into a real scholar. This school did that for me." After a few seconds' reflection, he adds, "Or maybe it taught me how to do it for myself."

These formal programs are important, but they reveal something more organic: OWU's ethos, an asset that no amount of programming could build. OWU's culture is defined by warmth and helpfulness. It doesn't have the hurry-up pace of competitive places or the small-fish-big-pond vibe of large universities. Dean of students Kimberlie Goldsberry gives perhaps the most compelling example of OWU's personality. In the middle of a fall semester, she began to think about how to help about fifty international students find homes for Thanksgiving break. But all of them already had plans, thanks to generous students and professors. "I shouldn't have been surprised," she says. "We are that kind of place. We take care of each other."

Ideas are welcome here, and the freewheeling exchange of them makes it a satisfying place for students and professors. So does the obvious mutual affection between students and faculty.

Students are eager to one-up each other with stories of teachers' kindness and mentorship: "A philosophy professor took me out after my final paper was done and graded to discuss my ideas," a senior says. Another senior says her Swahili professor arranged the final oral exam at an East African restaurant in Columbus. A freshman, near the end of her first year, can barely contain her zeal: "In high school, your teachers aren't really friends. Here, they are. They treat me like an adult. What I have to say is legitimate, like it's worth their time to talk to me. I think our professors really like spending time with students."

The university's collaborative spirit extends to the school's governance. The Student Government Association meets with university administrators once a month, and the SGA sets the agenda. It's a real meeting where students and administrators act as peers and students have power to influence their campus. "The university is unbelievably receptive. All you have to do is e-mail senior administrators with your ideas. That's the culture here," says the president of the student body, a junior from Washington, D.C.

All this magnanimity inspires service to others. About 80 percent of students volunteer for nonprofits, either during a service trip or as part of an ongoing commitment to a local organization.

An example: For more than two decades, Ohio Wesleyan students have traveled to the most economically depressed areas of Columbus to tutor and mentor students there, raise money for books, pack and unpack classrooms when the schools move into new buildings, and chaperone field trips. The program has inspired more than a few students to take jobs with Teach for America or pursue careers in education, nonprofit work, or advocacy.

As in their academic work, students thrive on possibility; they believe that they can, in fact, improve the world. Case in point: Two Ghanaian students founded a nongovernmental organization that raises money to help talented and needy students pay tuition at high-quality primary and secondary schools in Ghana. Five years after its founding, it is going strong, sponsoring nationwide meetings in Ghana about the public education system. For its hard work, in 2010 Ohio Wesleyan won one of six President's Higher Education Community Service Honor Roll awards, the highest federal award for civic engagement.

The character development that accompanies intellectual growth is exceptional. Few places pay so much attention to the whole person. Egos are small here, and hearts are big.

It's a desirable place to spend four years, and if you agree, you have a good shot at getting in. The university accepts about 70 percent of its applicants; the average high-school GPA of enrolled students is 3.4. The middle 50 percent scored between 1080 and 1300 on the SAT (critical reading and math) and between 23 and 29 on the ACT. About 30 percent were in the top 10 percent of their high-school classes, and 85 percent of freshmen return for sophomore year, up from 80 percent just a few years ago.

Ohio Wesleyan strives to make its education affordable. It awards scholarships not just for academic achievement but also for women who demonstrate leadership, legacies (children, stepchildren, grandchildren, and stepgrandchildren of alumni), ethnic minorities, children of Methodist ministers (a nod to its founders), and siblings of current students or alumni. Individual departments, including fine arts and economics, also give scholarships.

In total, 95 percent of OWU students get financial aid, merit awards or a combination of both. The university meets 83 percent of demonstrated need, and the average need-based aid award for the 2010–2011 year was $32,000, less than a quarter of which was loans.

What do you get for your time and money? Students here feel they're getting a better deal than their friends who went to brand-name schools. (Let's not forget that some of those schools' reputations were made by magazine editors.) They laud all of the things that make a college powerful: access to caring and gifted professors, a variety of well-developed courses and a strong curriculum, opportunities to use their passion and talents to help others, resources to support their ideas, and a residential community of people who genuinely like one another, even if they don't have much in common.

Many of them describe being "inspired" or, as one sophomore puts it, "activated, like someone flipped my 'on' button." The life of the mind matters on this campus. Unlike so many universities, OWU invests its resources in learning. (What a concept!) Consider this: Every year since the mid-1980s, the university has put on a major lecture-discussion series called the Sagan National Colloquium to explore a public issue. The program brings in noted speakers—best-selling authors, Nobel laureates, corporate and international leaders, and elected officials—who talk about the issue from their perspectives. Workshops and discussion groups with the speaker follow the keynote address, and during the fall semester, a series of speakers, most of them professors and researchers from other schools, present on the colloquium topic. Students can earn academic credit for their participation and related research and analysis. *This* is the stuff of higher education.

Students and professors at OWU cringe at the phrase "hidden gem" to describe their university. In their view, Ohio Wesleyan is doing the work more colleges should, with its cross-curricular learning and openness to collaboration among faculty and students. There's nothing hidden about what's happening here: It's progressive and thoughtful, a fine example of a university that didn't just assume that it was good enough—or that it should just do what thousands of other schools in the country do.

The president of the student government is an able spokesman: "I spent half my life in Egypt. I thought life would be so dull in small-town Ohio. But I was wrong: The world is here, through international experiences and people. The world is absolutely here."

St. Olaf College

Northfield, Minnesota

Aesthetically and academically, St. Olaf is Camelot. As visitors drive up and around the curving hill of the campus, they're struck by the beauty of the place, with its impressive light gray limestone-and-glass buildings, grassy expanses, emphatic shrubbery, and stately trees. The architecture might be called Norwegian modern, a blend of historical elements and contemporary touches.

This aesthetic is no accident: Norwegian immigrants founded St. Olaf in 1874 as a Lutheran school of liberal arts that would prepare students for work in the church and the world. The founders named their fledgling school for the patron saint of Norway, forever tying the college to its Scandinavian roots.

Today St. Olaf is a mainstream college with both a religious commitment and a commitment to the life of the mind. Officially, it is a college of the Evangelical Lutheran Church in America, but its commitment is to character, not creed. Students don't have to adhere to any faith tradition to enroll or feel comfortable here; 40 percent of the 3,100 students are Lutheran, and the rest represent other Christian denominations, Islam, Judaism, agnosticism, and atheism.

Students pointed out that the college's religious tradition enriches the community. "People are willing to go deep, and they're honest. If you come to St. Olaf, you will be up until two o'clock in the morning to talk about God—never in a coercive way," says a

Catholic student majoring in philosophy. "There's a comfort talking about these things that helps in our academic work. You can't understand some of the great questions about the life of the West without some familiarity with religion." Another senior, a biology major, adds, "People here are looking for truth. The conversations here teach you to embrace mystery."

Maybe this contemplative spirit is one reason St. Olaf is such a prolific producer of the country's scholars and scientists, out of all proportion to its size and selectivity. It ranks eleventh among the country's baccalaureate colleges (those that award mostly bachelor's degrees) in the number of graduates who go on to earn doctoral degrees. Its medical school acceptance rate is about 80 percent, a full 30 percentage points higher than the national average. And in 2011, St. Olaf seniors won an impressive nine Fulbrights, making the college's grand total a whopping seventy-nine since 1995.

The path to these achievements begins with a strong core curriculum, augmented by the Conversations, interdisciplinary programs designed to boost students' intellectual flexibility. The Conversations aren't required, but they are such a hallmark of a St. Olaf education— and a shining beacon of what liberal learning ought to be—that any student who enrolls at St. Olaf ought to take one.

There are four Conversations. The Great Conversation was established first; in a series of five courses taken over the first two years, students read great books and study works of art beginning with the ancient Greeks and passing through about thirty centuries of writers and artists. "It's the intellectual equivalent of drinking from a fire hose," says a senior, who says "the Great Con" was the reason he chose St. Olaf. "It teaches you intellectual humility. You learn to see how different pieces work together. I'm still talking about what I learned in those two years. I'll be thinking about it for the rest of my life."

American Conversations invites students to examine the people and ideas that define American values. During a series of four courses in freshman and sophomore year, students consider justice, freedom, and equality in the American context. Asian

Conversations, a sophomore-year program, dives into the forces—political, cultural, economic, linguistic, and environmental—that have shaped Asia; during the January term, students go to China or Japan for guided field study. And the Science Conversation, also for sophomores, is a three-course series that explores science's development in history, the relationship between faith and reason, and the sometimes-awkward relationship between society and science.

These programs give an added layer of life to an already vivacious campus. Everyone who participates—students and faculty—says that the programs feed curiosity and evoke rich discussion. "I love that students learn civility," says Dr. Karen Cherewatuk, an English professor and the director of the Great Conversation. "They learn to hear the other point of view. The rhetoric in this country is so inflated in terms of political discourse. In some small way, the Conversations are an antidote to that."

All students must take two courses in biblical and theological studies to learn how to examine the Bible as scholars, not adherents. Most students say they enjoy the courses—some are even shocked to learn that they don't know as much as they thought they did about Judeo-Christian history. A few students who grew up in Christian traditions grumble about the requirement, but a Muslim student says she finds them interesting and helpful in framing the kinds of conversations she enjoys at St. Olaf.

The rest of the curriculum reaches far across disciplines—and then around the world. Before studying abroad was in vogue, St. Olaf was sending students to foreign countries. That tradition has mushroomed into a cultural norm at St. Olaf: More than 75 percent of students study off campus in 110 programs, the vast majority of them abroad.

St. Olaf runs on a 4-1-4 schedule: A student takes four courses during each fourteen-week semester (fall and spring) and one intensive course during the January term, called "Interim"—a good time to go abroad if you're tentative or if your academic schedule doesn't allow you to leave for a full semester.

A senior biology major went to Peru during Interim with a team of medical professionals who gave medical and dental care to indigenous communities and children in orphanages. "It was phenomenal. I was blown away by seeing all of these people living lives of conviction in areas of great need," she says. "It's taking those ideals we have as undergrads and putting them into action. My life at St. Olaf has exploded since that experience. It expanded my ideas about what I can do with my life."

One of St. Olaf's most beloved programs is Global Semester, a five-month trek across Switzerland (in particular, the United Nations' headquarters in Geneva), Egypt, India, Thailand, Hong Kong, China, and South Korea. The trip, led by a St. Olaf professor, gives students an intimate look at these countries' cultures and pushes them to understand the prevailing challenges and riches of each place.

A recent participant, a political science major, is effusive: "Global was the most amazing experience ever. It's hard to talk about it and encompass those five months. It's not touring. It's living in these communities with real people and seeing the world as it is. It made me so much more thoughtful than I was, and so much braver. I feel the shift in my thinking. I remember my old self, but I couldn't ever be her again."

The State Department couldn't find finer ambassadors than St. Olaf students. They're self-assured but not pretentious or cocky. They'd probably cringe at the word "wholesome," but it's apt: Students display a genuineness that teeters on the edge of wholesomeness. And "they're bright," says dean of students Greg Kneser. "I mean that different from 'smart.' Bright is better. They are smart and they know a lot, but there's a buzz—an energy—about them." A recent survey of incoming students showed that for 90 percent of St. Olaf freshmen, the college was their first choice. People are happy to be here: An impressive 94 percent of freshmen return for their sophomore year, compared to about 69 percent of students at all four-year private baccalaureate colleges in the United States.

"Oles" love their community, and they're careful to protect it. Students live and study on their honor—guided by an honor system that asks them to pledge that they haven't cheated on their work and don't know of anyone who has. But that sense of honor extends well beyond the classroom. That's why bags sit deserted in the library and mailboxes in the student union don't have locks. (Every Friday, students stuff their friends' mailboxes with flowers, a charming tradition made possible by their collective commitment to respect.)

Free from worry about whether students are doing their own work, professors can focus on more productive and exciting tasks. They speak happily about how their students are up for any challenge. "[Our students] have energy for pursuing knowledge," says Dr. Julie Legler, a statistician. "I could tell it when I interviewed, and they're the main reason I came here. I could tell they were excited about learning and wanted to be here. To me, it's just what you want as a professor."

Dr. Legler leads the Center for Interdisciplinary Research (CIR), which matches statistics students with faculty from other disciplines to conduct research during the school year. The students—CIR Fellows—earn stipends and lend their statistical know-how to ideas far afield from their typical course work. In one project, a small team worked with a Norwegian professor whose great-grandfather was a famous author. The students quantified the style of the English translations of his work to understand the effects of different translators. In 2011 the program got a strong endorsement from the National Science Foundation: a $1.6 million grant to expand its work.

St. Olaf has long had robust math and science departments, but it's also a great place for artsy types, particularly music makers. The college's music program is one of the finest in the country, and young musicians who don't want to major in music can find a home in a long list of ensembles: eight choirs, two bands, two full orchestras, three jazz bands, two handbell choirs, and various chamber ensembles. The St. Olaf Christmas Festival features more than five hundred student musicians in one of the country's oldest and most beloved celebrations.

The music department also participates in Foreign Languages Across the Curriculum (FLAC), a program that allows students to take humanities and social science courses in Chinese, French,

German, Norwegian, Russian, or Spanish. These classes, a dozen or so a year, give students opportunities to exercise their foreign language skills outside the bounds of typical language courses.

St. Olaf students eat up these kinds of expanded learning opportunities. They beam when they mention how many students showed up to a recent dinner debate that examined pro-Palestinian and pro-Israeli viewpoints. They praise "STO Talks," modeled after TEDTalks, during which professors and students give panels on topics of interest. "St. Olaf students are legitimately interested in these events," says a junior. "People really want to know more. A lot of this has to do with the global perspective we get."

There's a lot of room for discussion and disagreement, students point out, because they know the value of community. A senior describes the student body as "smart, friendly people who genuinely like each other." He adds, "I visited some schools where people were clearly smart, but there was a competitive vibe on campus. There's not that same vibe here."

Instead, students say, they support one another. "We're always talking about community here," says a junior from Wisconsin. "My favorite way to explain it is that you're going to recognize a lot of people, almost everybody. And almost everyone will smile at you, say hello, ask how you're doing." Students highlight the college's single cafeteria, famous for its great food; they voted not to add a second one because they didn't want to break up their community. "It's great. You see everyone there," says a senior.

Since the first edition of this book, St. Olaf has become more selective simply because more people have discovered it. It still accepts 66 percent of students who apply; the middle 50 percent scored between 27 and 32 on the ACT and between 1200 and 1420 on the SAT (critical reading and math). And the college is one of few in the country that meets 100 percent of demonstrated financial need.

What you see is what you get—both from the college and from the people who live, work, and learn here. Proof of that coherence is that students and administrators say the same things about the college's work.

President David Anderson, PhD, an alumnus, explains the college's effect on students: "College is a laboratory where you have the freedom to try out versions of your future self. You come here as a student, and you are away from home with more discretionary time and more freedom to act than you've had ever before in your life. You have the chance to discover the type of fully formed adult person you'll become. 'What's my vocation?' is an important question, but so are questions about the nature and tenor of friendships, about your role in the community, about what you value. You can work at this here. You can go down a path and decide that's not who you want to be. We provide the best laboratory for students who are interested in delving into such questions."

And a senior speaks for many of her peers when she testifies to the kind of experience President Anderson describes: "St. Olaf doesn't prepare any student for what they're going to be, but for who they are. That can transfer to a lot of different vocations. I have so much more clarity about who I am, such a better understanding of humanity and the different challenges people face and how what I'm studying is relevant. I have so much passion. There's so much color to my life."

Wabash College

Crawfordsville, Indiana

"This is a clan with élan. Not a single student I talked to would be anywhere else. Wabash was their first choice, and one reason was that they'd been told, 'It won't be easy, but it will be worth it.' And if as a teenager long ago I'd known the luxury of comparison shopping, I'd have been one of them. . . . Long before the end of my overnight visit, I was wishing I'd gone here instead of to its co-ed rival, DePauw."

—LOREN POPE

Anyone worried about the future of young American men should visit Wabash College for a hefty dose of hope. Elsewhere, there's plenty of (merited) discussion about the losing battle for male college students, as women enroll and graduate at higher rates than men—and the gap is growing.

Wabash makes even a casual observer wonder if perhaps one answer is in single-sex education. On a handsome campus forty-five minutes from Indianapolis, this happy band of 850 brothers takes pride in working hard, developing their minds and their characters, and building friendships they'll enjoy for the rest of their lives.

It is a place that turns young men with even mediocre high-school records into clear-thinking men who lead the life of the mind and who have the confidence to take risks. And they go on to become high achievers and contributors to society at a rate that puts very selective and famous colleges to shame.

"We take pretty good guys and then turn them into absolute world beaters," says President Patrick White, PhD. "Our alumni are tremendous."

The students insist that the peculiarity of not having women in class fades after a semester or two. Occasionally, the discussion about going coed bubbles up, and some faculty members believe the college ought to enroll women. But the majority of professors see this educational option as an important part of the spectrum of colleges available to young men. "They're more willing to be vulnerable in the classroom," says Dr. Ann Taylor, a chemist. The risks are smaller in this tight-knit community, adds Dr. Tobey Herzog, an English professor. "They're not competing to impress women; they're competing to impress themselves, to see what they're capable of."

Students agree. "It's not about women being a distraction," says a senior chemistry major from Indianapolis. "I'm just more comfortable talking about emotion, talking about art, being creative." Another student chimes in: "We can explore all contours of masculinity; it's good to see the spectrum so each of us defines what a man should be. I don't think college guys get to do that at many places."

Dr. Kay Widdows, an economist, suggests that part of Wabash's transformational power comes from the lack of women. "Typically, women serve as the nurturers in a community," she says. "But here, the men take care of each other. We live in a [broader] culture that discourages this kind of interaction among men, but I think it makes for wiser, more thoughtful leaders."

Of course, Wabash isn't an island. DePauw, with 2,400 students, and Purdue, with 30,000 undergraduates, are only thirty miles away. A bit farther away is the cluster of universities in Indianapolis with thousands more. Women come to campus frequently; no one complains of not being able to find a date.

But during the week, Wabash students trade the typical coed social scene for three elements that define campus life: academics, fraternities, and sports. It's an academically serious place, rigorous but not overly intellectual. "Students won't appreciate you if you don't push them," Dr. Herzog says. "The fastest way to fail [as a teacher] is not to challenge them enough."

Professors boast about students' work ethic and willingness to engage with the material and one another. "I've never seen a harder-working group of students," says Dr. Rick Warner, a historian.

In an upper-level sociology of religion class with Dr. Jonathan Baer one spring morning, the students are fantastically adept at swinging from good humor and outright hilarity to very serious conversation about the development of selves in light of religious views. Everyone is prepared. Everyone participates. Later, Dr. Baer, who earned his PhD at Duke, says his best students are "absolutely on par" with the best students he knew in graduate school. "Wabash men aren't uniformly perfect [when they arrive], but the amount of growth here is a testament to the good work everyone does here. It's a privilege to teach here."

It's easy to see why: The young men are genuine, funny, and driven. They came here for "the prestige," "the family," "the fact that they take me seriously." The curriculum is no flash, all substance. (The college proudly eschews a business program for the more theoretical—and fastidious—study of economics.)

You might not find greater advocates of liberal arts education anywhere. Students here are convinced they're getting the best type of education to equip them for their lives. Even those who are on preprofessional tracks are fervent defenders of liberal arts. A premed student explains: "I feel like here, I'm examining what it means to be human. That's what doctors should deal in—humanity. Not just biological life but the value and purpose of life. You get that here. I'm going to be a better doctor for that knowledge."

Unlike almost every other college in the country, this is a collaborative community of learning because of the fraternity, not in spite of it. About 60 percent of men join one of the nine Greek houses on campus, and the goal of every house and dorm is to have the highest grade point average on campus. "There's no 'in crowd.' It's very communal, even among independents and fraternity brothers," says a junior. His peers nod emphatically.

Wabash men aren't stereotypical jocks, but they're fierce

competitors: 40 percent of them compete on Division III teams and 90 percent are involved in some kind of athletic competition. Long ago, Wabash's football team was dubbed the "Little Giants" for their ability to best big-name teams. (Of particular note is a 5–0 win over Notre Dame on a fateful fall day in 1905.) The Little Giants still take their sports seriously. For more than a century, Wabash's football team has met DePauw at the Monon Bell Classic, one of the best small-college rivalries in the country. Students here are quick to mention that Wabash has the winning record.

Intramural sports include mainstays such as basketball, tennis, touch football, and soccer, plus a few less common sports, including badminton, Frisbee golf, and table tennis. Faculty members are equally competitive, mounting teams in almost all intramural sports.

Because athletics are such a central part of student life, the college recently invested six million dollars in facilities. There are new baseball and soccer stadiums. The football field got artificial turf, and the college added pristine practice and intramural fields. Students boast about the facilities, new and old. "We have training facilities as nice as places ten times our size," a three-time all-American runner says.

This community of scholars, athletes, and brothers is governed by only one rule, the Gentleman's Rule: "The student is expected to conduct himself at all times, both on and off the campus, as a gentleman and responsible citizen." That's it.

"At other places, students learn to tiptoe along the line of what's acceptable. Here, it's much more real world. CEOs don't have someone else defining behavior for them. They know how to act, how to make decisions. That's how it is here," says a junior studying political science.

With this freedom comes inevitable responsibility: Resident Advisors, students who oversee the dorms, don't just have to prescribe punishment for infractions; they have to define what behavior doesn't measure up to the Gentleman's Rule. The same goes for fraternity houses. "It definitely sets the bar high," says a junior from Mississippi. "You want to live up to the community's expectations.

You definitely don't want to put your friends in a position of having to decide your punishment. There's this feeling of, 'Aren't we above this stuff?'"

Students warn that Wabash isn't for everyone. Wabash men have a lot of fun, but they're serious about their futures: They believe they're heading somewhere, and Wabash is helping them get there. "If you're the kind of guy who just wants to float through school and who isn't interested in forming relationships, you shouldn't come here," one student says. "People know you here, and they expect you to participate. Your professors will be on you if you don't show up or if you're not doing the kind of work you should. On the other hand, if you even think you might be interested in Wabash, you should visit. The men here will persuade you. You'll want to be a part of what we have here. It sounds so clichéd, but it's a brotherhood."

If you're convinced by the substance of this place, you might like to know that Wabash accepts about 58 percent of applicants. (As its fame has grown, so has its selectivity, but its goal is not to exclude students who want and deserve to be here.) Of the students who enroll, Wabash retains 89 percent—a ringing endorsement when you consider that nationally, about 67 percent of freshmen return to their colleges for their sophomore year. The middle 50 percent of admitted students score between 22 and 28 on the ACT and between 1040 and 1280 on the SAT (critical reading and math). The student body comes from thirty-four states and thirteen foreign countries; 20 percent of students are ethnic minorities.

Another key reason to consider Wabash is its generosity; it has one of the highest per-student endowments in the country. What's more, its resources benefit students—not the case at every flush college or university.

Wabash meets 100 percent of demonstrated need of students who meet the deadline for completing their financial-aid forms. Loans make up 13 percent of the average aid package. It gets better: Wabash's scholarships are abundant and hefty. Every student in the top 10 percent of his high-school class earns $15,000 a year in scholarships; a student in top 20 percent of his high school class gets $12,500 a year. The Honor Scholarship competition brings admitted students to campus each year to take exams in English, math, science, and history or a foreign language. Top performers earn anywhere from $5,000 to $20,000 a year in scholarship money. And there are awards for excellence in fine arts and for students who attended the Boys State program.

In one issue of the alumni magazine, a senior said: "Wabash is the kind of place where the sons of doctors and lawyers discuss Plato and Aristotle with the sons of steel workers and mechanics." It's as egalitarian a place as you'll find. "You can't tell the rich kids from the neediest," Dr. Warner says. Part of that spirit is the culture the students uphold; they're not interested in besting one another with fancy cars or daddy's yacht. They're too busy sharpening and testing themselves to worry about such things.

And the college's generosity virtually eliminates distinctions of wealth. Career Services maintains a room of suits in all sizes, which students can borrow for interviews if they don't have their own. Wabash offers a series of cross-cultural courses that include immersion trips across the United States and to foreign countries: three weeks in Quito, Ecuador; a trip to Europe to study the European Union; another to Mexico to study Mayan ruins. All of the travel costs, except the occasional meal, are covered by Wabash. And the student senate manages a budget of four hundred thousand dollars a year—the highest in the state—to award to on-campus organizations.

This support extends to faculty as well. At a time when state schools' budgets are cut to the bone, Wabash's support is "unbelievable," says Dr. Widdows. For their first two years, the college provides funding for professors' research, freeing them from time-consuming grant applications so they can focus on teaching and scholarship— and welcoming students into their research. They also get money for travel and professional development. Wabash knows that invigorated teachers make for dynamic classrooms and strong student-faculty relationships—essential for the kind of life-changing work that the best schools do. It also goes a long way toward attracting and keeping top-notch faculty.

One of the not-so-secret elements of Wabash's success is its alumni. "They're everywhere," jokes Dr. Warner. Wabash ranks among the top twenty colleges in the country in alumni giving, a key indicator of graduates' satisfaction with their education long after they've left campus.

And you shouldn't underestimate the role alumni play in helping students find internships and young graduates find jobs. The career services office gets high marks from students, thanks in large part to alumni who are eager to help graduating students find work. Alumni enter their information into the student mentor network, an online database, and students can log in to find alumni in particular geographical or professional areas.

Wabash also gets high marks from the annual National Survey of Student Engagement (NSSE), which reports on how frequently students are engaged in high-impact activities that influence learning and personal development: 69 percent of freshmen report collaborating with classmates outside of class to prepare class assignments, compared with only 45 percent of students at participating colleges nationwide in 2010; 66 percent of seniors report discussing ideas outside of class with faculty members; only 28 percent of students elsewhere do; and 79 percent of seniors say they talk about career plans with a professor, compared with 43 percent nationally.

It's not surprising that Wabash produces remarkable graduates: 13 percent of its alumni have PhDs, a higher figure than most of the Ivies. An amazing 12 percent of alumni hold the title "president" or "chairman," and a full 75 percent of graduates enroll in graduate or professional school within five years of finishing their work at Wabash.

Graduates sound a lot like current students. A 1997 graduate says, "Wabash students display a rabid pride in their college. And they're quick to include you in their club. As a freshman you immediately become immersed in a feeling of brotherhood, an all-for-one-one-for-all mentality. An extraordinarily deep bond forms between the men of Wabash. The studies are rigorous, and if you meet those challenges you will reap rewards. But Wabash has something else to offer its students: family."

Another, a 2003 graduate who went on to med school, says that Wabash showed him that "accountability, honesty, and hard work are the most important values one can have. It changed my life by making me realize and accept what my gifts were, and that I am obligated to share those gifts with others in making this world a better place the best way I can contribute."

President White says he thinks often about the current fight for male college students—to get them into and through college. "Young men want to believe their lives matter. We help them believe that and see how they can change the world. We pay attention to them. We teach them how to be the heroes in their own lives. There are so many examples in the media of men as feckless losers. We fight that image in a million ways every day."

The magic of this or any other place is not in what it does; it's in how it does it. Every college in this book achieves its goal by different methods. Here, the "how" is the pride the whole community takes in its commitment to learning for its own sake. It's the common enterprise—and a noble one.

Wheaton College

Wheaton, Illinois

"Wheaton is often called the Harvard of the evangelicals, but that moniker does not do it justice because it is head, shoulders, and heart above Harvard in its concern with good moral compasses and strong value systems, as well as in the percentage of future PhDs it turns out."

—LOREN POPE

An hour's drive west of Chicago, beautiful Wheaton College attracts young men and women who are professing Christians and sharp thinkers and turns out not only droves of future PhDs but also citizens who care about and understand the world's problems. What's more, they have the skills and the heart to fix them.

Wheaton's motto is "For Christ and His Kingdom." Unlike schools in this book that are loosely affiliated with founding Christian denominations, Wheaton is a school where nearly everyone has a Christ-based worldview.

Within that context, Wheaton is a community of about 2,400 undergraduates and 500 grad students that embraces at least fifty different stripes of Christianity, from liberal Episcopalians to literal fundamentalists. It is also a place that produces many highly respected scholars and scientists. It ranks among the nation's top producers of future PhDs, as well as teachers, missionaries, authors, political figures, and business leaders.

Students do not sign a statement of faith, but faculty and staff do, and the application for admission asks prospective students about their faith. The college is guided by its Community Covenant, which not only outlines permissible behaviors—dancing is okay, drinking on campus is not—but also encourages students to rely on the Bible for guidelines for right living, in keeping with their collective mission of glorifying God.

But don't assume that Wheaton is a center of dogmatism; quite the opposite is true. The college is a rigorous, thoughtful place where scholarship matters.

This might surprise skeptics, who wonder how a college with a biblical worldview can teach geology, which deals in eons, or biology, with its evolutionary focus. Dr. Jeff Greenberg, a geologist, explains: "I tell my students, 'There are no young-earth atheists.' We don't allow people to distort science to support their beliefs. We present the science to them and then tell them they'll have to make up their own minds about how they reconcile their faith and the science."

It's not just science classes where indoctrination is absent; every department is focused on the inquiry, analysis, problem solving, and critical-thinking skills that make a college valuable to its students and the world.

"We don't feel obligated to slap a Bible verse on every lecture," says Dr. Jeffrey Greenman, the college's associate dean of biblical and theological studies and a professor of Christian ethics. "Wheaton is not a gigantic four-year Bible study. Yes, we emphasize Christian engagement in the world, but we also emphasize academic engagement. We're talking about as wide a range of issues and ideas as any other strong liberal arts college." Wheaton welcomes guest lecturers and speakers without restriction, and the students packed the house when an atheist philosopher showed up to speak, Dr. Greenman adds with glee.

A sophomore double majoring in anthropology and English says he has taken two anthro classes in human origins. "A lot of Christian colleges tend to avoid such study, but I love that Wheaton goes there. I like the room to explore," he says. Professors frequently leave it up to their students to draw conclusions from facts. Some students say that ambiguity surprised them as freshmen, but as upperclassmen they appreciate it.

The faculty at Wheaton could be switched with that of almost any other in this book and no one would be able to tell the difference in regard to their affection for their students, their scholarly standards, or their sense of humor. "I came back to Wheaton because I don't find relativism to be much fun," says Dr. Sarah Borden, a philosopher and Wheaton alumna. "If students have a stake in something, if they're ready to fight for something, discussion is much more interesting." At other colleges, she explains, students are often willing to give in to whatever the professor seems to want them to say or do. Here, students' beliefs make them less willing to swallow whatever the professor says.

Political scientist Dr. Sandra Joireman laughs about the first call she got from Wheaton when the college was hunting for a new poli-sci professor. "I thought, 'No way. You guys are that fundamentalist school.'" But after she came to give a lecture about African politics, she was so smitten with the students and their thoughtful questions, she decided Wheaton could be the place for her. Like her colleagues, she talks about how much she enjoys teaching, how challenging and fulfilling it is, and how fond she is of her students.

As a whole, those students are studious, earnest types who arrive with strong credentials. They come from fifty states and fifty foreign countries, but the majority are conservative, middle-class Americans.

The college accepts about 66 percent of its applicants. Admitted students' average high-school GPA is 3.7, and the middle 50 percent of them scored between 1240 and 1400 on the SAT (critical reading and math) and between 27 and 31 on the ACT. About 80 percent were in the top quartile of their high-school classes.

When they arrive, new students discover a friendly and rigorous place. Many students describe Wheaton as "jolting," "surprising," or "overwhelming at first." One sophomore wonders if she'll ever feel successful again, but other students say they learned how to research, write, and think at a collegiate level within the first year.

"But you should tell [prospective] students that this place is intense," says a sophomore from Southern California.

When students are asked what kind of person would be happy at Wheaton, the most common answer is that he or she should be motivated and disciplined, interested in learning, and eager to be part of a community. They are assuming, of course, that the person is a Christian. But "don't assume that Wheaton is a place where people will just confirm your beliefs," a senior says. "We're a Christian school, and we agree on a few basic truths about Christ, but you'll be challenged here—academically and spiritually. That's probably the difference between Wheaton and other small private schools. We realize that your intellectual life impacts your spiritual life, and vice versa. But this isn't a place where we go around high-fiving each other for having figured it all out. We encourage and push each other, and there are definitely some intense conversations. I love it."

With surprising frequency, students also mention—with what appears to be sincere awe—how bright and driven their classmates are. "You get the feeling that people here are already doing something with their lives. I feel like so often, college is a cop-out, but it's not here. That lights a fire for everyone," says a sophomore from Grand Rapids, Michigan.

Wheaton's impressive retention and graduation rates suggest she's right: Students are happy and focused here. About 96 percent of freshmen return for sophomore year, and 80 percent graduate in four years; 88 percent finish in six years or fewer.

While they're here, students must take a series of courses that serve as a foundation for conversations about theology: Freshmen take "Gospel, Church, and Culture," an introductory course that helps students understand biblical studies in a liberal arts context. Students also take one class each in the Old and New Testaments plus an upper-level course called "Christian Thought," which delves deeply into Christianity's basic beliefs.

In a dynamic New Testament class one spring morning, Dr. Gary Burge talks about the cultural climate of first-century Corinth, an ancient Greek port city. "If LA and Las Vegas got married, you'd have

Corinth," he jokes. The class divides its time between lecture and discussion, as Dr. Burge gives historical, economic, and cultural context for 1 Corinthians, one of the Apostle Paul's letters to the church at Corinth. Dr. Burge challenges the students: Are the issues that were present in Corinth germane to twenty-first-century American culture? The discussion, thoughtful and honest, isn't for the faint of heart. Students bring up issues of moral courage in the church and outside it, drawing from their knowledge of history, Scripture, and personal experience.

It is no wonder that after class, a group of students from the class agrees with a woman who says, "I love classes at Wheaton because of what you saw in there. You're actually applying what you learn and asking yourself and other people tough questions about theology and life and what God is saying. Sometimes, growing up, I felt like church was all about easy answers and just being in agreement, but here, finally, you get to get to the meat of something, I mean, the parts that are complicated." What's even better, she says, is having professors who are able to listen and offer guidance one on one, whether students want to talk about spiritual, personal, or academic issues. "Usually, you go to talk about an assignment, and then you're saying, 'So remember how we were talking about XYZ in class? That's really been on my heart lately.' And you kind of swing back and forth between the academic and spiritual sides of a topic," she says. Her peers murmur their agreement.

Wheaton is also home to a conservatory that focuses on performance, composition, teaching, and scholarship and offers six different bachelor of music degrees, so music majors can select the focus that's most important to them. The faculty are impressive not only for their credentials—many hold doctor of musical arts or PhDs from such renowned places as Juilliard, the Eastman School of Music, and Northwestern—but also for their diversity of talents and interests. "One of the things that makes it possible for us to do what we do in the conservatory is the breadth: We're not just pointing students in one direction. There's a richness in the variety of courses available and in faculty's mentorship," says Dr. Daniel Paul Horn. "Many of our students have a background in a particular liturgical tradition, but they come here, and it's expanded. They're studying ethnomusicology; they're breaking from a Western tradition to study the marriage of music and culture. I'm tremendously happy with the breadth of study here. It's satisfying as a teacher, and I believe it's satisfying and probably surprising for a student."

Students and professors aren't the only ones who believe that Wheaton is doing important work in the world: The college's loyal alumni and friends are incredibly generous in their support. It's notable that in 2010 Wheaton completed a $260 million capital campaign, the largest in its history and a hefty sum for a small college. Coupled with smart stewardship of its resources, this support has built a very healthy endowment.

Wheaton shares its abundance with students. It is an exceptional value compared to its academic peer group. For the 2011–2012 school year, tuition plus room and board equaled slightly more than $37,000; for the same year, the cost of attending an Ivy soared well over $50,000. What's more, Wheaton meets, on average, 90 percent of a family's demonstrated need, and grants and scholarships make up about 80 percent of the typical financial-aid package. Wheaton's endowment allows the college to be generous with need-based grants and merit-based scholarships.

It has also invested in facilities, which are lovely across the campus. The student center, with its open, airy spaces and cozy nooks warmed by fireplaces, is the hub of student life. It's also home to a cafeteria that might serve the best food of any college or university cafeteria in the country—influenced, perhaps, by Chicago's foodie culture?

A state-of-the-art science center, opened in the fall of 2010, houses the applied health science, biology, chemistry, computer science, geology, health professions, math, and physics departments. Its 128,000 square feet include twenty-eight teaching labs that open to research labs, making it easy for faculty and students to collaborate on research. It's also home to the Perry Mastodon, one of North America's most complete mastodon skeletons and a reminder that the college is fully engaged in the intersection of faith and science.

Wheaton stands on a strong legacy of scholarship and teaching, and prospective students should expect to see that legacy extend even further into the world beyond campus, guided by the college's eighth president, Dr. Philip Graham Ryken, who began his presidency in the summer of 2010. An alumnus son of an English professor and a pastor with a PhD from Oxford, President Ryken has a vision for the college that includes expanding and organizing Wheaton's engagement across the globe. Certainly Wheaton's alumni live and work around the world—many of them are missionaries—but President Ryken is beefing up the college's commitment to immerse students and professors in other cultures and languages. To that end, the college recently added a dean for global and experiential learning, who oversees both curricular and cocurricular opportunities for students to learn about the world, on campus and off.

Wheaton will be building on a number of strong programs. Since 1976 its Human Needs and Global Resources (HNGR) program has taught students about the economic, cultural, and political circumstances in developing countries—particularly those in Africa, Asia, and Latin America—and then sent students to intern with organizations and learn how to confront and meet human need. The object is to learn about the culture so as to be able to help intelligently within that cultural context. Before many colleges were talking about service learning and immersion study, Wheaton was sending students to work in some of the world's neediest places, and lucky for the world, many HNGR alumni are working in developing countries as missionaries or for international or nongovernmental organizations.

The college has more conventional study-abroad programs as well, including opportunities to travel during the summer and school year. Students can trek to an archeological dig in southern Israel; to Germany and Switzerland to study how the invention of the printing press influenced politics, economics, religion, and technology; to Asia, where each year the college selects a different city to study; to Belize for an immersive introduction to marine biology; or to D.C. to get an up-close understanding of how government agencies work. Wheaton also sponsors trips to the Holy

Lands, Latin America, Spain, England, and Chicago (for an urban studies program), and encourages students to participate in partner programs with colleges and universities across the globe.

Wheaton's mission is clear—and its students absorb it wholly. They want to serve others, to improve the world, and they're hoping their time at Wheaton helps them figure out how to do that. Alumni stories suggest it will: Wheaton's community of alumni includes a former COO of Wal-Mart; a former CEO of John Deere; former Speaker of the House Dennis Hastert; President George W. Bush's former chief speechwriter; the president of Global Strategies for HIV Prevention; the chairman of surgery at Emory University; former chief of the thoracic division at Harvard Medical School; more than three dozen college presidents and provosts; evangelist Billy Graham; authors John Piper and Elisabeth Elliot; Grammy Award–winning musicians; countless teachers, business leaders, attorneys (the good kind, one would presume), and missionaries.

Its legacy, mission, and community add up to a hopeful place. Students learn that their abilities aren't just for their own self-interest, and that perspective adds a layer of sincerity to their studies and their treatment of one another. President Ryken, who remembers Wheaton students wandering in and out of his home when he was a child, thanks to his father's job, gives an explanation echoed by students and professors: "Vocational education prepares you for a career. Liberal arts education prepares you for all of the things God will call you to do."

College of Wooster

Wooster, Ohio

"The College of Wooster is my original best-kept secret in higher education; for thirty years, I've been telling clients that. As I have gotten to know what it accomplishes, I can testify that there is no better college in the country. Its record is unmatched in turning out scientists, scholars, and other kinds of achievers and contributors to society by multiplying the talents of B and C as well as A students."

—LOREN POPE

Forty miles south of Cleveland, in a beautiful, hilly part of eastern Ohio, little College of Wooster is a hotbed of creative and analytical thinking. Its 2,100 students are energized; its faculty, devoted. They walk around with smiles on their faces because they've discovered one of the country's finest educational establishments. You should discover it too.

One of the reasons for Wooster's power is its Independent Study, dubbed "IS," a senior-year project that influences all four years of a student's career. IS is "the worst name for the best program," says Dr. Paul Edmiston, a chemist, because the program is actually mentored undergraduate research. It's a collaborative effort.

Each student plans and creates an original project with input from a faculty adviser: conducting research in the lab, writing a collection of short stories, analyzing historical documents, you name it. The adviser guides her as she progresses, helping her define methodology or resources but also giving her room to take some risks. The culmination of IS is a thesis—often about one hundred pages long—and an oral defense. And one day each spring, classes are canceled and the campus becomes a giant undergraduate research conference where seniors share their projects through panel discussions, performances, and poster sessions, which allow students to showcase their work on elaborate posters and explain their research in a conference-style setting.

The project fosters creativity, resourcefulness, and self-reliance in every student. Unlike many places, where opportunities to conduct original research are exclusive to the top performers, Wooster sets the standard high for everyone. "About a third of our students come because they know about IS and they want that experience. Another third come simply for the liberal arts experience, and the last third come because they connect with something else on campus—a sports team, or maybe a parent came here," says Dr. Hank Kreuzman, a philosopher and the dean for curriculum and academic engagement. "But no matter why they come, the college proclaims loudly, 'You can take on this significant academic work and succeed.' That's powerful in a student's life."

Because everyone must complete an IS to graduate, professors infuse every course with a set of skills students must master to be successful researchers: They learn to frame questions, identify reliable sources, analyze primary documents, practice methodologies, and write cogently—precisely the skills that are invaluable in the workplace and graduate school. In essence, the curriculum is built backward, starting with a clear vision of what students need to complete IS successfully. That vision guides how professors teach even introductory courses.

IS began in the mid-1940s, imported by President Howard Lowry, who arrived from Princeton. More than sixty years later, current president Grant Cornwell is a fervent believer. He earned his doctorate at the University of Chicago and taught for twenty years at St. Lawrence University before taking the helm at Wooster in 2007. "What I learned about teaching [here] set me on a new course," he says. "Professors have to approach students as if they must ask their own questions and find their own answers. Other places, you study the research of others so you have knowledge. Here, you're not just consumers of other people's ideas. You generate your own ideas."

As you might guess, the level of interaction between students and professors is sky high—the primary reason faculty members say they came to Wooster and stay here. But it's taxing to teach and advise students on such an intimate scale. To keep its faculty invigorated, Wooster offers a sabbatical program unmatched by its peer institutions (and even those with ivy on their walls). Every fifth year, a professor can submit a proposal to a faculty committee for a year of study at full pay. The vast majority of them are approved. The idea is to give professors the same kind of soul-satisfying, mind-blowing opportunities for research that Wooster gives students. And with a cadre of eager young researchers on campus, professors must stay on top of the latest ideas in their own fields to be most helpful to students.

This schedule poses a challenge at a small college that hangs its hat—quite rightly—on student-professor interaction, but Wooster has created a few safeguards to make sure that the student experience comes first. Never more than 10 percent of faculty is gone at one time, and the college doesn't just hire replacements for a single year, says Dr. Carolyn Newton, the provost. Instead, the college looks at which departments will have professors taking leave in consecutive years and hires a replacement for two or three years, so visiting professors are better able to understand and support the college's mission. Wooster also adds tenure-track positions as it can so that departments can absorb the leaves without needing to hire adjunct professors.

In several dozen conversations with students, not a single one gripes about professors' absences, even when asked directly if they have ever had a hard time getting the adviser they wanted or needed for their IS.

Instead, students emphasize how collaborative their professors are, how eager to help, how interested in student work. "They grade us, but in most ways we're colleagues," says a junior from Pennsylvania. Professors agree. "Students don't always choose topics in your wheelhouse," says Amy Jo Stavnezer, a psychologist and neuroscience professor, referring to IS projects. "I'm always familiar with their topics, but we're working together to read and learn. I love it."

The expectations at Wooster are high, but nobody expects you to arrive as a perfect student. In fact, the college is built on the idea that every student has untapped potential and that the college—by way of teaching and mentoring—helps identify that potential and draw it out to its fullest form. "Students stumble. Our role is to teach them to be better people—better academically and personally, more passionate about their futures," Dr. Kreuzman says.

Professors relish the chance to talk about the students who weren't the shining stars from day one. Dr. Edmiston describes a D student who slowly worked his way to becoming a top student and is now a practicing chemist at Procter & Gamble. Dr. Stavnezer talks about a student who "would not have done an honors thesis at another school" because he was not a standout in the classroom but churned out an IS project that shocked her with its thoughtfulness and depth.

The college has figured out how to foster students' ambition (and in some cases, to unearth it first) without generating an atmosphere of competition. One person's victory doesn't come at another's expense. In other words, every IS project could earn honors. (They don't, but they could. There's no quota on praise, and there's plenty of attention to go around.)

More than one student mentions that the college's vibe is a welcome relief from high school. "I'm the only one of the top ten students from my class who didn't go to a brand-name school," says a senior from Jamaica. "I told my parents that I wanted to explore, and for me, Wooster reaffirmed my interests in diverse fields. Engineering is my passion, but I am also interested in politics and music. We're all multifaceted. Academics are only sixty percent of the experience, and I mean, who wants to be defined by their major?"

When he was a high-school student, a sophomore from San Francisco applied to highly selective places including Amherst and

Williams. He got wait-listed at most of them, but he says he considers that a stroke of good fortune. "You get the academic version of those places here without the competition." The summer after his freshman year at Wooster, he took a couple of summer classes at Berkeley. "It was sink or swim, and I realized how much professors here want you to succeed. The pace and method at Wooster are different, but I learn as much here, maybe more, as I did at Berkeley. I wouldn't trade this place for an education anywhere else."

Not only have they freed themselves from the frenzy of competition, but students say that by coming to Wooster they have also freed themselves socially. "I feel like I fit in here," says a junior from Michigan. "I was super-straight-laced in high school, and now I feel like I'm pursuing my own interests instead of letting other people decide what's valuable or what I ought to be doing." Another student says: "It's a trend here to be what you are." They call the student body "clever," "quirky," "sassy," and "involved." The student body president, a woman from Pennsylvania, sums it up: "People here are secret geniuses."

And their home is a campus straight out of central casting: You can almost hear the Frisbees flying across the quad before you see them. It's the quintessential college campus, beautiful and evocative—and getting better every day. In early 2012 the college opened a gleaming new athletic facility with four intramural courts for tennis, volleyball, and basketball; a two-hundred-meter track that meets NCAA standards; a fitness center with the newest weight-training and cardio equipment; and new locker rooms and athletic offices. It's all topped by an expansive array of solar panels, covering twenty thousand square feet and capable of producing 271,000 kilowatt-hours of electricity every year. Wooster believes it is the largest solar installation at any college facility in the United States.

In the spring of 2012, Wooster also revealed an innovative model for its library. Designed by one of the architectural firms responsible for the sleek Apple Computer retail stores, the library became the Academic Research Center. "Our library, at least in its look, feel, and function, was very much a twentieth-century resource, built for a time when libraries were repositories of knowledge, spaces one had to visit to consult and retrieve all that was currently known," President Cornwell says. Now, of course, access to knowledge is digital and ubiquitous, so Wooster asked: What is a twenty-first-century library? "Our answer is that it is a space not where knowledge is archived but where it is created, and created through the smart, critical, and creative use of information and communication technologies." In form and function, the Academic Research Center fosters research and collaboration—with a little help from an espresso cart, the nectar of the undergraduate gods. No doubt Wooster's model will inform conversations at other high-caliber colleges about how technology changes the ways students and professors access, analyze, and create knowledge.

Wooster is a forward-looking place, but the campus comes with a long list of quirky traditions. At first snowfall, students fill Kauke Arch, a rather large archway in an academic building, with snow. (A campus myth says that if the arch is filled with snow, classes will be canceled. So far, no luck.) When seniors turn in their IS reports (all together on IS Monday in the spring), the registrar gives each of them a Tootsie Roll. And before each home football game, a band of merry bagpipers leads the team into the stadium.

This esprit de corps is a hallmark of the Wooster experience; it's an all-for-one-and-one-for-all kind of place. And to that end, the college has established thoughtful mechanisms of support for students. Much like many of the schools in this book, it requires freshmen to take a First-Year Seminar to sharpen their writing and critical-analysis skills, the first steps toward academic success. The courses are topical, and "in many cases, the topics are outside the faculty members' expertise, so professors can model the kind of learning behavior they want students to emulate," says Dr. Newton, the provost.

An innovative and labor-intensive plan for new-student registration, launched in 2009, is another example. Each student sits down with a staff member from the student affairs office and a professor to register for classes. It's the kind of attention you will never get at a large university, and it sets the stage for the kind of support you can expect throughout your Wooster career.

And as a small but notable example of Wooster's care for students, the college's wellness center is open 24-7—a rarity these days—and provides an excellent spot for students to recover near their peers and professors but away from campus. A student might spend his last days recovering from surgery there or his first days of the flu hiding out, an option that helps contain sickness on campus.

All of these elements of the Wooster experience—dedicated faculty, an opportunity to conduct original research, a spirited culture, and administrators who prioritize student well-being—contribute to a happy student body: 89 percent of freshmen return for their sophomore year, and more than three-fourths graduate in four years. (Nationally, about 67 percent of freshmen return for sophomore year and about 47 percent of students at four-year, private, colleges graduate in four years.)

They come from across the country and around the world; a third are from Ohio, and the rest come from forty-six other states and forty-two foreign countries. One in five is Pell eligible, and 95 percent of students receive financial aid. "This looks like a country club, but it's not," says a junior from inner-city Atlanta. "People here are real. They just love you for what you are."

Wooster accepts about 60 percent of its applicants. In general, the middle 50 percent of enrolled students scored between 24 and 30 on the ACT and between 1110 and 1320 on the SAT (math and critical reading combined). Their high-school GPAs range from 3.3 to 3.9, meaning that a quarter of them are below the B+ range. Most of all, Wooster is looking for people who seek the thrill of this kind of education. "It's not a place to be quiet or uninvolved," says Dr. Scott Friedhoff, vice president of enrollment and college relations. "We want students who will contribute to this campus and make the most of their opportunities here, and we expect to see some reference to these points on students' applications."

If you're fortunate (and wise) enough to enroll at Wooster, you'll get to spend four years with people who expect a lot of you and who believe that learning is one of life's great thrills. And then you'll join the ranks of Wooster alumni, who have long been an impressive group. The college ranks eleventh in the country in the percentage of graduates who go on to earn PhDs. This achievement is nothing new: Wooster has been an incubator of future scientists at least since 1920, when the National Academy of Sciences started keeping tabs.

The College of Wooster produces educated—not trained—people. That sounds like a catchphrase, something the marketing department might work up, but it's an important distinction in a marketplace of higher education where the emphasis on preparing for a job suffocates the idea that students ought to learn how to think. That's not a risk here: Wooster students are well prepared for the real world precisely *because* they know how to think—and, of course, they've gained tremendous self-confidence from mastering a rigorous academic program with faculty advisers cheering them on. It should be a well-kept secret no more.

Austin College

Sherman, Texas

"[Austin College] is one of those [communities] that is doing the essential work of producing the enlightened, responsible, creative people with moral compasses who make democracy work. We need many more colleges like it."

—**LOREN POPE**

Anyone feeling disheartened by the state of the world, anyone wondering how we're going to yank our collective bootstraps and solve this century's most pervasive problems, should visit Austin College in northern Texas for a hefty dose of hope. There's plenty of optimism here, and rightly so.

The curriculum pairs in-depth study of liberal arts and sciences—helping students hone their problem-solving, communication, and critical-thinking skills—with a focus on international study that's hard to find anywhere else. The result is a group of 1,350 students who are thinking carefully about what they can do right now and for the rest of their lives to make the world a better place. And they're thrilled.

"I thought I'd come here, plow through the premed program, and go to med school and become a dermatologist. It was such a superficial plan," says a senior biochemistry major. "Now I want to work for Doctors Without Borders. AC shows you that we all have humanitarians in us. I had these things in me, but they were brought out by this campus."

How does this happen? First, through a kindhearted, entrepreneurial faculty. They're an unusually collaborative group, eager to help students make intellectual leaps across disciplines "because that's how problems get solved," says Dr. Michael Higgs, a computer scientist who worked for Texas Instruments and IBM before joining the college's faculty more than twenty years ago. "It fosters creative thinking; if our first attempt at a solution fails, we must be able to say, 'What else do I know that I could apply to this scenario?'" This kind of thinking makes for lively classrooms—and a good bit of fun. (Yes, fun.)

A five-year, $500,000 grant from the Mellon Foundation supports faculty collaboration. The grant funds "partnered courses": Taught by two professors from different departments, these courses marry seemingly disparate subjects in fascinating ways. For example, a biology professor teamed up with a communication-studies professor to create a course in nonverbal communication among animals and people.

The freedom to explore topics outside of their formal disciplines thrills faculty—and one must never underestimate the power of an enthusiastic professor. The life of the mind matters here. Dr. George Diggs, a biologist, says he has taken students to seventeen different countries in his thirty years at AC. "I've learned that there are many ways to teach, and I've gotten a chance to teach outside of my formal discipline. When professors are learning, that's incredibly beneficial for students."

Dr. Michael Imhoff, the vice president for academic affairs, came to Austin College in 1970 from Princeton to teach chemistry. "The first thing that surprised me was how national the faculty were. This isn't a sleepy little regional school. The second thing was how polite the students were. There's an initial warmth and openness, an egalitarian spirit, that was very different from Princeton," he says. That spirit hasn't changed.

Dr. Imhoff planned to stay only a few years. More than forty years later, he can't decide if the faculty or the students exerted the greatest pull on his heart. "I would not be dean of any other faculty," he says. "They're aligned; they share a mission. I don't think people outside of academia realize how unique and important that is."

This top-notch faculty is backed by an administration led by the college's beloved new president, Dr. Marjorie Hass. Young and vivacious, she is as far from a typical college administrator as you'll find for a thousand miles, and to say she is charismatic is like saying that Mark Zuckerberg has some cash. But lucky for this community, beneath that charisma is a deep sense of mission and an intense love for Austin College.

It was an unlikely fit: Dr. Hass, a philosopher, had never been to Texas before her interview on campus. She's Jewish at a school founded by Presbyterians, and she's Austin's first female president.

But across campus, Marjorie—few people call her "Dr. Hass"—is a kind of rock star. It's easy to see why. Her first commitments are to students (current, former, and prospective) and to faculty. Under her watch, in 2011 the college broke ground on its long-anticipated IDEA Center, a 103,000-square-foot, $38 million center for the sciences, mathematics, and computer science departments. The building will double the college's classroom space and add thirty-two high-tech labs, plus a 108-seat auditorium. At the same time, the college is building new dorms at the edge of campus for upperclassmen. The cottages and "mansions"—a kind of triplex—incorporate smart green-building elements, show off Craftsman and Victorian architectural details, and give students their first taste of quasi-independent living while preserving a spirit of community. The only problem, of course, is that most students' first apartments postcollege won't be nearly so lovely.

Dr. Hass would like to see all of AC's students study or intern abroad; currently, the college sends 70 percent of its students abroad, putting its program among the top programs ranked by the Institute of International Education. And she's very thoughtful about supporting faculty because "our curriculum is so relationship driven. I want our faculty to have the resources and energy to keep giving to and supporting our students."

In short, she wants Austin College to be better at the things it already does very well. "One thing I like best [about Austin College] is that I've never once heard anyone say, 'We need to be more like X College,'" she says. (Many colleges are plagued by the grass-is-greener-on-that-quad syndrome.) This confidence frees AC from chasing the latest shortsighted educational trend to focus instead on helping students hone their skills and boost their confidence.

To this end, the college has made a few changes in recent years. Every student must complete a major and a minor; minors used to be optional. The goal of this new requirement is to give coherence to a student's general education requirements. Many students choose "pure" academic subjects for minors, but the faculty have added or expanded the college's interdisciplinary offerings to meet the increased demand. With options such as Film Studies; Global Science, Technology, and Society; International Economics and Finance; and Western Intellectual Tradition, it's no wonder many students choose a double minor or double major to satisfy their curiosity.

The new Center for Global Learning brings together all of the college's opportunities for international travel, study, and internships. AC's approach to study abroad should serve as a model for colleges and universities across the world; the emphasis is on living and learning immersed in a culture, not acting like a kind of supertourist who spends a few hours a day conjugating French verbs with other American twentysomethings.

For semester- or yearlong study, students can choose from dozens of programs across the world run by third-party organizations, either other colleges or well-established groups that manage such opportunities. "We're looking for providers [of study-abroad experiences] who help students establish roots in a place—volunteering to coach swimming for local youth or singing with the community choir," says Dr. Truett Cates, the center's director. Austin College professors also offer twelve to fifteen off-campus classes each January term.

These experiences tend to inspire students to dig even deeper, so the college offers a couple of other impressive programs. Each summer, Global Outreach (GO) Fellowships support ten to fifteen students who want to volunteer abroad; students write a reflective paper at the end of their service work and share their experiences with the campus through video diaries, presentations, and articles in the school paper. In fact, one of AC's newest programs helps students who have been abroad "unpack" their experiences in a multiday creative workshop where they create digital stories with photos, video, audio recordings, and music that help them reflect on what they have learned.

For students who want to intern in the United States or abroad, AC's Career Study Off-Campus (CSOC) provides an excellent avenue for charting one's own course. With input from a faculty adviser, students write their learning goals and decide how they'll be assessed. Internship sites are as diverse as you can imagine: a Nepalese rehabilitation center for children, Parisian public schools, and the Sherman paper's newsroom.

As you might expect, students who are turned on by such opportunities are eager learners. They're also good-hearted, down to earth, and passionate. They're proud of the college's diversity— 35 percent of students are minorities, and the religious plurality is a rich part of college life. A junior from Oklahoma explains, "AC attracts a certain type of student. They're here not because their parents made them come to college. They're here to get something out of it." And if you're lucky enough to join them, you'll get a community of people who take care of their own. Every single one of dozens of students—prompted or not—says that when challenges arise, whether academic or personal, students and professors get them through. "We care about everyone. This is our mini globe," a sophomore from Plano says.

Uniformly, students feel they have powers they didn't have a few years ago. Professors agree. Dr. Diggs says: "I've realized that one of my most important jobs is to help the kids in the middle of the pack. AC opens their eyes to what they do well. It's amazing what happens when you tell a kid, 'You are talented. Strive for more.'" Every teacher has handfuls of stories about students who blossomed: those who came from rural schools and took their first plane trips when they crossed the globe on January term courses; type-A students who would have withered at competitive places that didn't give them room to step off the path and take a few risks; tough guys who cried when they got accepted to top-tier graduate programs.

"They're not a ritzy, wealthy bunch," says Dr. Patrick Duffey, dean of humanities and a professor of Spanish. "They're not trendy, and they're much more diverse than you would expect in a small Texas town." They're not interested in résumé building or grade grubbing. "Most of them are driven by passion." Dr. Higgs, who earned his PhD at Stanford, adds, "Some of our good ones are as good as the best I saw at Stanford."

He knows because, like his colleagues, he has seen students work in class and in the lab. Student research is a big deal at AC, and students' names often appear right next to professors' in academic journals. Dr. Stephanie Gould, a chemist, estimates that 95 percent of chemistry and biochem majors conduct research before graduating. You can't earn a degree in physics without doing two semesters of research with two different professors, so you learn multiple methodologies. The Scarborough Summer Research Program funds independent student research (guided by a faculty member) in the humanities and social sciences.

This relationship between professors and students begins with the freshman course Communication/Inquiry—or "C/I"—a required class in the fall that eases students into the college's expectations. Professors take turns teaching, and each fall delivers a new batch of interesting courses on topics like innovative architecture, the truth and myth of genetic engineering, and personal diaries of literary giants. C/I emphasizes time-management skills, oral and written communication, and critical inquiry. Best of all, the professor who teaches a student's C/I is her faculty mentor for all four years. Students call these relationships "authentic" and "secure." One young woman, a first-generation college student, says that her mentor gave her the courage to stay at AC when she got a serious case of home-sickness her freshman year.

As more students and parents have discovered how wondrous and powerful an Austin College education is, the college has gotten slightly more selective, but it still accepts about 70 percent of its applicants. About 95 percent of them come from the top half of their high school classes, and more than 80 percent come from Texas (but remember, Texas is a diverse land unto itself). The college's commitment to financial aid is admirable: 75 percent of students earn merit-based scholarships, and more than 90 percent receive some kind of financial help. "Scholarships aren't just a nice thing to do," Dr. Hass says. "They're part of who we are, part of our responsibility to students who are qualified to be here."

Financial access to college is a tough issue for most families and most colleges, but Austin College sees its investments grow tenfold or more when its students graduate. Primed for adventure and confident in their own abilities, they pursue the kinds of experiences many adults wish they had. An analysis of a recent cohort of five consecutive graduating classes reveals that about 18 percent of students serve in AmeriCorps, 7 percent go into the Peace Corps, 15 percent go on to Teach for America (famously competitive), and 8 percent earn Fulbrights. In fact, per capita, for the fifteen years leading up to 2009, Austin College students earned more Fulbrights than Rice University, UT Austin, Baylor, Southern Methodist University, or the University of North Texas. Another 35 percent enroll in graduate or professional schools immediately after AC.

Current students say they feel very confident pursuing the things in their postcollege lives that would be satisfying to them and of service to others. "AC teaches you to trust yourself. You'll figure it out," says a junior. Thanks to a two-and-a-half-month internship in a small Thai village, a senior plans to spend her life working with developing communities to help them preserve their cultural identities. "In high school, I could never have imagined loving any kind of work as much as I love doing this," she beams.

It's easy to admire Austin College's spirit. At other schools in this book, students grumble occasionally about their schools' under-the-radar status. Here, students are primed to show anyone with Ivy envy just how remarkable Austin College is. "I love that we're getting a global education in a town that nobody's ever heard of," says a senior from Dallas. Given AC's momentum, it won't be that way for long.

St. John's College

Santa Fe, New Mexico, and Annapolis, Maryland

"[St. John's] is a hard-working Shangri-La for the life-of-the-mind teenager who may hate or is bored by high school or is disgusted with education's stupid SAT system. St. John's has the courage to reject all that stuff; it's who you are and what you want out of college that counts."

—LOREN POPE

St. John's is a school for the intellectual explorer. If you're looking for someone else to tell you the right answer, skip it. But if you're game for an adventure that equips you to think and communicate about complex ideas with a collegial community of scholars, St. John's might be your nirvana.

The college has no majors, one mission, one catalog, two campuses, two presidents, two faculties, and two student bodies that may move freely from one campus to the other. The unusual duality is the result of the expansionist mood of the sixties, when education was a booming industry and the college's keepers in Annapolis decided to clone the college on a mountain in Santa Fe.

St. John's charming tidewater colonial campus of 450 students in Annapolis, with its ancient trees and mix of historic and modern buildings, is on a Severn River tributary. On another dramatically beautiful campus on the other side of the country, nestling on the shoulders of Monte Sol in the southeast corner of Santa Fe, a student body of like size wrestles with the same questions of the human condition.

Students on both campuses follow the Program, a great-books curriculum entirely deserving of its capital *P*. Students take four years of language (ancient Greek and French, and a close look at the nature of languages), four years of math, three years of lab science, one year of music, and four years of the queen mother of all courses, seminar—an intellectual journey with some of Western thought's most interesting and influential authors as guides. It's a cross-curricular investigation of literature, political science, religion, philosophy, history, economics, and psychology.

The curriculum is based on original works of literature, art, music, language, math, and science. You learn geometry by reading Euclid. You learn astronomy from Copernicus. You learn about democracy from Tocqueville, Lincoln, and Hamilton.

That means there are no textbooks, except in the ancient Greek and French courses. Students love it: "You get to see the personalities of the people you're reading," says a junior from New Mexico. "You don't get that from a textbook."

St. John's lacks other mainstays of typical college education: There are no midterms or finals; the only quizzes or tests happen in ancient Greek and French classes. Grades are based on class participation and papers, but the college doesn't issue report cards and nobody talks about grades, which are recorded for graduate-school purposes only. (New College of Florida might be the only place on the planet that cares less about grades.)

There are no fraternities or sororities; all the Greeks on campus are ancient philosophers or epic poets. And there are no intercollegiate sports, but Johnnies can be fierce intramural competitors. If you enroll at the Annapolis campus, you'll be powerless to resist the Gatsby-esque picnic that surrounds the annual croquet match against its neighbor, the Naval Academy.

What's more, there are no faculty ranks. All professors are "tutors" because they do not profess; they stimulate learning. There is no need to publish, and they all teach everything. That is, a tutor with a PhD in philosophy might be teaching Euclid's geometry one year and music theory the next. It's as honest a community of learners as you'll find.

At the end of each semester for a student's first two years, she meets with her tutors for the "Don Rag"—a frank conversation about the student's work. (The term comes from Oxford, where professors, called "dons," would "rag"—or challenge—their students during oral exams.) It's here that students learn whether they can continue in the Program. By junior year, the student prepares her own self-assessment for the Don Rag. "I never had anyone express an honest opinion about my work," says tutor Guillermo Bleichmar, who earned his BA at Columbia and his PhD in comparative literature from Harvard. "I wish I had. You can't imagine how powerful these conversations are for students. They change and improve and take up the challenges we offer to them."

Intellectually demanding and intense, St. John's is not selective; it is selected. It accepts almost 80 percent of its applicants, who demonstrate whether they belong there by writing as many as six to ten pages about themselves. Most come from the top quartile of their classes, and plenty have B averages in high school. "We're looking for a few things: an understanding of the Program, evidence of a reading life, and an appreciation for this type of education," says Santa Fe's director of admission, Larry Clendenin. You don't have to submit ACT or SAT scores, but you'd better be ready to explain why you want to study at St. John's.

Your enthusiasm and understanding matter because there is no middle ground: It's excitement or misery. The miserable leave; the excited flourish. "I love the generality of the program," says a junior from Albuquerque. "It gives me time to discover what I enjoy without having to narrow it down before I know the possibilities." Many students—particularly women—point out that they disliked math and science in high school, but St. John's uncovered the mathematicians and scientists in them. Maybe that's one reason St. John's ranks among the top fifty American colleges in producing future PhDs in science and engineering, according to data from the National Science Foundation.

Students are almost fanatical about their learning. But in typical Johnnie fashion, they don't spew superlatives; they give thoughtful analyses: "I knew if I came here, I could discuss the perennial

political and human problems. That opportunity is not taken seriously other places," says a freshman from Minneapolis. "I'm more
confused than ever"—he laughs—"but I've never had this much fun
or fulfillment from learning."

"I'm better able to observe my own thoughts and know when I'm
being honest," adds a junior from Albuquerque. "My learning folds
into everything I am. It's not just academic; it's how I approach
everything in my life. I feel so capable."

"I've learned to talk less," says a junior from San Francisco. "I'm
not interested in 'winning' a point. Here, it's about getting to a place
where you can learn something. For example, we discussed the
phrase 'We the people of the United States of America' for an hour
in our last seminar. Three years ago, you could have asked me,
'What's a country?' and I would have looked at you like you were
missing some brain cells. Now I realize how significant a question
that is, and I have some ideas about a good answer. Maybe this is
kind of melodramatic, but I really think that if more Americans had
to think about these questions, we'd have less ideology, more com-
promise, and fewer problems in the country, probably in the world."

The self-confidence that comes from this kind of learning is
unmatched. No amount of parental cheerleading or straight-A
report cards can persuade a student of her own powers like thinking and writing about history's greatest ideas and the people who
gave them life.

In a sophomore language class one late spring afternoon, students sit in "Johnnie chairs"—the custom-made, simple wooden
chairs are everywhere on campus—and discusses Shakespeare's
The Tempest—or more specifically, the source of Prospero's power
on his tiny, barely populated island. Students discuss his roles as
father, deposed politician, and slave owner with an earnestness
Supreme Court justices would admire. Can they separate his
sources of power from his true nature? If his sources of power are
good, does that make him virtuous? And if they're not, can they
dismiss him as evil? It doesn't take long for a student to get here: "I
think we're talking about the definition of evil in humanity." And
all of a sudden, they are pulling ideas from Aristotle's *Nicomachean*

Ethics and Shakespeare's *A Midsummer Night's Dream* and Chaucer's *The Canterbury Tales*. If discussion were an Olympic sport, these students would be gold medalists in training.

Then a most unusual thing happens: The tutor (who happens to have a PhD in comparative literature) says he's curious about a particular passage in the text. A student responds by acknowledging that yes, that passage is interesting, but what she really wants to examine is this other passage. Another student picks up her comments—and the discussion rolls again.

It takes a gifted teacher to know how to guide a class—and when to let go—and St. John's faculty is exceptionally good. "A classroom of fifteen people who are coming from fifteen different places constitutes a whole far more powerful than any one individual, including the teacher," says tutor John Cornell, who earned his PhD at the University of Chicago and came to St. John's because an exceptional teacher there had been a tutor at St. John's. "Tutors orchestrate that music. The kind of discourse we see is missing in our country today."

Tutors are a happy group. They're enthusiastic about what St. John's has done for them—namely, released them from the shackles of minutiae to enjoy the Big Picture, to connect their advanced learning with the context from which it's often removed. Topi Heikkerö, who earned a PhD in social ethics from the University of Helsinki, was deeply entrenched in the philosophy of technology before he came to St. John's. "All those years of studying, and I didn't know about the classics of math and science," he says. "I was missing so much, and I feel like every class, I have a reawakening."

The college prepares tutors for the unusual task of teaching—and learning—outside of their primary disciplines with a variety of resources: weekly tutor study groups–cum–prep time; intensive summer workshops; Friday Night Lectures, open to the entire campus, when faculty lecture in their fields. New tutors move through the program chronologically—the same path students take—to give them the ultimate perspective. And best of all, St. John's gives each tutor a sabbatical at full pay every eight years—a benefit that's not always provided at institutions of higher learning. "It's a time to rest and recharge, to prepare for deepening work in the Program," says Victoria Mora, the former dean of the college in Santa Fe. "Tutors take time to delve into a particular area that interests them most with the ultimate goal of learning more. It might be Maxwell's equations or ancient Greek."

Tutors are obviously fond of their students, who are quirky, witty, and earnest. You won't find a college cafeteria anywhere where eavesdropping is more fun. Because they've all read the same texts, and because they're a thoughtful group, the repartee is irresistible— even if the food isn't.

If you long to be one of them, students advise, don't let the school's reading list dissuade you. It looks daunting, and the reading is significant, but motivation matters most. So what if you once thought Molière was a kind of mosquito-borne disease? "Nobody here judges. We expect a lot of each other because the best classes are the ones where everyone is prepared and amped up, but we're protective of each other. There's a lot of room to grow," says a senior from Chicago.

St. John's does a good job helping prospective students discern whether the Program is for them. When you schedule your visit, you'll get the reading assignment in advance, but you may not participate in the discussion. It's the perfect litmus test: If staying silent makes you crazy, St. John's might be the place for you.

And to parents worried about the practicality of this kind of education, the college's keepers—and its students—have a solid answer: There is no more practical education anywhere. "By focusing on fundamental things, young adults develop intellect, imagination, habits and practice, and communication skills in various ways. Those are the things necessary to be successful at anything else," Dr. Mora says.

A student put it another way: Without knowledge, she said, "You are at the mercy of popular thought. What if popular thought is wrong?" Just a guess: The world economy shrivels up, natural resources grow scarce, and we recognize bronzed beachgoers from Jersey but can't figure out who our local elected officials are.

This is why St. John's is as valuable an education as any in the country. Sure, its outcomes are impressive: 80 percent of students go to graduate school, and it has produced six Rhodes Scholars—a rate that outpaces plenty of "big name" schools, such as Cornell University. Among its alumni are notable writers, researchers, and thought leaders, including Ray Cave, the former editorial director of *Time*; Lee Zlotoff, creator of *MacGyver* and a successful screen-writer and director; author Andrew Krivak, nominated for a National Book Award; and Margaret Winter, head of prison proj-ects for the ACLU. But it's also doing a great public good in produc-ing the kind of college graduates who hold their communities accountable to ask and answer significant questions.

Alumni agree. A 2004 graduate writes, "In many ways, the school has helped me articulate the fundamentals of my own being. I'm not a different person than the student who stepped onto the campus four years ago, but I'm a much better version of who I've always been. I feel like I can go into the world and hold my own in any environ-ment, something the eighteen-year-old from a small West Virginia town may not have been able to do as well as she thought. . . . We've managed to identify ourselves in the huge and rich context of this culture we live in; how many colleges can claim that?"

And in perhaps the most literary explanation of what St. John's does, alumnus and author Salvatore Scibona penned an article titled "Where I Learned to Read" about his alma mater for a June 2011 *New Yorker*. He wrote: "By senior year at St. John's, we were reading Einstein in math, Darwin in lab, Baudelaire in French tutorial, Hegel in seminar. Seminar met twice a week for four years: eight o'clock to ten at night or later, all students addressed by sur-name. On weekends, I hung out with my friends. The surprise, the wild luck: I had friends. One sat in my room with a beer and *The Phenomenology of Spirit*, reading out a sentence at a time and stop-ping to ask, "All right, what did that mean?" The gravity of the whole thing would have been laughable if it hadn't been so much fun, and if it hadn't been such a gift to find my tribe."

If his description stirs something in you, if you long for a salve from the pop-culture ballyhoo that distracts from clear thinking, you'll likely find your tribe at St. John's too.

Southwestern University

Georgetown, Texas

"Southwestern is a warm and friendly place that evokes in its teenagers and in its teachers a pride in belonging, and for good reason. It will do the same for those who come from the North, the Midwest, the West Coast, or the Northwest. True, they might as freshmen find their classmates a tad more conservative than themselves, but also probably kinder, more tolerant, and more considerate. Four years later, as seniors, they'll probably have found some common ground, and those from afar may have acquired some of the warm virtues of their Southwestern friends, as well as an exceptional four years of growth."

—LOREN POPE

Southwestern University has an unusual mission in Texas: In the shadow of the University of Texas at Austin, this small, private liberal arts university in lovely Georgetown is delivering high-quality, life-changing education in a culture that doesn't quite know what to make of a university that doesn't even have a football team. Its 1,370 students are bucking the trend—and loving it.

"The students have already set themselves apart by coming here," says Dr. Emily Niemeyer, a chemistry professor. "They're primed for an experience that's unlike the majority of higher education in Texas." That is, nurturing, challenging, and attentive to undergraduates.

The school has had an exciting few decades. Chartered in 1840 and established by the Methodist Church, it has benefited from a series of strong presidents—beginning with Dr. Roy B. Shilling in the 1970s—each of whom has asked how the university can be more effective and more engaged in students' lives. Successful fund-raising and a few hefty grants in the late nineties and early 2000s beefed up Southwestern's endowment nicely. The money attracted a solid group of young faculty and paid for several new and impressive buildings on campus.

In 2000 alumnus Dr. Jake Schrum became the university's president—and Southwestern continued to grow and change. An $8.5 million grant from the Priddy Charitable Trust enabled the university to launch the Paideia Program, a distinctive interdisciplinary adventure. Senior professors meet with cohorts of ten students each to discuss ideas of civic engagement, create service-learning projects, conduct undergraduate research, and engage in creative works. Paideia scholars meet with the same cohort through their sophomore, junior, and senior years, and each scholar gets a thousand-dollar stipend to use toward one of his experiences in service, leadership, creative, or intercultural projects.

As one student explains: "[Paideia] is the ultimate liberal arts experience because it forces us to make connections between ideas and reality. We don't just get to sit around and think—even though we do that too. We have to take action and respond, whether it's a service project or our own research or some kind of artistic expression. It's awesome."

She sounds a lot like her classmates, all of whom use superlatives to describe their campus. "I couldn't have asked for a better school," says a freshman theater student who is painting sets in the smaller of the two theaters in the Sarofim School of Fine Arts building. (Southwestern comprises the Brown College of Arts and Sciences and the Sarofim School of Fine Arts—hence the "university" in its name.) A sophomore from Albuquerque adds, "People here show up for each other; we're all interested in what's happening on campus. More than once, I've gone to a play and I'm surprised to see who's performing. It's a chem genius or one of the lacrosse guys. And I'm like, 'This place is amazing.'"

His classmates agree: In the 2010 National Survey of Student

Engagement (NSSE), 78 percent of first-year students said that they frequently got prompt verbal or written feedback from Southwestern faculty members (compared with 70 percent nationally for similar institutions) 92 percent of freshmen felt that Southwestern placed substantial emphasis on academics; and 83 percent of seniors would choose Southwestern if they could start their college careers over again. Compare those numbers with the fact that more than 50 percent of American college students transfer at least once in their college careers, and you realize how satisfied Southwestern's students are.

They're also polite and friendly; they lack pretense, and they seem to relish the fact that they've traded the typical Texas university experience for this unique opportunity to learn from professors in lively classrooms. Students aren't afraid to lob their ideas into class discussions and see what happens, and professors give plenty of room for students to ask questions and share their own ideas—an art far more sophisticated than simply lecturing to a classroom of warm bodies.

A strong majority of students comes from Texas, but don't be fooled into thinking this is a homogenous student body: Texas is a vast and varied place. Consider that, as the crow flies, Dalhart, in Texas's northwest corner, is closer to Bismarck, North Dakota, than it is to Brownsville on Texas's southern tip. And Brownsville is closer to Cancún, Mexico, than it is to Dalhart. This is expansive country. Plus, about 30 percent of students are minorities, and the students who aren't from Texas come from thirty-three other states and four foreign countries.

Many of Texas's public high schools are larger than Southwestern's student body, but the students here insist that the small size is one of their favorite features. "At a place this size, you get to know a lot of people you wouldn't get to know if you were at a big school and just hung out with your fraternity brothers or a few kids from your major," a sophomore from Houston says. "I know because I visit my friends at UT, and they each have, like, ten friends. Here, I have friends on the lacrosse team, from the politics department, from my freshman dorm, from the service trip I took. I've heard so many perspectives I never knew existed."

The students who enroll have solid academic records: Almost 50 percent of them are in the top tenth of their high-school classes. The middle 50 percent scored between 24 and 30 on the ACT and between 1110 and 1340 on the SAT (critical reading and math combined). But if your test scores are weak, don't fret: The admissions office does not turn away applicants simply because of low test scores.

In recent years, the university has continued to expand its resources for students and faculty, even during the financial crisis near the end of the last decade. It built ten new buildings between 2000 and 2010, the last of which was the Prothro Center for Lifelong Learning, which brings student-centered services, such as the registrar, student health center, and career-services office, all under one roof. Students rave about it. The fine arts building got a ten-million-dollar renovation, making it worthy of the college's excellent programs. And the university isn't done: A strategic plan for the next decade calls for a new science building, among other improvements. Students are clearly proud of their beautiful campus; it's nearly impossible to find a piece of trash anywhere.

What hasn't changed is Southwestern's greatest virtue: its ability to foster close bonds between students and their teachers. In institutional surveys, year after year, students report that the top reason they came to Southwestern and stayed were connections with faculty. Students from two dozen departments say the same thing in person: Professors push them and guide them—and sometimes give them the proverbial kick in the pants—and every single student expresses gratitude.

And nobody says it's easy to get an A. Most laugh at the question. "Teachers expect a lot from you, but they give a lot back to you," says a junior. "The resources are available for you to succeed, but classes definitely require a lot from us." Students are also unanimous in saying that they wouldn't have it any other way. "I'm definitely thankful for the rigor," says a junior political science major. "I would not have known what I'm capable of otherwise."

Most of the professors chose Southwestern over larger, research-driven universities, and they all say they love the teacher-scholar model. "The vitality of being around twentysomethings who are excited about the trajectories of their lives—it's great. I'm never going to get old." Dr. Niemeyer says. "We all take pride in our one-on-one interactions with students. It's at the heart of our work."

Dr. Carina Evans, a young English professor who arrived on campus straight from earning her PhD at a large university, adds, "That's the thing that makes me feel inspired here—the classroom feeds my research, and vice versa. I don't have to choose between the two."

Professors call their students "very engaged," "eager and likable," and "very present in class." Dr. Evans gives this example: "In a midterm evaluation I gave the students during my first semester, one student wrote, 'You can ask more of us.' So I did, and the student was absolutely right." Only real teachers get joy from this kind of challenge.

Dr. Evans's example points to another distinctive element of this campus: Faculty, students, and senior administrators are very willing to discuss what works and what doesn't. It can be tough to change an organization—to release it from ideas about "how we've always done things"—but somehow Southwestern seems very able to preserve what's best about it while assessing how it could do better. In other words, there are no sacred cows, so leaders are able to respond to students' and professors' needs and ideas—a hallmark of a college that is preparing leaders to do the same for their colleagues one day.

Students clearly feel safe on campus—not just from roaming thugs (or heavy-handed administrators) but from the emotional and social daggers that can damage teens' psyches. "High-school labels don't apply here," says a young woman. Another adds: "I'm doing a lot here that I wouldn't have ever done at any other school. It's less scary to try things because everyone's trying things."

The foundation of this unique risk taking is the Honor Pledge: "I have acted with honesty and integrity in producing this work and am unaware of anyone who has not." The pledge tells students that the campus community trusts them; it lets them decide whether their word is good, and it sets the tone for healthy relationships between students and teachers. Students pledge all of their work, and the benefits are sweet: unproctored exams and take-home tests. If a student cheats, an Honor Council of students and faculty decides the appropriate consequence, from a failing grade on the assignment to expulsion from school. Students say cheating is taboo—a kind of insult to the whole community. It's not just an academic offense; it's a good way to be ostracized socially too.

But since cheating rarely happens, and students are uplifted and curious and adventurous, the whole campus purrs with eager optimism—and fun. Students work hard, but they are also quite good at playing. About 90 percent of students participate in Division III or intramural sports (including a Quidditch team, no broomsticks necessary). As many as 50 percent of students study abroad. Students are pondering politics, planning events for their fraternities and sororities, and interning at organizations and government agencies in Austin. In fact, professors say they sometimes have to persuade students to cut down on commitments.

One of the most popular—and beloved—elements of campus life is the arts. Maybe something wafts up from Austin to inspire this kind of passion. Or maybe it's the university's pride in being one of a handful of small liberal arts communities that supports a separate school of fine arts. No matter the reason, students and professors from across departments laud the Sarofim School of Fine Arts, home to the theater, music, studio art, and art history departments—where every student takes at least one or two courses. (Students who wish to major in these areas must first gain admission to the university and then audition or submit portfolios to apply to Sarofim.)

"I love that Southwestern requires every student to interact with his or her creative spirit," says Dr. Rick Roemer, a theater professor. "One of my favorite classes is 'Theatre for Non-Majors.' We help them think and respond in new ways." Students from all disciplines perform in the school's theatrical and musical performances each year. Generous scholarships for Sarofim students emphasize the university's commitment to the arts.

And if the arts aren't your thing, you're bound to find something that is among the university's many extracurricular learning opportunities. The chemistry department's Welch Summer Research Program pays as many as twelve students to stay on campus for eight weeks in the summer and collaborate with faculty members on their research. The business and economics department offers the Financial Analyst Program: Student portfolio managers manage part of the university's endowment (with great success). Or you can create your own adventure through the King Creativity Fund, established in 2000 with a $500,000 gift from an alumnus. The fund awards grants to students who want to take on their own creative work; previous King projects include the construction of an electric cello, performances of Shakespeare's *A Midsummer Night's Dream* outdoors (rather, "out of the box"), and the assembly and study of solar chimneys to see if they're viable sources of alternative energy. "Our school does a good job of allowing us to personalize our education," says a senior majoring in economics and psychology, who conducted his own research on driver fatigue and then took an internship at Dell in Austin. "I never would have considered grad school, but I can't stop now. I have to see how much more I can do."

The quality of a Southwestern experience translates into a broad and enthusiastic alumni network, which is one of its greatest assets. One alumnus led and funded a recent shift in the alumni structure, from a less organized mass of eager professionals to a strong chapter-based model. (The chapters in Texas are robust, of course, but their peers in LA, Chicago, and the Pacific Northwest will not be outdone. The benefit to current students is tremendous.) Alumni are more available than ever to sponsor internships, offer networking help, and give advice on the transition from college to career.

It's a good and exciting time to be at Southwestern if you're looking for a place that helps you discover your passions and develop them. A senior communications major sums it up: "I wouldn't say that Southwestern changes your life. I'd say that it gives you the tools to change your own life."

WEST

University of Puget Sound

Tacoma, Washington

Don't let the weather fool you: The University of Puget Sound is a bright spot on the map of American higher education. Students searching for thoughtful professors, a lively interdisciplinary vibe, friendly classmates, and a beautiful setting ought to add the university to their short lists.

Trees that would give shade to giants dot the ninety-seven-acre campus, and everywhere shades of green, vibrant and varied, are a gorgeous reminder of Puget Sound's spot in the Northwest. On a sunny day—and there are plenty of them, despite the meteorological stereotypes of Washington—Mount Rainier is visible from campus. Amid this natural beauty stand handsome buildings so classically collegiate that they might have been plucked from a New England college. The campus "expresses the college's soul," says President Ronald Thomas.

It's a happy soul, say the 2,600 students who share it. "I couldn't have found a better place," says an English major, singing a common refrain. "I love the atmosphere. We want to be here and have productive discussion. Judgments I've had of other people have come undone. I've been humbled and then built up." Her classmates agree that Puget Sound boosts their confidence, sharpens their skills, dissolves their assumptions, and gives them a community of scholars and friends.

Puget Sound has an unusual and valuable history. It begins in the usual way, with a small and determined group of clergy (Methodist) who founded the college in 1888 to be "a praise in all the land." The college grew steadily—with the exception of the war years, when enrollment floundered. After World War II, the university exploded, adding a law school, evening programs, and vocational programs, which cost the college its focus and academic rigor. Here's the remarkable part: In the 1970s, when other universities were embracing the idea of a "multiversity," being all things to all people, the faculty and trustees here agreed that the college must return to its liberal arts roots. They reduced enrollment, earned a chapter of Phi Beta Kappa—the country's most prestigious academic honor society—and in 1993 the Carnegie Foundation reclassified Puget Sound as a liberal arts college.

As a result of its history, Puget Sound is both an old college and a young one. Its devotion to the liberal arts feels less like the assumed love between an old married couple and more like the passion of newlyweds: exciting and enchanting, hopeful and forward looking.

"We have courage to try new ideas," says President Thomas. "We have an entrepreneurial spirit." For proof, look at the college's curriculum, which is full of interdisciplinary programs, valuable for their emphasis on connecting ideas from different fields. Students learn to pull together information from disparate sources and analyze it in the context of a central question or idea. It would be easier for the college to adhere to clean-cut departments where professors teach the same courses over and over again, but the faculty here like to dream up new courses and expand offerings as their fields grow, change, and overlap.

For example, International Political Economy (IPE), one of the college's popular interdisciplinary programs, examines the social, political, and economic factors that contribute to global issues and events. Students in the 1980s told professors in these departments that they were seeing connections among the courses' content and wanted a formal program. In true Puget Sound fashion, the professors responded and wrote a textbook, now in its sixth edition and used at about two hundred other colleges.

Other examples abound: In Science, Technology & Society, students examine the intersections of science and history, technology, politics, and philosophy—and then look at how these factors influence decision making and values in public and private realms. Environmental Policy and Decision Making applies a similar interdisciplinary lens to issues of environmental policy. Students who take courses in the Global Development Studies program dive into the macro and micro issues and theories that influence development across the world. And if a student can't find what she wants among the college's thirty-nine departments and programs, she's free to design her own major with guidance from a faculty adviser.

Even the business program gets an injection of interdisciplinary juice. Puget Sound's approach to its program might win over even the liberal arts purists who believe business courses are too vocational and narrow, sacrificing the analytical skills so central to liberal learning. For starters, Dr. Jeffrey Matthews, a historian, directs the Business Leadership Program, an honors program for business students. "We are not set apart; the faculty in the business school see our curriculum in the context of the liberal arts," he explains. So the course on strategic planning examines the Lewis and Clark expedition, and a marketing course requires students to do presentations in foreign languages. "If you want to be a CPA, the business program here probably won't be a good fit for you," says Dr. Matthews. But if you want to graduate with the precious skills liberal learning bestows and with some context for understanding business principles, Puget Sound is a good choice.

One of the college's other shining stars is its Pacific Rim/Asia Study-Travel Program. Every three years, a group of students, led by a professor, spends nine months living and learning in Asian countries (not all of them on the Pacific Rim), including Korea,

Nepal, Vietnam, Japan, India, and China. Like St. Olaf's Global Semester, the Pac Rim experience strips away a student's assumptions and gives her powerful academic and personal experiences. She sees for herself the cultural, political, and economic influences of each place and expands her understanding of global affairs.

It's clear that Puget Sound has a smart, fascinating curriculum grounded in the liberal arts. But students say their experiences hinge on the quality of teaching here, and professors earn shining endorsements. "I have academic crushes on my professors. I have loved every class I've had," says a junior from Portland. A senior from California brags, "If more people knew how good the teaching is, it would be as hard to get into Puget Sound as it is to get into Harvard." Students also volunteer how frequently and easily they get good advice from professors, whether about where to study abroad or how to find a worthwhile internship. "They'll drop anything to help us," says a sophomore from Washington.

Professors come—and stay—because they want a place where there is no equivocation about whether their primary responsibility is teaching or research. Six of them have been crowned Professor of the Year by the State of Washington—a record unmatched by any other school in the state.

Faculty members speak with affection for their students and a clear vision of their purpose. "None of us wants to prove how smart we are," says Dr. Priti Joshi, chair of the English department. "I'm here because my job is to help you see what you can do with the tools you have and we develop together." Dr. Sunil Kukreja, a sociologist, adds, "My measure of my own success is seeing where we can take a C student. The top students are often very easy to teach, and we do a very good job with them, but the real measure of our talent as teachers is reaching the ones who need to be drawn out."

The university has room for these students. It accepts 76 percent of students who complete their applications. The middle 50 percent of enrolled students scored between 1130 and 1340 on the SAT (critical reading and math) and between 26 and 30 on the ACT. Their average high-school GPA was 3.51. The school provides merit- or need-based aid, or both, to 90 percent of students. "This place attracts and supports students who are independent thinkers and creative," says Dr. George Mills, vice president for enrollment. "We can work with students who come with talents and help them develop rather than forming them into a predesigned mold."

Students concurred. "Everyone brings different interests to campus, or you find new interests here. What we have in common is passion," says a senior biology major. A sophomore majoring in international political economy adds, "I'm always saying to people, 'I didn't know that about you.' You're constantly discovering new things about yourself and your friends. It's not like high school, where maybe you were just a jock or just the music guy or just the kid who wrote for the paper. You can explore here, academically and in extracurriculars."

A pass through the handsome student union reveals a bit about the student body's personality: A student has hung a sign for the "Minnesota Club" in the hallway. He sits at a table beneath the sign and calls out to his classmates passing by—many of whom are laughing—that the club accepts students from any part of the world, as long as they're willing to listen to A *Prairie Home Companion*. He gets a few takers.

Another student shrugs and smiles: "We're kind of quirky here." Students also describe themselves as "happy," "respectful of others," "social," and "interested in academics but also in life outside the classroom." An impressive 88 percent of freshmen return for sophomore year, besting the national average at similar colleges by about 16 percentage points.

Students enjoy a rich and open community where they feel heard and respected. President Thomas has open office hours between eight and ten every Monday morning, and once a month he and his wife host a fireside dinner for students. An e-mail goes out to the whole student body with an invitation; the first ten students to respond are in. "It's a random group of students," President Thomas says. "They get along well, talk eagerly. We have very few boundaries here. It's as true a community as I've ever seen."

Students have opportunities to transform the environment that transforms them. Three-quarters of Puget Sound students volunteer, many of them through civic-engagement projects established by the university. An example: The Civic Scholarship Initiative provides support for collaboration among students, faculty, and the local community to solve problems, influence policy, and expand public knowledge on important issues. One professor and a small group of students worked on developing "market mechanisms" that promote smart urban planning while protecting the area's open space. Another team developed a series of educational programs for local physicians that offer insight into social, cultural, scientific, and political issues that influence health care and patients' lives. The theater department teams up with local theater and playwright groups to produce an annual festival of new works, with students, faculty, staff, and alumni working with theater pros from the region. And Puget Sound's highly competitive physical and occupational therapy graduate programs, remnants of its history, have an on-site clinic where professors and students provide free therapy to community members.

These experiences influence students long after they graduate. The college has ranked in the top ten small colleges for producing Peace Corps volunteers since 2001, when the Peace Corps began issuing its annual report. In 2011, Puget Sound tied for seventeenth among small schools for the number of graduates who joined Teach for America. (That year, Teach for America accepted 11 percent of applicants, making acceptance to the program nearly as tough as getting into Dartmouth or Brown.)

Puget Sound is also a robust producer of scholars and scientists. In the 2010–2011 school year, the university had four Fulbright Scholars, ranking it among the top thirty small colleges in the country. It is one of forty schools to participate in the Watson Fellowship program, which gives $25,000 stipends to fund a year of travel and independent study for recent college graduates. And it is among the top 15 percent of PhD producers in the country.

Alumni express deep gratitude for what the college did for them. "Puget Sound taught me that really, it's up to you to choose your path," says a 1992 alumnus, an executive at Netflix. "It gives you opportunities and makes the consequences of failure low. It taught me to take chances and be an outside-the-box thinker. I preach to anyone who asks me that it doesn't matter what your major is. You want to learn how to think critically, how to be a member of society, how to communicate effectively. The people who are going to solve the problems of the world are the ones who see the problem differently from anyone else. Puget Sound helped me with that, and I look for people who can do that too."

A 2010 alumna, a magazine editor, praises the college's strong emphasis on writing. "I came in knowing I was a decent writer. I was probably a little too confident. My professor ripped to shreds my first paper, but it was done in such a tasteful way. It showed me how much I had to learn, but it wasn't discouraging. All my professors were nurturing in a powerful way. To sum it up, that didn't stop—the criticism and endless notes—and eventually, the university helped me blossom into a writer."

Alumni from three decades speak with gusto about their enduring friendships with classmates and professors. "I'm still extremely close with my adviser," says a 2008 graduate. "She's an amazing woman, and I look up to her so much." A 1980 graduate, an entrepreneur, says, "I'm going on a trip this weekend with my college roommate and my big brother from the fraternity. My former classmates are fascinating people, and I've had so many interesting experiences because of them."

They all say, in so many words, that the college has given them plenty of pats on the back and the occasional swift kick in the pants, a healthy combination. They draw direct lines from the skills they developed—risk taking, critical thinking, strong leadership, and clear communication—to their success and their postcollege happiness. Puget Sound will do the same for anyone who shows up ready to embrace its abundant offerings.

Reed College

Portland, Oregon

"If you're a genuine intellectual, live the life of the mind, and want to learn for the sake of learning, the place most likely to empower you is not Harvard, Yale, Princeton, Chicago, or Stanford. It is the most intellectual college in the country—Reed in Portland, Oregon."

—LOREN POPE

Let's begin by addressing the obvious: Reed is more selective than the other schools in this book, accepting less than half of its applicants, and its academic profile reveals that the students who enroll here are talented: 88 percent of admitted students were in the top fifth of their high school classes, and the middle 50 percent of them scored between 1300 and 1470 on the SAT (critical reading and math). Their average high school GPA was 3.9.

So what is Reed doing in this book of colleges that take B students? Despite its increasingly selectivity, Reed still takes risks on students who demonstrate intellectual potential and passion for learning, even if their test scores or GPAs fall outside the college's profile. You don't have to look far at Reed to find a student who was the brilliant-but-bored high-school student, the one who read *Ulysses* because he wanted to or designed and built his own computer for fun.

Philosophically, Reed aligns perfectly with the schools in this book: The college isn't hanging its hat on how many students it can deny, and it takes no pleasure in the rankings game. Reed's leaders have long stayed out of the rankings fray by refusing to participate when magazines request data for their tabulations. Its admissions staff reviews each application carefully and takes seriously the job of finding people who have the intellectual horsepower to handle Reed's academic program.

That's because Reed is not for everyone. It's the foil to the Hollywood-inspired college scene, where football and fraternities define the ideal. Instead, Reed exists for the life of the mind. Learning is the central activity and a thrilling adventure here, and the college displays a steadfast commitment to the liberal arts.

Reed's 1,400 students engage in one of the country's most rigorous academic experiences for undergrads. Freshmen begin with Humanities 110, a yearlong survey of works from ancient Greece, Rome, Egypt, and Persia and the Bible. It serves to prep new Reedies for the writing and critical-thinking skills they'll need to do well at Reed. (In Humanities 110 alone, each student writes seven papers.)

Every student must then fulfill distribution requirements that provide the framework of a liberal education. He must take a junior qualifying exam given by his major department or interdisciplinary committee before he can begin the major task of his senior year: the thesis.

Under the guidance of a faculty member, the student defines a problem—"experimental, critical, or creative," the catalog says—and spends the year resolving it in his thesis. He integrates all aspects of the academic experience and produces new knowledge. There's no mere summing up of other people's ideas.

As you might expect, the labor and pressure to create theses are intense. More than one senior has told his or her adviser, "I just can't do it." The response: "Yes, you can." On the final day of classes in April, seniors march in the much-anticipated Senior Thesis Parade. As befits all the sweat, tears, and pressure, every thesis is bound and housed in the hallowed Senior Thesis Tower in the library.

But that's not all: The last step in a student's academic journey is a two-hour oral examination that may cover his entire academic career but emphasizes his thesis and major. Professors from his major department, another department, and even from outside the college may sit on his committee of examiners.

Reedies have a split identity: They describe themselves as iconoclasts, free spirits, and rebels, but they're also serious learners who enjoy achievement and rise to the very high expectations their professors set for them. Students call their education "humbling," "intense," "difficult," and "satisfying." A junior history major from Santa Fe says, "I loved high school, but Reed has changed the way I approach work. It's given me diligence, and it has turned me into a scholar." Adds a senior chemistry major from Vermont, "I understand how my brain works now."

A majority of students say they love the academic experience but not necessarily the accompanying "culture of stress," as one of them describes it. Attrition is higher than at schools with similar academic profiles—about 60 percent graduate in four years—but about 90 percent of freshmen return for their sophomore year. The thesis scares some away, but so does the culture. As a former student body president explains, "With all its wonderful qualities, Reed is not perfect, and I nearly left freshman year. Here were a lot of bright kids not knowing who they were and trying to find their identity. But whatever I did, people didn't care, only did I have integrity, was I intelligent, did I cheat, and it was really hard. . . . Here you make your own choices. They expect you to be an adult, and that's hard. . . . The adjustment is difficult. What kept me here was the faculty. One counseled me to find a dorm situation where I'd be comfortable. I went on a twelve-mile hike in the summer with a couple of others and I realized I'd have a hard time finding that kind of concern anywhere else."

Perhaps it's fitting that every hour on the hour during finals week, a sound system in the library lobby blasts "Eye of the Tiger." "We get pumped up. It's geeky, but it works," says a senior music major.

The program is intense, but Reed mitigates some of the angst by deemphasizing grades. Students earn grades but don't see them unless they ask. It's a brilliant plan designed to keep the focus on learning and analyzing information, not on getting a gold star and checking a course off the list. "It intensifies the way you communicate how students have done," says Dr. Keith Karoly, a biologist. "Feedback is of a different quality; nobody is asking, 'Why did I get a B+ and not an A–?'" Instead, professors give students specific written feedback on their strengths and weaknesses.

A junior psych major on the premed track speaks for a lot of her classmates when she says, "I was very grade oriented in high school. Coming here has calmed me down in a good way. It has helped shift my priority away from my grades." She also mentions that students collaborate much more readily than in high school because few people are most motivated by grades. "We're all on the train together. It's not like you can get to the destination first. We like to discuss and learn together. I think Reed does a good job of cultivating that." Reed's bright and airy cafeteria is one of the best places in the country to eavesdrop. On one fall morning, students at one table are chatting about China's relative economic strength while the students at the next are discussing whether pop culture is a legitimate area of academic study.

As you might guess, the distance between students and faculty at Reed is slight. Students call their professors by their first names, and many Reedies spend summers working in the lab or library as professors' research assistants. For their part, professors say they feel the intensity of the culture and love teaching Reed's students. "I cannot imagine that there's a better place in the universe to teach than here," says Dr. Pancho Savery, an English professor. "I do not view my place in the classroom as the source of knowledge. The primary educational energy comes from the students." Dr. Kimberly Clausing, an economist, agrees. "The culture here is very intellectually curious. I don't have to do any jumping jacks to get people interested."

Just like the students, professors talk like members of a family involved in a common endeavor, one that teaches people to think critically, to present and defend their views in discussion groups and conferences, and to learn about themselves. Learning at Reed is a communal affair.

Why does all this happen here? Reed has always been a place to come not for a degree or a job but to become an intellectual novitiate. It has never wavered in its conviction about what constitutes a liberal education, even in the sixties when Amherst, Brown, Oberlin, and others abandoned required courses so kids could satisfy their own desires for "relevance." As Jacques Barzun, former provost at Columbia, said, "If students were competent to decide matters of curriculum, they'd be in the faculty, not in the student body." True to that spirit, though Reed has a reputation as a progressive place, its curriculum is relatively conservative—no trendy courses designed to pander to students.

What has changed over time is more support, both academic and personal, for students. "There's less and less of a stigma here tied to getting help," says dean of students Mike Brody. Nearly two hundred Reedies are trained tutors, and as many as a third of students take advantage of free peer tutoring. The college's recently expanded health and counseling center gets high marks from students. Students can get free therapy, learn how to meditate, or visit the mind spa, an oasis with a massage chair and computers with biofeedback software.

Some students say the college's hundred-acre campus, quintessentially beautiful, provides a natural antidote to the program's rigor. Handsome brick buildings stand amid lush, green spaces that typify the Pacific Northwest's landscape. A small canyon cuts through a stretch of campus; in the outdoor amphitheater near the canyon's edge, the college community performs a traditional Greek play each year.

This tradition is worth mentioning because it represents Reed, which gets labeled simply as quirky. But the college's brand of quirky differs from that of other schools that share the descriptor: New College, St. John's, and Marlboro, among others. "It's hyper-academic," says a junior from northern California, "but I love that Reed has a sense of humor about itself." A senior theorizes, "On the scale of weird people, we're centrist but we're not all the same. I love punk music and chemistry, and I also own some sweater sets." Several students say they were surprised to find that the lore surrounding Reed didn't bear out: "I was expecting more of an extreme place. I thought it would be freakish. I was pleasantly surprised," a junior says.

When they describe the campus culture, Reedies express unanimous gratitude for the freewheeling conversation and creativity that mark the community. "One of my favorite things about Reed is having intellectual conversations about nonintellectual things," says a senior chemistry major. Another student describes it this way: "There's not as sharp a division between the intellectual and the fun sides of campus." So if you happen to visit campus when the Defenders of the Universe, an on-campus club, build a human-scale hamster wheel or a seesaw made of couches, you'll understand. (And if you don't, Reed might not be for you.)

A few distinctive elements of Reed might help prospective students understand its culture: It has one of largest private comic-book collections in the Pacific Northwest, and it's the only liberal arts college in the world with its own research reactor, providing students and faculty a neutron source to perform scientific research. Undergraduates run the reactor, after taking a noncredit course and passing the Nuclear Regulatory Commission's licensing exam. Though most of them are science students, any student from any discipline can learn how to operate the reactor. Reading the comic books, on the other hand, requires no advanced training.

The Honor Principle governs the whole campus. Rather than a code, which could easily be quoted and posted, the Honor Principle at Reed is an idea. A student handbook entitled "Living with the Honor Principle" describes it this way: "Any action that causes unnecessary pain or discomfort to any member of the Reed community, group within the community, or community as a whole, is a violation of the Honor Principle." In other words, "We do not tell them what to do and what not to do," says Dean Brody. "We encourage them to think deeply about the consequences of their actions." Of course, the college has policies on significant matters—drug and alcohol use, cheating, and sexual assault, for example—but Reed has very few hard and fast rules.

The result: Students have a lot of control over the campus culture. Individuals must self-govern, an essential part of a democracy.

Reed expects honorable conduct, and students must reflect daily about how they define honor. All of these outcomes are tremendously important not just to the college but also to the development of thoughtful citizens.

Reed's financial-aid program is distinctive among colleges in this book and among private colleges in general. The college has no merit aid; instead, the sole aim of its financial-aid program is to enable qualified students to enroll. The college meets 100 percent of demonstrated need for every admitted student who meets admission and financial-aid deadlines. About half of Reed's students get financial aid, and their average loan debt at graduation is about sixteen thousand dollars—more than nine thousand dollars less than the national average. "[Our program] enables us to get the highest caliber of student we can," says Keith Todd, the college's dean of admission.

The college's investment is well spent. Reed graduates are among the country's most remarkable. As of 2011, its students had earned sixty-four Watson Fellowships since the program started in 1968 and twenty-four Goldwater Scholarships (for students interested in careers in science and math). Reedies have amassed 139 National Science Foundation Fellowships and seventy-nine Fulbrights. Three alumni have won MacArthur Foundation "genius" grants, and only one other liberal arts college has produced more Rhodes Scholars.

The research experience and having so much responsibility for one's own education have a lot to do with the large percentages of alumni who go on to graduate school. Students and alumni speculate that once a person has tasted the richness of intellectual inquiry, she can't resist it.

So Reed alumni head for academia with great success. Per capita, Reed ranks third among all colleges for its production of future PhDs, according to the Higher Education Data Sharing Consortium (HEDS). It ranks first in turning out future history PhDs, second in life sciences, and third in math and physical sciences.

A Reedie who graduated in the early nineties and ended up on the Yale faculty says he's run into three other Reed alums teaching in other departments. A graduate student at the University of Chicago says there is a covey of other Reedies there. Another grad from the early nineties, who earned a PhD from Harvard and went on to teach Buddhism at Amherst, says Reed is "one of the few truly intellectual colleges in the country, unencumbered by the follies of collegiate athletics and fraternities, where people who are genuinely intellectually curious can explore the ideas for their own sake."

A thread that runs through alumni's comments is the discovery that they were neither the eccentrics nor the whiz kids they'd been in high school. They were surrounded by "gloriously freaky people" and humbled by the knowledge and intelligence of classmates. One of them writes, "I vividly recall when my first Hum 110 paper, which would have garnered me an A+ in high school, was returned to me covered in red ink. It was wonderful."

A 1996 alumna writes, "It was probably the hardest four years of my life, but so worthwhile." An actress sums up her paean: "Reed was very difficult in every imaginable aspect. I suffered and I grew. I wasn't fond of the place when I left, but now I look back with gratitude, respect, and longing. I think Reed is the best community I've ever known, and the world could learn a lot by mirroring its ways."

St. Mary's College of California

Moraga, California

Tucked against a hill twenty miles from San Francisco, St. Mary's College is a beautiful place. White Mission Renaissance–style buildings with terra-cotta roofs stand out against the lush green hillside. Covered outdoor walkways connect well-maintained academic buildings. It looks like a place of privilege, but it's actually a down-to-earth college where 2,600 undergrads and 1,300 graduate students make the connection between learning and life.

St. Mary's is a Catholic college run by the Christian Brothers, a lay teaching order that has its roots in seventeenth-century France. The college's educational principles grow from the writings and teachings of St. John Baptist de La Salle, who worked doggedly to establish schools for poor and working-class children.

The Lasallian tradition fuels the college's perspective on teaching and learning: Education is powerful, and it comes with a deep responsibility to improve the world. It's a mechanism of change. "You come with a desire to get something out of it. You get everything you can from the school because it's a privilege to go to a school like this," says a senior majoring in music and business. "You leave with the skills to examine and solve the world's problems." When asked if that description seems lofty, a bit pie-in-the-sky, he answers, "Of course. Why would you get a college education if you weren't hoping to do something good in the world?"

Like many of the colleges in this book, St. Mary's doesn't have the typical private-college crowd. One-third of students are Pell eligible. About half are ethnic minorities. The vast majority—87 percent—come from California, but it's important to remember that California is a large and varied place, so if you're an out-of-state student, you won't feel out of place. Slightly more than half of students are Catholic, but the college welcomes students of any (or no) religious background.

Everyone takes the Collegiate Seminar, a four-semester series of intimate classes that covers major works of Western civilization, starting with Homer and Aristotle and passing through about 2,700 years of philosophy, history, literature, art, and science. The course asks big questions: What is goodness? What is death? Does evil have to exist? Students learn to read carefully, draw sharp conclusions, listen to other people, and disagree civilly.

One early spring morning, a group of freshmen reading St. Augustine's *Confessions* struggles with questions about the nature of God and sin. Prompted by the author's analysis of his spiritual journey, some students reveal their own religious histories as a way of relating to St. Augustine; others are eager to ask bigger questions about how and whether God reveals himself to people. They don't agree on answers, but they are diligent about listening to one another and referring to the text. They answer one another's questions to the best of their abilities, and even when the conversation flags, they stick with it. After class, a student says, "This is the first time in my life someone else hasn't told me exactly what to learn. It's hard. I get frustrated, but when I finally understand something, I feel like I've accomplished something. I can feel my brain growing."

Professors rave about what the seminar does for their students. "Many students have gotten this far because they're good at 'duck and cover,'" says Dr. Myrna Santiago, chair of the history department. "They give all authority to the teacher. They can't in the seminar program. We're colearners. We look them in the eye and say, 'What do you think?' Eventually, they learn to negotiate and discuss and own their ideas. They realize they're no longer doing well by staying silent." The content matters, professors argue, but the process of learning matters more: "[During grad school] at Purdue, I taught a class of 450 students. The content was great, but there wasn't a way for students to sort it out with their peers or me," says Dr. Shawny Anderson, associate dean and professor of communications. "I find a lot of joy in seeing our students engage honestly with difficult texts and each other."

The other unifying experience is January Term, an intensive four-week session when each student takes only one class. The offerings each year are new, as faculty design courses based on a broad theme. "My first Jan Term opened my eyes to what's happening here," says Dr. Robert Bulman, a sociologist. "It's an opportunity to explore topics outside our particular realms of expertise. When I realized that professors got to be learners too, and that the college wants us to model intellectual exploration for our students, I decided I never wanted to leave."

About 55 percent of St. Mary's students travel abroad, many of them during Jan Term as participants in courses led by professors. In 2011 courses traveled to Yosemite National Park to study the effects of altitude on physiology; to Haiti to perform direct earthquake relief work and produce multimedia projects; to South Africa to examine its culture and nature; to Israel, Palestine, and Jordan to examine the history, religion, and politics of the Holy Land; and to other spots in the United States, South America, Europe, India, and Southeast Asia.

Professors willing to trek around the world with students are rare, and St. Mary's attracts the precious few whose ideas about education align with the college's mission. Of these, 95 percent have terminal degrees in their fields, many of them earned at some of the country's most renowned graduate schools: Princeton, Stanford, Brown, Harvard, and Berkeley. And professors here enjoy working with students who arrive with a breadth of skills and preparation. "Teaching is an exercise in a kind of prospective friendship," says Dr. Steve Cortright, a philosopher, speaking on behalf of many colleagues. "You can go anywhere and get your opinions challenged. What we do here is get to know students, get them to find out what they love, what sparks them. That is a kind of friendship."

Dr. Denise Witzig, a women's studies professor who earned her BA at the University of California at Berkeley, says, "As an undergraduate, I didn't see an adviser until my senior year. I wonder: What would have happened if someone had said to me, 'Here is what I see in you'? That's what we do here. I would never want to teach at Berkeley. The students are better prepared, on the whole, but there's no connection that compares to the bond between professors and students here."

Unlike many of its neighbors, St. Mary's isn't an exclusive place. It accepts 69 percent of its applicants. The middle 50 percent scored between 1010 and 1210 on the SAT (critical reading and math) and between 22 and 27 on the ACT; they earned high-school GPAs between 3.2 and 3.8. About three-fourths of students get financial aid.

The college has a robust academic advising staff and strong support services for all types of students. The college's free tutoring gets high praise both from students who identify themselves as quick learners and from those who admit they are struggling. Staff members at the Tutorial and Academic Skills Center also give small-group and one-on-one workshops to boost study and time-management skills, teach note-taking strategies, and enhance reading comprehension.

For first-generation and low-income students, St. Mary's offers an impressive High Potential Program (HPP) that smoothes students' transition to college. For two weeks in the summer, about forty incoming students live on campus and sample collegiate courses so they understand what's expected of them. They learn about on-campus resources and get to know one another. In addition to a regular faculty adviser, each student has a specially trained HPP adviser. Upper-class peer mentors help with social adjustment.

Without exception, students of all academic stripes say they feel well supported by the college and their professors. "I wasn't sure what I wanted to do when I got here, but there are steps in place to help us figure that out," says a senior political science major. "St. Mary's helped me find direction. I feel comfortable and prepared." A sophomore biochemistry major adds, "It's worth the money. Professors are super close with us. My calc professor is one of my best friends." A freshman nearing the end of his first year and planning to follow the college's 3-2 engineering program can't stop bragging about his teachers: "Professors are not drab. My classes are very interesting. Our English professor reads our essays five times before he grades them. He wants us to get better. My physics professor makes it easy to learn. My calc professor makes it fun. I never liked classes [in high school] like I do now, and I never worked as hard either, so it's not like I'm just kicking back and relaxing here."

Another thread running through the students' comments is love for their community and a fierce sense of school spirit, bolstered by little St. Mary's Division I athletics and its basketball teams in particular. Nobody complains for want of friends, and everyone brags about being a little school with a reputation for frustrating big schools' sports teams. "It brings us all together," says a sophomore who describes herself as "allergic to playing sports." "There's a sense of community on campus anyway, a base of friendship among people just because we all attend St. Mary's, but that's blown up and magnified when we start cheering for our teams."

The college underscores the value of its community with weekly "Community Time," ninety minutes around the lunch hour when there are no classes, no meetings, and no service in the cafeteria. Instead, St. Mary's hosts a barbecue on a terrace near the center of campus, and students, faculty, and staff gather for casual conversation.

And when students need a little break from St. Mary's—as all undergraduates want from their campuses occasionally—the Bay Area has something for just about everyone. Students are less effusive about the relative charms of Moraga. Some say the little town is too sleepy. Plus, "you need a car to get out of here," complains a freshman. A bus picks up students and takes them to BART, the public transit system, where they can get almost anywhere in the Bay Area. For a quick run to Target or an off-campus meal, students say they carpool. (The upside of car ownership, besides instant popularity, is that parking on campus is free.)

But this little inconvenience doesn't dull students' enthusiasm for St. Mary's and the changes it has wrought in them: "I've become hesitant to form opinions too quickly," says a junior majoring in biology. "If I'm going to have an opinion, I have to be able to support it." A sophomore muses, "A big change happens freshman year. Your priorities change. You can't ignore problems in the world anymore, and you start to understand your own power to do something about them."

The college gets high marks from seniors who complete the Cooperative Institutional Research Program (CIRP), an anonymous survey conducted by the Higher Education Research Institute at UCLA. The survey asks about specific learning outcomes, and St. Mary's outscores its peers in several key areas, including:

- More than 61 percent of seniors say their general knowledge is "much stronger" than it was when they arrived as freshmen, compared with 51 percent of students at other four-year private colleges.
- About 56 percent say their critical-thinking skills are much stronger than when they were freshmen, compared with 47 percent of students at peer colleges.
- More than 41 percent say they are much more able to get along with people of different races and cultures as graduating seniors than they were as freshmen. Only about 27 percent of seniors at similar schools report the same.

Alumni say these numbers tell only part of the story. "You can't quantify what St. Mary's does," says a graduate from the late nineties who now runs his own business. "It makes you see the bigger picture and raises your expectations of what you can do and what a community can do—not just can do, but should do. It makes you accountable to yourself. I really miss it."

A 2001 graduate, now an industrial-organizational psychologist, says, "Academically, it was phenomenal. I felt very prepared when I left for graduate school. I loved the community; I love my friends. We're still very close. Probably the biggest shift for me came from the women's studies program. I realized what was happening, these horrible things, to women around the world. It opened my eyes and forced me to contend with hard stuff, but not without people who helped me process it. St. Mary's is like my family."

Students and alumni like that St. Mary's isn't a power-driven place. The college isn't sacrificing its history or mission for a whirl at the latest educational trends or a spot higher up the rankings. Its faculty and staff work diligently to do a few things well: uphold high expectations, challenge and support students, and guide them through these formative developmental years.

It's no coincidence that the first thing a visitor sees when she drives up to St. Mary's beautiful campus is the chapel and a statue of St. John Baptist de La Salle, where the college's motto is inscribed: "Enter to learn. Leave to serve." It's not terribly sexy, especially for the typical eighteen-year-old. But St. Mary's sticks with it. It's a guiding principle important to twenty-first-century students and alumni—and to American culture.

Whitman College

Walla Walla, Washington

If you're eager to blend what you learn with how you live, Whitman might be a good place for you.

Its 1,500 students come here with an interest in service and eagerness to be part of their community. In dozens of interviews, they credit Whitman with helping them develop ideas in the classroom that they want to act on outside of it.

They're also eager students who come for the academic program, a rigorous liberal arts curriculum that debunks the myth that students ought to know exactly what to study when they're eighteen years old. Instead, Whitman students sharpen their skills against new research, difficult texts, and big ideas from all disciplines as they fulfill their liberal arts requirements. Each student homes in on a major, and everyone must sit for an oral defense and either produce a senior thesis or pass a comprehensive exam. It's not an easy education, but it's incredibly worthwhile—and, if Whitman's students are to be believed, a lot of fun.

"There's a sense of purpose in our education here," says a senior from northern California. "It goes beyond getting an A. It's more like, 'So you have this amazing education. What will you do with it?' We feel like there's a lot we can do."

President George Bridges, PhD, puts it another way: "There's a sense of congruity and focus here. Unlike research universities, which have a lot of missions, this is a place that has just one: enabling undergrads to contribute to the world." Those contributions are defined broadly, but Whitman alumni must believe the college does what it promises: About half contribute financially to the college, ranking it among the top twenty or so colleges and universities in the country in alumni support.

In many ways, that focus is common among all of the schools in this book. Whitman takes it a few steps further by building support structures that foster student development. For example, the majority of residential colleges use resident advisers to help freshmen adjust to life away from home; upper-class students, RAs emphasize the social and emotional well-being of the student. To this structure Whitman adds student academic advisers, upperclassmen who live in the dorms with freshmen for the first semester and help them navigate the academic scene. They discuss classes, recommend their favorite professors, give tips on using the library and academic support services, and keep an eye on how the freshmen in their sections seem to be adjusting to the pace of academic work.

Another example: Freshmen begin their college careers with Encounters, a yearlong survey of the great thinkers in Western and Eastern cultures. Each class is capped at sixteen students, and professors from all disciplines teach it. You're as likely to be discussing Descartes or the Bhagavad Gita with a physicist as you are with a philosopher. Students say they love having a shared academic experience, and professors say they enjoy the act of learning alongside their students, since they're covering topics that aren't necessarily in their wheelhouses. Ideas and texts from Encounters pop up again and again as students dive more deeply into their majors.

Better still, the community displays warmth that couldn't be manufactured by even the best administrative policies. At most colleges, when asked how to describe their college communities, students immediately offer up "diverse" and "eclectic." (It's enough to make you wonder: If everyone's eclectic, is anyone?) At Whitman, students never once say these things—though the college community is more diverse than most in this book. Its students come from forty-five states and thirty foreign countries; about 20 percent are ethnic minorities, and 12 percent are first-generation college kids. It's telling that instead of holding up diversity, which they value, students say things like "We respect each other" and "Students are very supportive of each other." A senior from St. Paul, Minnesota, says she visited thirteen schools during her college search. "There's a sense of community here unlike any other place I visited," she says. "I felt it when I visited, and it's even better than I imagined."

Students also speak fondly of Walla Walla, a town of about thirty thousand people in the southeast corner of Washington, just a few miles north of the Oregon border. It escapes the typical weather of the Pacific Northwest, thanks in part to its fortuitous spot on the east side of the Cascade Mountains. Good sun and soil have given life to a booming wine industry, and local entrepreneurs have helped build a charming and busy downtown with wine-tasting rooms, coffee shops, and a few very good restaurants. Students can drive from Walla Walla to Seattle in four and a half hours or to Portland in just over four hours.

Students from big cities admit that they worried about coming to Walla Walla. Would they be giving up urban amenities—culture, arts, good food—for a little town near the Blue Mountains? But nobody admits wishing for something else. A senior from New York City says, "I love Walla Walla. I don't feel at all like I traded down. You don't end up here by accident, so it feels like everyone has a sense of purpose. Plus, it's beautiful here, so that doesn't hurt."

Whitman is as active a place as you'll find: The theater department produces eight shows a year in its impressive, newly renovated Harper Joy Theatre. (A typical liberal arts college puts up three.) The busy Outdoor Program hosts day and overnight trips to sea kayak, mountain climb, hike, raft, paddle, and play in Whitman's beautiful backyard. The radio station, KWCW, is student owned and operated, and it's not hard to find someone on campus with his or her own show. There are musical events, speakers—politics are always a popular topic—and the queen of them all, intramural sports, popular with about 70 percent of Whitman students. You can even join the annual Quidditch tournament, complete with broomsticks and cross-country players who act as snitches.

Whitman strikes the right balance: Its academic program is

serious; its focus on social justice, earnest; and its playfulness, healthy. It's a near-perfect formula, if Whitman's statistics are any measure: about 92 percent of freshmen return for their sophomore year, and more than 80 percent graduate in four years, 85 percent in five years. Most colleges would give their mascots' firstborn to have such excellent numbers.

Whitman has room for all kinds of people. The college likes to celebrate its lack of pretense, without a hint of irony, for good reason: Students and faculty say that what you see is what you get. "I just wanted to find my people and do what I want to do," says a senior from Connecticut. "You don't have to try to be something you're not here." She says she felt nervous in high school. "I was always trying too hard. I'm so much more relaxed now." The student body president, a first-generation college student, agrees: "Elsewhere, everyone is trying to be an idea. Not at Whitman."

Dean of faculty Timothy Kaufman-Osborn, PhD, makes an apt comparison: "Whitman students are surprisingly decent. I taught Princeton undergrads, and in a heartbeat I'd choose Whitman students. I noticed a sense of entitlement among at least some of the students at Princeton. There's none of that here."

Instead, faculty say, students are motivated and hardworking. Case in point: Whitman's library is open 24-7, as is its wellness center. Few college facilities across the country keep such hours. In the library's Allen Reading Room, the silent space in an otherwise bustling building, students hunker down for late-night studying and a strange incentive: On the fireplace mantle sits a small book, and the last person in the room for the night (or morning) signs the book. That students' honors theses are bound and shelved in this room is no coincidence.

Since the first edition of this book, more and more students have discovered Whitman's special blend of education and community. It now accepts about half of its applicants. The middle 50 percent of its admitted students had high-school GPAs between 3.7 and 3.96; they scored between 1230 and 1430 on the SAT (critical reading and math) and between 28 and 32 on the ACT. But admissions reps insist the college still has room to take a chance on

WHITMAN COLLEGE ✦ 319

a student who hasn't yet hit her prime but reveals a deep and abiding interest in learning and getting involved in the college community.

Eighty percent of students get some kind of financial aid. The average merit-based scholarship was just over $9,000 in 2010; the average need-based grant, about $24,000. Add in work study and loans, and the average financial-aid package was about $32,000. The average debt at graduation was $14,285—about $11,000 lower than the national average and significantly lower than most of the schools in this book.

Whitman knows what it does well—teaching, mentoring, and inspiring undergraduates—but it's not resting on its laurels. In recent years, it has turned its focus to interdisciplinary courses. With the help of a $350,000 grant from the Mellon Foundation, Whitman faculty members learn how to develop team-taught courses. The college emphasizes helping students look at issues from multiple perspectives because no one area of study has information to solve the world's biggest problems.

One of the most successful and unusual interdisciplinary courses is Semester in the West, a field program in environmental studies. Every other autumn, a group of twenty-one students and Dr. Phil Brick, a politics professor, travel through the American West to explore its politics, culture, and ecosystems. For three and a half months, they road trip through Oregon, California, Nevada, Colorado, Idaho, Utah, New Mexico, and Arizona, doing fieldwork, writing about nature, studying public policy, and talking to leaders on every side of public lands conservation. They sleep on tarps and travel with a sixteen-foot trailer outfitted with desks and a library.

Westies, as they're called, say the experience transformed them. A senior says her "brain exploded." Another says, "I see the holes in arguments now. I can analyze so quickly, and say, 'We actually need to find out that little piece of information to know if our ideas are on the right track.' I just feel so capable. It feels like running a marathon with your brain."

You can get that kind of cerebral workout plenty of other places at Whitman. "We maintain the seriousness of book learning and discussing," says Dr. Shampa Biswas, a political scientist. "I think of my upper-level seminars as graduate school–level work." She adds that many students come with political viewpoints that have never been tested. "I tell my students, 'My contract says to give you sleepless nights,'" she laughs. "Students come to my office hours completely worked up about something they've learned. Knowledge brings responsibility and obligation. Whitman students understand that."

On balance, the faculty at Whitman are young, due to a wave of recent retirements. They're coming out of some of the best graduate programs in the country and bringing their research programs with them. "[New professors] learn quickly how to incorporate students into their research. It's an institutional norm, not a requirement, which makes it more powerful," says Dean Kaufman-Osborn.

Aspiring scientists should talk to professors and neurobiologists Ginger Withers and Chris Wallace. Drs. Withers and Wallace run Team Dendrite, their research program on brain science. They split a teaching load and run the lab together. "We know the research and we run the classes," Dr. Wallace says. "There is no middleman. We're building a scaffold to get our students to the relevant info."

Dr. Withers adds: "The experience in the lab is transformative for students. They're constantly encountering the lack of certainty in the world. You can't just refer to the textbook for the answer." Both professors traded in work at a research institute for Whitman, where they might not have as much fancy equipment but they have more interaction with people from other disciplines and the benefit of students who bring their cross-disciplinary learning to the lab. "The hardest thing in a lab is developing good judgment. The liberal arts build good judgment more effectively than anywhere else because they force students to take a novel approach to ambiguity," Dr. Wallace says.

Echoing professors at every school in this book, Dr. Withers adds, "When it comes time to go into the world, we can advise them. We write honest letters of recommendation because we know what our students do well." She tells the story of a student who was mediocre in class but brilliant in the lab. "He put things together in ways I never would have thought of." Had he been a student at a huge university, he never would have set foot in a professor's lab—and probably never discovered his talent. As it turns out, this student went to work at the prestigious Woods Hole Marine Biological Laboratory because of the opportunities and guidance his professors gave him.

These opportunities to collaborate with professors are available in every department, courtesy of several generous grant programs that support student-faculty research. Faculty-student teams who apply must show how the project will involve the students' intellectual power. Students aren't mere laborers in professors' research programs; they are colleagues.

Dr. Sharon Alker of the English department and her student researcher earned an eight-thousand-dollar grant to study James Hogg, an early-nineteenth-century Scottish writer, at the National Library of Scotland for a summer. "We worked in the library every day, and then we'd go for coffee afterward to talk about what we discovered. I wanted her to see the ebb and flow of research. Some days, you find nothing; others, you are awash in new information. I also teach [my student research partners] to criticize me and to give feedback because the work benefits from our cooperation. It changes how students think and how they define learning, and I just love having students with me. It enriches the whole experience." Other faculty eagerly testify to Dr. Alker's claim: "These partnerships are happening all over campus." These close-working friendships with faculty help open students' eyes and encourage them to take any new roads that beckon.

Once a year, on a springy April day, the college cancels class and hosts the Whitman Undergraduate Conference, a celebration of students' scholarly achievements. Students display their research and original work in poster sessions, performances, and presentations. A group of seniors helps students prepare for the big day, and according to students and President Bridges, "everyone shows up." The event aligns with Whitman's clear view of the liberal arts as a vehicle for inspiring lifelong learners. As a senior rhapsodizes: "I fall in love with something new every week, and I don't understand people who don't have that problem. Fortunately, those people aren't at Whitman."

This "problem" manifests itself in many ways: As of 2011, graduates had amassed thirty-nine Watson Fellowships, and between 2000 and 2011 they earned a whopping forty-two Fulbrights. Whitman ranks among the top fifty producers of PhDs in science per capita, and a full two-thirds of alumni head for graduate and professional schools, which welcome them eagerly.

At the start of his last year on campus, a senior from New York City reflects on his Whitman journey: "I applied here with a sense of purpose. I had a desire to improve the world, but I didn't know how yet. Professors mentored me, and students inspired me. Now I care a lot about voting rights, and I can communicate my ideas in a much stronger way. I think colleges should be evaluated by a new standard: It's not just whether you're changing students' lives; it's whether you're producing people who can change other people's lives. Without question, Whitman does."

Willamette University

Salem, Oregon

Willamette University is far away from the East Coast prestige machine in both geography and philosophy. It's a place where you will grow, if you take advantage of the university's abundant offerings and active community.

The sixty-acre campus is an attractive blend of red brick buildings, huge trees, and sweeping, expansive green space. It's home to the College of Liberal Arts and three graduate schools: law, education, and management. The undergrad program enrolls two thousand students from thirty-nine states and thirty-eight foreign countries. The majority come from the Pacific Northwest.

Unlike megauniversities, where professors tend to defend their disciplines against all others and where turf wars are legendary, professors here see themselves as part of the whole. Before they talk about the specific curricula in their departments, they talk about how a Willamette education changes a student. It is no wonder that ten Willamette professors won Oregon's Professor of the Year award between 1990 and 2011—a record unmatched by any other school in the state.

"The thing we do is not about specialization," says Dr. Amber Davisson, who teaches in the rhetoric and media studies department. "We don't let students confuse a degree and a career. We focus on analysis, and we expect a lot of critical thinking. We teach our students how to ask questions and answer them. It's hard, but it's really good for them."

Across campus in the art history department, Dr. Ricardo De Mambro Santos shares a similar vision: "A big university is like a knowledge machine. At the University of Washington, I had four hundred students and four TAs in a single class. They were shadows in the arena, and I was the gladiator of knowledge. It drove me crazy. I wanted closer relationships with students. I wanted to help them analyze and solve problems, not just memorize. A book can give you information. We help students learn to do something good with that information."

A senior majoring in history says she loves this emphasis on applying knowledge and building skills: "In high school, you're asked to demonstrate that you can do busywork. You can just jump through the hoops. At Willamette, there are not hoops to jump through. Everything you do has a purpose. In my department, we don't learn facts and dates. They teach you how to write, present, and think critically. It's no longer just about filling in the blanks."

Part of this magic comes from abundant hands-on learning opportunities. Students from across departments rave about how easy it is to participate in faculty research or design their own special projects.

One tremendous source of these opportunities is the University Forest at Zena, a beautiful plot of land comprising three hundred acres of forest and five acres of farmland. A twenty-minute drive from campus, it is a rich and diverse outdoor classroom, where professors of art, environmental science, biology, English, theater, politics, and history teach classes that tie the local landscape to academic exploration. As many as four hundred students a year spend time at the forest.

"Zena encourages professors to be creative," says Dr. Joe Bowersox, a professor of environmental policy. "It's a great place for students to test their ideas. They learn that it's one thing to embrace a theory; it's a quite a separate thing to have to apply it."

Students help maintain the land: They prune trees, thin the forest, and build trails as part of their education in sustainable forestry. One group used predictive models to determine whether they could control invasive species with hand labor. Another group built the greenhouse and a wind turbine that provides energy for the electric fence that surrounds the farm, where the college grows organic vegetables for the campus community. Each week during the harvest, the veggies are sold on campus at a farm stand; the campus bookstore sells honey from the beekeeping practice.

In the summer, the university offers a six-week program in sustainable agriculture at Zena. A small group of students live at and tend to the farm. They take two interdisciplinary courses that examine how our food system influences and is influenced by ecology, society, ethics, and the economy, and they travel to local dairies, farms, food-processing plants, and markets.

"Students aren't just learning how to do research here. They're actually doing it," says Dr. Emma Coddington, a neuroscientist. "That's key because they're developing such important skill sets: how to filter information, how to observe and synthesize. That translates into being a great thinker. I don't care if they go to graduate school. I want them to be able to go into the world and actually think for themselves."

The biology department makes sure that its students know how to communicate their research to a broad audience by sponsoring a "reverse science fair." Middle- and high-school students from Salem attend the fair, where Willamette students present the research they conducted for their theses. The younger students vote on the "best" project.

And it's not just science students who get these opportunities. When Dr. De Mambro Santos discovered a collection of 106 unpublished drawings from the Renaissance, he arranged for the college's lovely art museum to host the first-ever exhibition of the art. Then he enlisted the help of his students; together they analyzed the drawings, attributed them, and created explanatory labels to give visitors context. "My students were young scholars," the professor says. "They went beyond the boundaries of the slim academic realm and into the community. Every single line they wrote had very serious consequences. They started providing ideas and analysis that I never would have imagined. I was learning alongside them. We were on fire."

The college has funds to support several dozen student-faculty collaborations for nine weeks each summer. Professors post descriptions of their ongoing research, and students apply to join their programs. In the fall semester, students present their research in a campuswide symposium. Science students travel to a regional conference for undergraduate research and present their findings. Many students, from all disciplines, have the chance to coauthor papers and present their work at full-blown academic conferences.

Maybe this collaborative spirit is born of Willamette's oft-quoted motto: "Not unto ourselves alone are we born." Students mention it. Professors point to it. It's a guiding principle, not a marketing mantra. Professors demonstrate its essence by being generous with their time and encouraging their students. As students benefit and grow, they begin to think about their own powers to do good in the world.

So it is no surprise that Willamette's sense of community is deep and dutiful. Students take community service seriously, and they talk a lot about their own responsibilities in light of the world's challenges. Most of them want to develop a meaningful philosophy of life. A senior explains, "We are concerned about living the best life we can. That goes beyond finding the best jobs we can."

They see themselves as tolerant, liberal, diverse, involved, and compassionate. The happiest say they took on leadership opportunities early—an easy option, given the wide range of student activities on campus. They're zealous about sports, particular'y intramural athletics, and the outdoor program, which takes full advantage of the Pacific Northwest's natural playground. The program hosts as many as fifty trips a year to take students hiking, camping, white-water rafting, mountain climbing, whale watching, skiing, snowboarding, ice-skating, fishing, and more.

Sustainability is also a major topic on campus. Not only do most students embrace sustainability as an important political topic, but the college also has made commitments to reducing its environmental impact. It has large-scale commitments, like cutting its energy consumption in half by 2020 and constructing LEED-certified buildings when it needs more space. And across campus there are small changes too: Students get free city bus passes (rather, the cost is included in their fees). A campus bike shop, staffed by students, offers free loaner bikes to students. The college recycles everything it can, including cooking oil and garden debris. For its work, Willamette has garnered praise from the growing cohort of organizations calling for eco-friendly practices in higher education, including the Sierra Club and the National Wildlife Federation.

Politically active (or interested) students can cross the street to Oregon's state capitol, where many of them intern for elected officials and state agencies. "I do casework for constituents in the governor's office," says a junior majoring in politics and Spanish. "It has made me even more interested in politics, but it has also shown me the limits of political theory. It's pretty common for us to be talking about an idea in class and for someone to bring up practical issues from their internship at the capitol. You learn both sides here, the theoretical and the real-life side."

In academic and extracurricular offerings, Willamette gives students opportunities to explore. Students who say they were dreading the liberal arts requirements when they arrived have discovered what students at other innovative schools find: an array of courses that testify to professors' creativity and boost students' curiosity. A chemistry major who "hated history" in high school was worried about taking a history course until she discovered a class about the history of Western medicine. Many students say they underestimated how valuable the exposure to wide-ranging topics and ideas would be. "The things you look for [during your college search] aren't the things you end up appreciating most," says a junior majoring in rhetoric and media studies. "I complained about my liberal arts requirements, but I'm most grateful for the liberal arts vibe here. Even if you come here wanting to do one thing, you won't be disappointed if you fall in love with something else."

A student who grew up wanting to be a graphic designer—and had the portfolio to get into design school—chose Willamette because he had a hunch he wanted to learn more than "how to do one thing." He says he made the right choice: "I feel vindicated now. I have an awareness of the world that I didn't have. It's only the educated person who can speak the truth, and I want to use my art to speak truth. The perception is that you can't get good at art if you don't go to art school. I want to challenge that."

When students arrive, professors say, they're still in high-school mode. They expect to be spoon-fed the information. "They've had the curiosity beat out of them in many cases," Dr. Coddington says. "We help them fall in love with biology—or whatever their discipline is—and then we refine, refine, refine. By the time they're seniors, they can read widely and discern reliable knowledge. They know how to challenge each other without getting emotionally charged. It's a lovely thing to see. It's why we teach."

This transformation happens to students who say they were "average" and "low B" students in high school as well as to students who were valedictorians and salutatorians. The college has room for many of them: It accepts 60 percent of its applicants. The middle 50 percent have SAT scores between 1160 and 1340 (critical reading and math) and ACT scores between 27 and 30. Their median high-school GPA was 3.7. The college meets an impressive 91 percent of demonstrated financial need; 65 percent of students get aid.

Eighty-eight percent of freshmen return for their sophomore year, beating the national average for similar schools by 16 percent, and 70 percent of students graduate in four years. Nationally, only 46 percent of students at private four-year schools that grant master's degrees manage to finish in four years.

Each year, Willamette students add to the college's respectable list of awards. Between 2006 and 2011, graduates won thirteen Fulbrights, putting Willamette among the top fifty or so colleges in the country in production of Fulbright Scholars. Between 2005 and 2011, Willamette students won eight National Science Foundation Graduate Research Fellowships, which support three years of graduate study toward a master's or doctoral degree in science, math, or engineering. And between 2000 and 2011, eight students won Goldwater Scholarships, which also encourage students to pursue careers in STEM (science, technology, engineering, and mathematics) fields.

The sense around campus is that Willamette is a rising star—a place that does its work well and has momentum to claim its rightful spot among the few colleges in this country that prioritize undergraduate education. Its students happily skip the prestige mill in exchange for honest mentorship, a rich array of hands-on experiences, and liberal learning that cultivates critical thinking and values. You would do well to join them.

COLLEGES' CONTACT INFORMATION

Agnes Scott College
141 East College Avenue
Decatur, GA 30030
800-868-8602
www.agnesscott.edu

Allegheny College
520 N. Main Street
Meadville, PA 16335
800-521-5293
www.allegheny.edu

Austin College
900 North Grand Avenue
Sherman, TX 75090
800-KANGAROO
www.austincollege.edu

Beloit College
700 College Street
Beloit, WI 53511
800-9BELOIT
www.beloit.edu

Birmingham-Southern College
900 Arkadelphia Road
Birmingham, AL 35254
800-523-5793
www.bsc.edu

Centre College
600 West Walnut Street
Danville, KY 40422
800-423-6236
www.centre.edu

Clark University
950 Main Street
Worcester, MA 01610
800-GO-CLARK
www.clarku.edu

Cornell College
600 First Street SW
Mount Vernon, IA 52314
800-747-1112
www.cornellcollege.edu

Denison University
100 West College Street
Granville, OH 43023
800-DENISON
www.denison.edu

Earlham College
801 National Road West
Richmond, IN 47374
800-EARLHAM
www.earlham.edu

Eckerd College
4200 54th Avenue South
St. Petersburg, FL 33711
800-456-9009
www.eckerd.edu

Emory & Henry College
30461 Garland Drive
Emory, VA 24327
800-848-5493
www.ehc.edu

Goucher College
1021 Dulaney Valley Road
Baltimore, MD 21204
800-GOUCHER
www.goucher.edu

Guilford College
5800 West Friendly Avenue
Greensboro, NC 27410
800-992-7759
www.guilford.edu

Hendrix College
1600 Washington Avenue
Conway, AR 72032
800-277-9017
www.hendrix.edu

Hillsdale College
33 East College Street
Hillsdale, MI 49242
517-437-7341
www.hillsdale.edu

Hope College
69 East 10th Street
Holland, MI 49422
800-968-7850
www.hope.edu

Juniata College
1700 Moore Street
Huntingdon, PA 16652
877-JUNIATA
www.juniata.edu

Kalamazoo College
1200 Academy Street
Kalamazoo, MI 49006
800-253-3602
www.kzoo.edu

Knox College
2 East South Street
Galesburg, IL 61401
800-678-KNOX
www.knox.edu

Lawrence University
711 East Boldt Way
SPC 29
Appleton, WI 54911
800-227-0982
www.lawrence.edu

Lynchburg College
1501 Lakeside Drive
Lynchburg, VA 24501
800-426-8101
www.lynchburg.edu

McDaniel College
2 College Hill
Westminster, MD 21157
800-638-5005
www.mcdaniel.edu

Marlboro College
2582 South Road
Marlboro, VT 05344
800-343-0049
www.marlboro.edu

Millsaps College
1701 North State Street
Jackson, MS 39210
800-352-1050
www.millsaps.edu

New College of Florida
5800 Bay Shore Road
Sarasota, FL 34243
941-487-5000
www.ncf.edu

Ohio Wesleyan University
61 S. Sandusky Street
Delaware, OH 43015
800-922-8953
www.owu.edu

University of Puget Sound
1500 N. Warner Street
Campus Mailbox 1062
Tacoma, WA 98416
800-396-7191
www.pugetsound.edu

Reed College
3203 SE Woodstock Boulevard
Portland, OR 97202
800-547-4750
www.reed.edu

Rhodes College
2000 North Parkway
Memphis, TN 38112
800-844-5969
www.rhodes.edu

St. John's College (Annapolis)
60 College Avenue
Annapolis, MD 21401
800-727-9238
www.sjca.edu

St. John's College (Santa Fe)
1160 Camino Cruz Blanca
Santa Fe, NM 87505
800-331-5232
www.sjca.edu

St. Mary's College of California
P.O. Box 4800
Moraga, CA 94575
800-800-4SMC
www.stmarys-ca.edu

St. Olaf College
1520 St. Olaf Avenue
Northfield, MN 55057
507-786-3025
www.stolaf.edu

Southwestern University
1001 East University Avenue
Georgetown, TX 78626
800-252-3166
www.southwestern.edu

Ursinus College
P.O. Box 1000
Collegeville, PA 19426
610-409-3200
www.ursinus.edu

Wabash College
410 West Wabash Avenue
Crawfordsville, IN 47933
800-345-5385
www.wabash.edu

Wheaton College
501 College Avenue
Wheaton, IL 60187
800-222-2419
www.wheaton.edu

Whitman College
345 Boyer Avenue
Walla Walla, WA 99362
877-462-9448
www.whitman.edu

Willamette University
900 State Street
Salem, OR 97301
877-LIBARTS
www.willamette.edu

College of Wooster
847 College Avenue
Wooster, OH 44691
800-877-9905
www.wooster.edu

INDEX OF COLLEGES